9/85

OP
10.20

EMERGENCE

EMERGENCE

A TRANSSEXUAL
AUTOBIOGRAPHY

Mario Martino
with harriett

CROWN PUBLISHERS, INC.   NEW YORK

Printed in the United States of America

Published simultaneously in Canada by General Publishing Company Limited

Library of Congress Cataloging in Publication Data

Martino, Mario.
  Emergence.

  1. Transsexuals—Biography. 2. Martino, Mario.
I. harriett, joint author, . II. Title
RC560.C4M37 1977   616.6   77-3329
ISBN: O-517-52952-1
Second Printing, August, 1977

TO *Dr. Harry Benjamin*

> *Pioneer in the field of transsexualism,*
> *who gave respectability to the gender-disoriented.*
> *Through his caring and constancy,*
> *many of us have experienced rebirth.*

AND TO *Becky*

> *of whom the poet wrote:*
> *"Who can guess the potency*
> *of woman's love and patience,*
> *her precious influence,*
> *her sweet strength?"*
> *Without her support this book*
> *would have been more difficult to live*
> *and impossible to write.*

Acknowledgments

For their guidance we are gratefully indebted to our loved literary representative, Ruth Aley, and her associate, Bobs Pinkerton.

Our readers—Violet Bell, Charles Kingsford, Al Tannenbaum— gave their valued critiques and three varied perspectives. Judy Granger gave us a fourth perspective, along with her happy and unceasing support.

Jim Davis and Doug Anderson worked with us on the jacket, accommodating—with admirable diplomacy—our wishes.

We cherish the sensitivity of Marian Behrman and appreciate the arduous task still facing her.

Sig Moglen deserves all the accolades ever awarded an editor. With modesty, and unequaled acumen, he has explored and focused our thoughts while shepherding and sustaining our spirits. Since that first meeting, he has been our constant friend.

THE AUTHORS

Foreword

Emergence is fascinating in many ways, often touching, and quite dramatic.

I have long felt that there is a real need for the detailed autobiography of a female-to-male transsexual. I know Mario Martino's history will create sympathy. It will certainly dispel a great many wrong ideas—principally the notion that these people "could change if they want," and that they can be treated and "cured" by psychotherapy.

A highly important book, *Emergence* will clarify the minds of female transsexuals and their families, and help them find themselves and their position in life. The narrow-mindedness of people, which has endured on this subject for so long, will be counteracted by *Emergence* as much as it can be by any book. Mario Martino and his collaborator, harriett, should be proud of this book.

Harry Benjamin
M.D., retired
April, 1977

Preface

I am a transsexual.

I have undergone sex change, crossing over from female to male.

Mine has been a painful life to live, a painful story to write.

I have written to lay my own ghosts to rest and to help others to exorcise their demons.

Legally male, a happily married husband, I ask only to be accepted now as an average man.

It has been a twisting road from that home of my childhood in which sexuality was a closed door, as secret as our parents' off-limits bedroom. The word *sex* was never used in our home or in our schools. In both, the atmosphere was rigid and self-justifying, and we lived in genuine fear of sinning.

My life was a series of distorted mirrors. I saw myself in their crazy reflections as false to the image I had of myself. *I was a boy!* I felt like one, I dressed like one, I fought like one. Later, I was to love like one.

Unless you have actually experienced transsexualism, you cannot conceive of the trauma of being cast in the wrong body. It is the imprisonment of body and of soul, and for some transsexuals life is largely a succession of disapprovals, disappointments, rejections. I have been far more fortunate. I have emerged from that labyrinth into sunshine.

I can report, therefore, with candor—and, I hope, even humor—the circumstances of what will seem superficially to be a bizarre and humiliating sexual past. I wish to make available the facts and feelings of my life, for too little is yet known about transsexuality—by doctors, by academic theorists, by transsexuals themselves, and certainly by the public.

I trust my book will offer, however modestly, authentic firsthand evidence which will be of some use. I have changed names to be able to tell the truth more fully about myself and about others—friends and foes, family and professionals, my lovers and my wife. The merciless shadows of contempt and tragedy still fall on transsexuals. While clinging to a hope of anonymity for myself, I hope that exposing my full and true story will help create an atmosphere of greater understanding for all.

PART ONE

THE
LABYRINTH

1

The Early Years

Till I was nine, I didn't know that I wasn't a boy.

My father knew I wasn't, but I didn't.

My father, indeed, was certain about everything. My father was cast from the same mold as the Godfather. An Italian immigrant, Pa was the patriarch, his word undisputed. When he called, we did not ask why, we went to him on the run.

Short and stocky, he always smoked a long cigar and carried his gun. A policeman, Pa's beat was in one of the worst ghettos in the Midwest, where killings and worse were part of his workday. Ma said this explained his hard exterior, his short patience, his terrifying temper. Yet he had buried sensitivities, for once he admitted to us there were two things in life that bothered him: going to a home to tell a mother her son or daughter was dead, and that one time when, in the line of duty, he had shot and killed a man.

What Pa could not give his family in expressed affection, he gave to cronies from the Old Country, who came to him for

advice and camaraderie and to share his homemade wine. Still
he wore his gun, even while playing poker for fifty-cent stakes.

A man's man in the Italian tradition, feared by almost
everyone who knew him, loved by few, respected by all. And
that's what he wanted: RESPECT.

Like most children, we believed our mother loved us best.
She would intercede for us when we needed money for projects
at school or when we wanted to go to the movies. In her gentle
mother-wise way, she too kept us in line. She was the one to
buy our lemonade after we tried and failed one afternoon to
sell it to those who passed our stand. And her rebuke had been
as soft as a caress: "Giving to our neighbors—not selling—is
our way. . . ."

She saw to it that we were quiet when we were supposed to
be quiet. And it was Ma who got up in the night when we
were restless or coughing or simply wanted a glass of water.
Countless times, I'd call for water just to see her once more
before I fell asleep.

Anyone with a problem could come to Ma, or she'd go to
their home, cook, and help care for the whole family. She was
the angel of mercy on our block.

Italian-American, her face *and* her eyes smiled, and her
black hair curled in a pretty way. She was as warm and giving
as Pa was unbending. We could crawl onto her lap and get the
expected kiss at any time. About Pa's height, she was a heavy
woman and encased her ample bosom and hips in a long laced-
back corset. Her printed housedresses were freshly laundered,
and over them she always wore an apron that covered her
front, went over the shoulders and halfway down her back. On
special occasions she wore dark crepe or silk dresses.

Ma found satisfaction in her skill in cooking innumerable
dishes, always Italian. We were not permitted to have "American food" as Pa called it. Once I made the mistake of asking
why.

"Why can't we have Spam like our neighbors?"

Pa exploded. "You're stupid! You eat like a king. Now you
want to eat junk."

Dom, our half brother, was very special. He was the only

one in the family to whom Dad ever gave an affectionate pat or hug, the only one of us who could bring a glint of pride to Pa's eyes. But Janet and I were equally proud of Dom, and Ma loved him as her own. Somehow, none of us resented the favoritism.

Fourteen years my senior, Dom was always tall to us. Slim, as compared to my bulk, he was handsome and well-spoken, quiet and controlled. Perhaps too controlled: Were I suddenly to pull a hidden string, I sometimes thought, Dom would unravel. But he was an example to me of everything a young man should be, and everyone expected his sisters to excel as he excelled. I resolved that some day I too would be an achiever and then Pa would be proud of me.

Sometimes Ma sent Dom to discipline me and his words were sharp, not to be disobeyed. Once, and just once, he hit me under the chin and I almost bit my tongue in half, not only from the force but from the surprise of it. Against Ma's orders I'd run off alone to the park, and Dom was within his rights in punishing me. I loved him, worshipped him, and forgave him all at the same time. When he joined the Army and went away, the house seemed empty. When he sent me his old Army hat I folded and tucked it in the pocket of his hand-me-down shirts and this gave me a feeling of comrade-spirit with all men in uniform. I'd join their ranks as soon as I grew up.

Next to Dom, Pa favored Janet. Her cute little Italian face was olive-skinned, pert, and pretty, her braids a shiny brown. She was a tease. In her coquettish little-girl ways she charmed Pa in ways Dom and I could not. Janet was no threat to me, and I felt a love and protectiveness toward her and pride in her outmaneuvering our fiery father. Not that she wasn't punished on occasion. But her infrequent spankings were more or less on general principle rather than because of major infractions.

Fond memories and sad.

We lived in a substantial but unpretentious brick house, near the end of the bus line. Beyond were truck farms, expanding into fields and then the woods.

A grape arbor was at the back of the house, this side of the barnlike garage. We had grapes to eat as they ripened, grapes to pick for jams and jellies and for Pa to make barrels of *Dago Red*. We had grapes to share with friends and neighbors.

The garage was used to store gardening tools and paraphernalia, in lieu of the car we never owned. This was a good place to play: rafters to climb, discarded furniture to arrange according to whim. A rickety old table served as an operating table—with me always the surgeon!—during boy-girl war games and, oh, the miraculous cures I was responsible for: the reattached legs and arms, replaced eyes and noses and scalps, the impossible restoration of vital organs.

An older cousin of mine who was a nurse gave me a first-aid book from which I learned about the stethoscope. Following the diagram, I devised my own stethoscope from an old wire hanger, sliding on dried macaroni to cover the long part and attaching a soft red ball for the tip. I also traced pictures of skeletons and made proper notations on binder paper.

The family went in the back door of our house, visitors the front. Every visitor was made welcome. Our extra-large living room had off-white stucco walls, which were repainted every spring. Windows on three sides were covered with real lace curtains. We had an amply proportioned upholstered sofa and three matching chairs, all comfortably slipcovered and further protected by white crocheted doilies, starched and ironed to perfection. Family photographs were crowded onto the large mantle over our false fireplace. The furniture was heavy, bulky, oversized. Footed table legs were profusely ornamented with curves and turns, thoroughly disgusting when it came to Saturday cleanings.

It was the kitchen table that our adult visitors liked to sit around, sipping and praising Pa's wines and complimenting Ma's cake. Both Pa and Ma took great pleasure in having a well-stocked icebox, full pantry and cupboards. When friends came visiting, the men would gather at one end of the table, the women at the other, and the children were given something to eat and sent outside. If weather was inclement we ate from chairs against the wall, under fearful threats should we spill anything on the floor.

Family entertainment often centered around the wooden-boxed Philco radio with its ornate front resembling a small peaked stained-glass window. Nothing was more exciting to me than sitting beside Pa, listening to the fights. I imagined that our being together, sharing, was creating a bond between us.

Our parents' bedroom was off limits and we dared not go in even if the door was open. The fascination of the forbidden— and the unknown.

To the big mirrored door in our bathroom, I was secretly to reveal my true self as the male I knew myself to be. Here, behind locked door, I was to cover my face with Pa's shaving cream, work up a fine lather, and shave, fully convinced this would sprout a beard.

Pa had designated the basement as one of our play areas, but we were careful *never to ask permission* to reenact the Mass. Without his knowledge, I would set up an altar on a wooden orange crate, cover it with a clean white sheet, and act as the celebrant priest. A glass was my chalice and water or soft drink my wine, and the filled chalice was protected with a colored linen napkin. The host was from a roll of pastel candy wafers I'd bought for a nickel, one for each of my parishioners, Catholic or Protestant: I did not discriminate.

The Catholic Church was the pinnacle in our lives. We were often reminded that the highest religious aspiration for any Catholic girl was to become a nun, for a boy, to become a priest. Although Pa and Ma went to Mass only on Easter and Christmas, Dom and Janet and I went every Sunday.

But we were the only Catholic family on the block and this difference from our peers was especially noticeable on the Sabbath: By the time we had returned from Mass, our pals had left for Sunday school and church services with their parents.

The only work Pa ever did in the house was to indulge his passion and talents for cooking and wine-making. He gloried in the fame of his fruitcakes, made and brandied in July and set in the cellar to season until the Christmas holidays. On rare occasions he'd make pizza, not for a meal but for light snacking.

On Sundays Pa took over the kitchen. Sunday was spaghetti day. Preparations began around eight o'clock when, with a grand flourish, he tied a chef's apron over his expansive front, scrubbed his hands to a redness, and set about another week's-end triumph. Carefully he'd unfold a clean white sheet and spread it over Dom's bed (because his was the neatest), and on this sheet he would spread out to dry the flat spaghetti which he himself would make. Store-bought? Never. Only the best would do—and best was homemade as only Pa could make it.

Now the actual making would get under way. Pa would set the oversized breadboard on one side of the freshly scoured kitchen table and, next to it, a cutting square: a huge boxlike contraption with multiple wires, razor-sharp, reaching from one side to the other. He'd scoop white flour from the bin and form a mountain of it on the board, hollow it out in the center, crack eggs with style, and empty both yolks and whites into the hollow. And now, with what seemed to us a marvelously elegant ease, he began the elaborate process of handmaking the dough: mixing and kneading and flouring it, rolling it paper thin until it fell over the edges of the breadboard. Careful to keep it from tearing apart, Pa would transport this fragile, stretching sheet of dough from board to square, place it just so, and run the rolling pin across, cutting dozens and dozens of long dough strings, which fell through onto the table like magic. He'd pick up the strings in both hands and carry them in and arrange them on the white sheet, allowing two hours or more for drying.

We could scarcely tear ourselves away for nine o'clock Mass. To miss Mass was unthinkable. But just the thought of this noontime meal was enough to tickle our palates all the way to church, throughout the service, and all the way home. That last block our senses were newly alerted by the tanginess of garlicky sauce and meatballs. The sauce Pa had made from our own garden-grown, home-canned foods and dried stuffs: tomatoes, onions, bay leaves, garlic, basil.

By noon everything was ready, including a tossed green salad or tomatoes with oil and garlic dressing. One of Ma's great cakes. Milk. Only Pa did not drink milk. A quart decanter of wine was always on the floor beside his chair at table. He would fill and refill his glass throughout the meal and, miraculously, the decanter seemed to empty just as he finished.

Afterward he would refill the decanter, choosing from the barrels of his own homemade wines. Only at Christmas would he treat the rest of us to a shot glass of the bitter-tasting stuff, thus satisfying our curiosity and making us feel less denied.

We always thought of Sundays as feast days but, in all truth, we had good meals every day of the week. The anticipation was added incentive to hurry home from school and change from uniforms into work clothes. Together, we siblings marched into the dining room, sat down at table, ate everything on our plates—not a smidgen to be left over. All wordlessly. To talk, or to nudge under the table with a gentle kick, was a foolishness we knew better than to attempt: an invitation to a sound spanking. Supper finished, we asked to be excused, and the three of us trooped out together. After Dom left for the Army, I thought of myself as a soldier at home on furlough, marching protectively alongside my little sister Janet.

Sometimes we were allowed to invite a neighbor child in to Sunday dinner. But not often. Times were hard, Pa liked to remind us, and others could and should take care of their own.

Yes, Pa must have loved us. He fed us, provided for us.

Kissing was as much a part of our lives as breathing. Cheek-kissing. But we never saw Pa kiss Ma. Pa briefly kissed all women who came to our home, and all the men kissed Ma just as briefly. Women kissed each other, kids stood in line for their turn. Kids were kissed good night before going off to say prayers, for we were always alone when we talked with God.

Kissing was a part of growing up. After a certain age boys shook hands instead. I liked kissing the girls and women but not the men. I was a tomboy, proud of it, and preferred playing and fighting with boys, not kissing them.

A very pretty young woman, Barbara, lived next door. She was in her late twenties, tall, blond, married. I never thought of her husband. Rather, I'd go to sleep dreaming I was married to Barbara. To me, being married meant huggin' and kissin', nothing more.

Barbara's daughter Clare was about my own age and she went to a Protestant church. One Sunday (unknown to my family) I went with Clare instead of to my own church. And I became a momentary hero because I was the only one who knew that Peter was one of the disciples Jesus would make into a fisher of men, and what Jesus meant when He said: "Follow me, and I will make you fishers of men."

My fame was short-lived. It ended abruptly when the minister from her church came to my father and handed him my collection envelope and said, "I believe this should have gone to your church."

Pa was enraged. As soon as the minister was out of sight Pa chased me around the table, grabbed me, and beat hell-and-damnation out of me. At least, so he thought.

I will never forget Ann. We were about eight and often played in the garage. We'd make believe we were on a train and I was the conductor and Ann was the lady with the baby. In time we began touching, and eventually we were bold enough to undress. This led to exploring our bodies, even the "privates" (as our parents called that private part of us). Feeling some vague excitement I would cut playtime short and hurry home to explore my own body in the bathroom's mirrored door.

Masturbation must have started at about this time. It set me tingling, filled me with sensations I could never have imagined, would not have known how to describe, had I dared describe it. I didn't. I practiced this new thing secretly in my bed and in my bath. And once Ma caught me, fully dressed, touching my untouchables.

"Nasty!" Her eyes were searching, piercing my very private being.

I had displeased my mother. The best friend I had. I was torn between pleasing her and pleasing myself. Yielding to this frightening temptation of the devil (as the priest would have said), I doubly guarded my secret. But Ma's word stayed with me, nagging like a *nasty* little bee—yet the bite of it didn't always deter me from this inexplicable delight. But the word was imprinted on my mind and came to torment me with every tender secret touch.

I had very little association with girls. Rough-and-tumble games, aggressive leadership—that was my style. Gee, was I

proud of being a tomboy! I appropriated for my own a mil-
dewed hat that had once belonged to Pa, and walking around
in his old shoes filled me with manliness. It didn't matter that
they kept twisting and falling off my feet.

So I played with the boys. I was at ease with them, though
they were uncomfortable with a girl around. Being a girl, I
tried harder and they imposed every imaginable hardship on
me. I was their drudge: I supplied the old tire for the swing. I
had to find materials for the treehouse, pull the boards and
hammer and nails up into the tree, do most of the nailing
down. If they hammered at all it was for the pleasure of the
moment.

Being the family tomboy had one disadvantage: I was pressured into carrying buckets and buckets of water to the garden
on a vacant lot four houses away.

I yearned to sprinkle the lawn and the flowers that bordered
our curved walk but this privilege was Pa's alone. Could this
selfish attitude have been the seeding of a hostility yet to surface?

What a picture Pa made: massive, powerful, handling that
sprinkler with dignity and fierce possessiveness. I was to realize
many years later that this holding of the lawn hose, forcing the
spray into the receptive earth, had become a potent symbol in
my subconscious.

Pa liked to work without his shirt. Naturally, I did too. Because Pa did. Everything he did I aped—even to the way he
hitched up his jeans. And then, suddenly one day in my ninth
summer, he looked at my bare chest a second time and roared
out at me: "Go home! And put some clothes on!"

I was mad. Just as mad as Pa was. If he didn't have to wear
clothes on top, why did I?

No one explained why.

Could this have been the day our rivalry began?

Two weeks before Christmas our tree was always up, special
lights blinked at the windows, and evergreen branches decorated the house throughout. We kids were assigned the delicious
task of trimming the tree, and it was at this time of year that
Pa showed genuine interest in what we were doing. He would
sit with his cigar, supervising and directing—or give an oc-

casional assist when we couldn't reach a higher branch. And it was always Pa who positioned the angel with the silken hair. Ma had her work in the kitchen, but she'd frequently appear in the archway and smile approvingly at her well-behaved family. The last thing to place was the long strands of tinsel, each of which had to go on separately. Here I was likely to become too eager and throw up a handful—and, happily, Pa would not strike out. Perhaps touching the angel with the white silken hair had evoked lovely memories of his own childhood Christmases in his native Italy.

Family unity was at its best, and memory of the piney perfume was to pervade all the Christmases to come.

In my earliest years I was disappointed to get dolls and I promptly passed them on to Janet, leaving me one or two presents short. In time my parents caught on that giving me such toys was a waste, so, in their new wisdom, they switched to harmonicas and ball bats and dump trucks. My most successful Christmas was my eighth, when I found both ice skates and Yo-Yo under that tree! I was on the ice almost before it was dusted free of snow and all but broke my bones trying simultaneously to skate and twirl the Yo-Yo around my head.

One of my cheeriest and most exciting associations was with a dear neighbor woman, Grandma Thomas. Because I was a child, Grandma was old to me, if for no other reason than because of her abundant white hair, which she wore in a thick white silk net. In her mid-fifties, she stood four foot ten and weighed about ninety pounds. Her skin was tanned and somewhat wrinkled, her face creased, her smiling brown eyes twinkling. Large purple veins stood up on her gnarled hands and arms, hardened muscles sharply defined her arms and lower legs—all of which contrasted incongruously with her slight build.

Grandma Thomas feared nothing and no one and, like others in the neighborhood, never locked her doors. She was never sick, never complained. Grandma was loved by everyone, from the youngest to the eldest, and she left wonderful memories to all of us.

I think I got on so well with her because she did all the

My ambiguity was evident at an early age.

things men did and seemed not to care about women's goings-on. Maybe this was why I never thought of marrying her. Another reason I adored her was that she understood my boyish ways as others did not. Little wonder, then, that I rushed through my Saturday chores at home so as to run over to Grandma's and finish off the day in new excitements and real fun.

Just thinking of Saturday mornings made my blood boil. I fretted over the unfairness of it: Dom and Janet and I took turns doing the dishes, yet Janet never helped outside. And Dom certainly was not expected to condescend to cleaning house. Cleaning meant getting down on hands and knees and scrubbing floors—and going back a second time if corners were not spotlessly clean. It meant endless hours of dusting (drat those table legs!) and running the vacuum, to say nothing of changing linen on all the beds. By noon I was resenting both Janet and Dom, Pa—because I was on the verge of yelling—and even Ma for permitting this unjust distribution of work loads.

But my reward was to come: Once these miseries were over I was free to run to Grandma's house where working was play—and paid for in actual dimes and quarters.

Compliments from Ma and our relatives were my compensation for work at home. To be *paid* as well as *praised* was not a thought to be entertained: Hard work was a matter of course, one of life's hard facts. I was lucky if Pa forgot to nag that I was wearing jeans.

Even compliments to me were limited. Primarily, they related to my being a good worker. Personality ran second. Perhaps the nicest thing said about me came from a diminutive great-aunt. "Mari-a," she would say, "you could charm the snake."

Enough of black thoughts. I'd dismiss them—until next Saturday. No need fretting about that which I could not change.

Grandma Thomas lived in a white frame house set back from the street and near the alley. Stepping inside, I would run to the overstuffed sofa or one of the plump chairs, plop myself down and sink into such softness as I'd never known. The colors were bright, the yellow matching print curtains hanging at unpredictable lengths (a variance I attributed to her failing eyesight). A wood-burning, potbellied stove stood in the center of the room, and during the winter it generated enough heat to warm most of the interior of her snug house.

The atmosphere was one of an indefinable warm and rather happy clutter. Grandma was forever sewing together and braiding old rags into floor coverings. Her floors were over-lapped by these large and small multicolored rugs, which, in turn, caught and trapped the floating brown and white hairs from two Pomeranian dogs who had free run of the place.

The most delectable fragrances emanated from an ancient kitchen stove. Grandma was always canning produce or baking such marvels as her chocolate or peach pies, all the while antici-pating the joys of sharing with families on the block. The old wooden table ran the width of the room and a chair could always be found for one more person. No matter that the table-cloth was spattered with stains: Neither the good woman nor her regular visitors seemed to mind, recalling each stain as a memory of an earlier pleasurable meal or snack.

The most wonderful part of her house was the bedroom. A small closet and large chest housed her limited wardrobe and linens. A big rocker was always ready for a good swing. But the zinger stood in the middle of the room: that great double bed. The mattress was made mostly of feathers, honest-to-gosh feathers. My richest reward for helping Grandma—far richer than any monetary thing—was the treat of being invited oc-casionally to sleep with her in that feather bed. I felt loved—and privileged.

At the back was an old shed: home for a few egg-laying hens and sprightly young roosters, garden implements, and miscel-lanea. As the hens grew older they became less productive, and Grandma had an uncanny sense for keeping the stock strong. So, at rare intervals and on special occasions, she would kill a nonproductive hen for dinner. No qualms about going into their midst, grabbing one by the neck and, in a dancelike movement, wringing off the body—not the least dismayed that the body would wander senselessly around for a minute or two while she stood waiting with the lifeless head in her hand. I'd get a queasy feeling: a desire to run plus a choked fullness in

A boy's face in banana curls.

my throat while waves of nausea rushed over me.

Often we'd talk about doctors and nurses and medicine and one day, after work, she said, "Today we're going to the movies. Not only that, we're going to eat out beforehand."

Added to this was the excitement that my parents had said I could sleep over.

"Gol-ly-gee!"

I took out the two quarters she'd just paid me.

"No, no. This treat is on me."

We ate our dinner at Woolworth's. A first time for me, and nothing could compare with it. Then we went to see the life story of Sister Kenny, who had found a way to deal with polio. I came away from the picture fully determined to get into "doctoring," as we called it.

"Some day I'll do something as noble as Sister Kenny has done."

Grandma smiled at me as if she knew something I could not yet comprehend. Did she recognize something within me that I was not then conscious of? Or was it from my endless talk about bones and cures that she knew how I'd thrill at seeing such a heroic life story?

Back at her house again. Cookies and milk, then off to the feather bed. Because it stood so high from the floor, this tiny woman used a small tufted stool to hoist herself up and in, but I liked to make a run and jump for it. My first try was a miss. On the second I ran back to the door and, gaining this extra momentum, made it. How we laughed, how we hugged. We kissed cheeks and said good night.

What a great, great feeling: drifting down into that feathery warmth, next to this Grandma I loved most next to Ma, thinking of Sister Kenny. . . . Lightly, without my knowing it, sleep came.

Every summer Ma took us for a week's visit with Uncle Bill on his farm. I especially liked early evenings: cows to be milked, eggs to be gathered, chickens and ducks to be fed. We all wanted to help and did, with many restrictions and admonitions. One evening, on impulse, I ran into the kitchen for a glass of lemonade.

Uncle Bill's house had a sitting room off the kitchen. Hearing a sound like the turning of magazine pages, I turned and looked inside. My bachelor cousin Willie, a man in his early thirties, was sitting there wearing only a T-shirt, exposing his lower anatomy. This was the very first time I'd seen that half of a full-grown man. Since he wasn't the least embarrassed, I pretended not to be, yet I couldn't understand why he tried to draw me into conversation since he wasn't all together. I was as shocked as I would have been at the sight of my half-dressed father or mother, a sight I'd never witnessed, never expected to.

It was little more than an incident and soon forgotten. I was not to think of it again until my second encounter with an adult man.

Ken, a neighbor boy of about twenty, broke his leg. Olive-skinned, dark-haired, muscular and sinewy, he had a vague, detached air about him, even a hint of mystery. We fantasized about his comings and goings. Ken owned an old roadster with a rumble seat, and in our eyes he was a big cheese. Now, with his disabled leg propped high, boys and girls came from blocks around to view and examine at firsthand the plaster cast that was temporarily immobilizing him. And enhancing his image.

For some reason Ken had always shown a preference toward me and, admittedly, this sort of set me up. Out riding in his roadster, he'd often stop and ask me to hop in, but, as much as I craved to be special among the kids, I never did hop into that rumble seat unless several of us were together. We'd all had strict orders from parents never to get in anyone's car, even if we knew him.

Besides, I didn't really like the guy. I didn't quite trust him. But for some reason long forgotten, this particular afternoon I arrived at Ken's house to find none of the other kids there lining his room next to the front door. He lay there, grinning, a sheet pulled up to his T-shirt. The minute I stepped inside he grabbed my hand, pulled me to his bed, threw back the sheet, and tried to get me over and on top of him, all the time kissing me. I began pounding and fighting, but Ken was far, far stronger and he almost succeeded in getting me on top—but not quite. Enraged, he held my hand viselike and, in such a way that his was over mine, clamped both our hands on top of his privates and began pumping away, faster and faster, muttering and moaning.

Suddenly something happened: The iron pipe in our hands went limp. I was terrified, I didn't know what was happening —and now my hand was covered with a white sticky substance.

Abruptly he let me go, and I fell off the bed, scrambled to my feet, and ran out the door. I never in my life ran so fast to get home and to the bathroom, where I scrubbed my hands with soap until they were sore, stopping only long enough to start the tub water. I scrubbed my whole body in the tub then, feeling soiled, knowing that something was very, very wrong. I was smeared with guilt and all that soap and water couldn't wash it away. I dressed in all fresh work clothes, rushed off to the garden, and, for the first and only time, carried buckets and buckets of water without a grumble.

This was a thing I could tell no one. Not the priest, not the nuns. At school it was constantly drilled into us: "If you ever do anything sexual with one another—or if a girl does anything to arouse a boy—the girl is just as guilty as the boy of mortal sin."

So this was *sexual*. Instinctively, I knew. The word had meant nothing to me before—it was just a word.

Guilty. I was as guilty as Ken of mortal sin. But what had I done to arouse him? I couldn't figure it out. . . .

Since I could not confide this horrendous experience with sexuality to anyone, I had to continue as I always had: When the other kids went to see Ken I went along. But now I was afraid. Ken was the Devil, with whom I had committed mortal sin.

The guilt of my sin and the weight of carrying it alone became too much. Ann. Could I confide in Ann? We had long ago grown beyond the stage of our earlier explorations and now we were just good friends. She became my confidante.

"Well," she said at the end of my story, "Mom has a set of medical books. Maybe we can find something there."

We found a flashlight in the kitchen, took the books from their hiding place in an upstairs closet, secreted ourselves there. By the end of the third reading we felt the old arousal and were both in a sweat. Whether this was from answers we found to our questions or from the closeness of our bodies in the unventilated closet we did not try to determine. Neither of us wanted to revert to that phase of our lives, so we returned the books to their hiding place and removed ourselves from the closet, taking the flashlight downstairs and back to the kitchen drawer.

A hasty thank-you and good-bye. At home sooner than Ma had expected, I surprised her by asking what I could do to help with supper. She could always use an extra pair of hands, and this new show of willingness to work brought brightness to her tired face. Could this be atonement? Perhaps, in the very smallest way, making Ma happy was making amends, or at least lessening the weight of my sin.

Then there was that tough guy, Patrick Murray, in the fourth grade. He was about my size, maybe slightly larger, and we'd been competitive since the first day we met. On the ball field, the playground, in the classroom or our own backyards. I wanted his place in the sun and he wasn't about to give it up. The inevitable showdown erupted while we were swapping baseball cards: He grabbed my deck and ran. But I was faster and stronger and the poor kid ended up with a bloody nose and torn pants. I gloated over my victory and my black eye— until I reached home and took a real beating from Pa.

I kissed a girl full on the lips for the first time when I was eleven. She was Karen, my secret sweetheart, and I had a birthday present for her: a little gold finger purse which I'd bought with my own quarters earned at odd jobs for the neighbors and Grandma Thomas.

"I have a surprise for you, Karen. Close your eyes."

Karen closed her eyes and held out her hands and I leaned over and gave her a long, smoochy kiss. She was twice surprised, but smiled and thanked me for the present.

At the moment of the kiss I was almost overcome with a passion to hold her close. But I wasn't that brave. In spite of our being a kissin' family, this sudden desire for lip-kissing was somehow different. For a long time I puzzled over the difference between kissing Karen and kissing all the relatives.

I'd always wanted a bike. Pa said if I wanted one I'd have to work and pay for it myself. The news spread, and one day soon afterward, Mrs. Miner, who lived across the alleyway, called to say her son Bob had one he'd sell for twelve dollars. I ran into the house looking for Ma but couldn't find her. The door of the bedroom she shared with my father was closed. In spite of the off limits, surely today was an exception. And surely there'd be no harm in just looking in through the keyhole to see if she was there. She was not in sight. But Pa! Pa was on the bed, stretched out full length. *Naked.*

I ran straight to my room and shut the door. I sat on the edge of my bed and thought about it. My father—naked. The picture of him would not go away. And suddenly, he became three men: Pa, Ken, Willie. The shadows of guilt hit me full on and I fell back on the bed and my head spun round and round. Suddenly the full revelation came to me: the physical difference between male and female. Dabbing at my eyes, I went to the bathroom, pulled down my jeans, and accepted the real difference for the first time. And then the question: If I was the spittin' image of Pa, why didn't I have the same thing?

My body structure began to change.

It was quite a blow to my resolve to join the Army to be told by Ma that, now that I was going on twelve, it was time to go shopping for a bra. I looked down the front of Dom's castaway shirt and had to admit to a slight protrusion on either side of the buttoned closing. I hunched my shoulders and drew myself in, but Ma was not to be fooled. She made one concession: "We'll wait one month."

One day I deliberately hung behind the others going to work in our garden. When they were two houses away I went to the bathroom, locked the door, and reached for Pa's shaving mug. I made a thick lather, covered my pubic area, and neatly shaved off the unwanted hair. Now whether it was from the sense of doing something wrong, or the friction of the razor on the mons, I had no way of knowing—but suddenly I was sexually stimulated. Excitedly, I viewed my nude body in the mirror and then, on impulse, reached for the bag Ma used to give us enemas. The nozzle looked unfamiliar but that wasn't worth a second thought—besides, it was much longer and that, plus the peculiar shape at the end, suited my purpose admirably. I unscrewed the big nozzle from the bag, turned again toward the mirror, and maneuvered the nozzle into position between the lips by the clitoris. In my limited imagination, I supposed that, with my improvised penis, I could somehow feign the exhilaration Ken must have felt during my first terrifying experience.

Naturally I did not confide this flight of fantasy, even to Ann. About this I had no feelings of guilt. I felt good. I felt like a man.

The month was up. Hating the world, and myself even more, I went shopping with Ma for the bra.

The saleslady at the local department store smiled her forced toothy smile and chattered incessantly as she measured and congratulated me.

"Imagine! Your very first bra! Which do you prefer, dearie, white or tearose?" All this in plain view of everybody.

She directed us to a fitting room.

Almost instantly the curtains of the cramped fitting room parted and Miss Smiles bounded in.

"Aren't they pretty, dearie? Which shall we try first?" Without waiting for an answer, she added: "Strip to the waist for me now, that's a dearie!"

"Do as the lady says."

So this was "blooming womanhood"—and the tedious, hateful job of enhancing it . . . The tearose was revolting, so we tried on three white models before I blurted out: "Let's go, Ma!"

Ma said we'd take the first one, Miss Smiles disappeared, and we went back to the salesroom, everyone looking at us. Our beaming saleslady dropped the "pretty" into a bag and daintily handed it over the counter.

How could I keep that image of myself, as I saw myself in

the bathroom mirror, with this new image thrust upon me by virtue of a female form?

On a visit to my cousin's house in a large city I was expected to help with the housework. Detesting it at home, I liked it even less on a supposed holiday.

But cleaning the upstairs turned into an amazing adventure: Under my cousin Frank's bed I found magazines such as I'd never seen before—girlie magazines! They held me speechless, spellbound, yet put me in a sweat, and my blood pumped at an alarming pace. Automatically my hands found my genitals and I fantasized that I was making love to a woman. There was only one thing now that I wanted to do and this would have to wait until I returned home: put the douche nozzle between the folds of my labia and on top of the clitoris and make like a man.

For the duration of the visit with my relatives I was eager to help and offered to do the upstairs bedrooms all by myself.

Education in the Catholic schools of that era was strict, authoritarian, unbending, and painful, both physically and emotionally. If we did anything the sisters considered wrong, it was common practice to be punished in front of the whole class. How I remember kneeling while Sister slapped my backside, seemingly without mercy, with the pole designed to lower the windows. Hell-fire-and-damnation sermons took on new earnestness as we approached puberty with its great surge of sexual feelings.

My own feelings were focused on Marlene, a petite girl about my own age, already beginning to blossom. I taught her to play marbles, carried her books home from school. We shared our most intimate thoughts. She was an only child, and her ambition was to grow up and get married and have at least three children. My plans were to be a doctor, I told her, or a nurse. So long as it was medical. I would never marry. Marlene and I would be together for hours sometimes and I'd touch her face or arm at every opportunity.

Ma and Pa had made elaborate plans for my twelfth birthday party. The basement was transformed into a party room, with ropes of brilliant crepe paper dangling from the ceiling and bunches of balloons bouncing and popping all over the place. Ma had outdone herself on the chocolate frosted cake and we'd all helped turn the crank on the ice-cream freezer long before the guests arrived.

We ate the cake to the last crumb, the ice cream to the last lick—and Pa wore a satisfied grin as he went up the stairs, trusting us to behave ourselves in fun and games. To hurry things along, Janet and I helped Ma clear away the paper dishes and spoons and take them up to the kitchen.

Alone. All the kids, no chaperone. And Marlene was standing next to me. Everyone was clamoring to play spin-the-bottle.

We played and I was the first to be kissed. By a boy. Gosh, it was disgusting. And I was aching to kiss Marlene. Now it was another boy and another. I made each encounter a brief one. What did these boys, klutzy oafs, know about kissing? (I thought of myself as being exceedingly knowledgeable about such things, having read the magazines my cousin Frank hid under his bed. Now that I was educated as to how a woman should be treated, these other twelve-year-olds looked like infants to me. And I was dying to try out my newly found expertise on Marlene.)

I was shaken out of my fantasies when one of the kids suggested we turn out the lights. We stampeded toward the switch and the first one there pushed *off*. I'd waited only long enough to edge closer to Marlene and now I kissed her as I was sure no male in that room knew how, judging from the way they'd kissed me.

The darkness lasted less than a minute, for my parents sensed the sudden quiet and appeared at the top of the stairs. On went the lights. Everybody scrambled apart. Did Marlene know she was being kissed by me, or did she think it was a boy? Whatever she thought, her response was titillating: wiggling and squirming and fumbling at my fly. (As yet I hadn't begun to pad the front of my pants with a sock to give an impression of maleness.) Lights on, my face flamed red and instantly I moved away from Marlene. Pa yelled and ordered everyone to go home.

The party was over.

And that was the last of my birthday parties at home.

Some of the kids must have told their parents because Sister called me out of class the following morning and charged me as guilty for whatever part I played in turning out the lights. She did not mention that I was seen kissing a girl, but she said in no uncertain words that what we'd done was sinful and dirty and we must confess. Accordingly, I went to the priest for confession: I couldn't bring myself to say I was kissing a girl, only that we'd kissed boys. The priest went on at length about how if I ever allowed a boy to touch me "that way" before marriage I would be committing mortal sin, as would the boy. I promised him, with all my heart, that he would never have to worry about such a thing happening. (Never could I confess to him that I believed myself to be a boy!)

My unspoken romance with Marlene continued. It wasn't until years later that I was actually to touch a girl in a sexual way.

In my more literary moments I compared our father and mother with the fabled *Wind and the Sun*. Pa, the patriarch, would blow with might and main, chilling us with the fierceness of his blasts. Ma, soothing us with loving arms and warming kisses, was the winner.

Ma would often stand as a buffer between us and our father when, in a rage, he attempted to beat the one who had offended him. She'd take the punches from his clenched fists aimed at the child. And when Pa's fury had turned to dead ash, she would go quietly to their bedroom and we could hear the sounds of her grief. Since that room was off limits to us, there was little chance to comfort her other than to promise ourselves we'd try still harder to keep in line with Pa's demands. But once, after a particularly frightening time (and I was the offender), I waited outside the bedroom until her sobs ceased and she opened the door and smiled at me as though nothing out of the ordinary had happened.

"Ma," I almost shouted, "I hate myself. But more than I hate myself, I hate Pa. I'll kill him! Some day I'll kill that man."

"Oh, you must never, never say that. Pa doesn't want to

hurt me. Or any of you. It's just his temper."

"But it's not fair, Ma."

"He just doesn't think when he's like this."

"Why doesn't he love us?"

"Your pa loves you, and me, in his way. He's following the traditions of his own family in the Old Country. I'm sure his pa and ma were even stricter in bringing him up."

"Even so—"

"Pa wants you to be good children. A credit to all Italian families."

"But does he have to be so mean about it?"

"Well, look at the Italian families who come to visit us. Aren't their pas very much like your pa?"

"Not as strict as all that."

"You see them with company manners. Who knows what goes on at home?"

Of course Ma was right. Still my dark thoughts persisted. How, I wondered, could I ever have wanted to be like Pa? I was no longer proud of looking like him. Everyone said I did. "Just take another look at the family album," someone would say. "That picture of you could've been your pa at your age."

Knowing what he'd do to me if I dared such a thing, I resisted the impulse to destroy every picture that included the two of us. I could never trust Pa again. My love for him had changed. A bit of Oedipus, you think?

In October of the year I was twelve, my mother died.

2

Puberty

We'd gone off to school as usual that morning in October. Mom had kissed us good-bye, Janet and me, to the tune of Western country music.

Doc Hopkins was singing on the radio at that hour and his words (as I remembered) were to remain with me for all time: "I need You, how I need You, precious Lord. I need You."

We walked to school with Randy and Lorraine, who lived down the street.

"Look! The leaves are all golden. And they're falling, falling." Lorraine was going to be an artist and a poet.

"Dried autumn leaves on the ground always remind me of giant Post Toasties—and when the frost comes it's as if they're covered with sugar." I was not to be outdone.

"Oh, you kids. Always dreaming up fancy things to say." Randy was the realist.

Janet was on our side. "But it's fun to talk fancy."

Well, soon enough there'd be bushels of leaves on the ground and they'd have to be raked. I'd be realistic then. For now I liked the crunch of them under my loafers. The air was

brisk and cool, just right for playing hooky. Only we never
dared.

Sister Catherine was a mere five feet and only her face and
hands were visible from within her concealing black habit,
white wimple, and black veil. She was school principal, her authority unquestioned. *Pal* she was not. She had no interest in
the student's side of any altercation, and to be called into her
presence was tantamount to punishment. The pleasantness of
the morning was shattered when Janet and I were told at about
ten o'clock to report to her office. Something was very, very
wrong.

My fears intensified when she actually put an arm around
each of us and spoke our names in an unbelievably gentle
voice. Then she said, "Your mommy has died and gone to
heaven."

Heaven? I wanted to yell. *Heaven!* I don't want her in heav-
en, I want her here. Now! Had she listened too hard to Doc
Hopkins's words: "I need You"? Was her need so great she
must go searching for Our Lord?

Sister Catherine had to be wrong. When we went home
Mom would be there. Just as she always was. She'd welcome
us with her after-school kiss. Yes, Sister had to be wrong.

Only yesterday Aunt Concetta, the sister in whom Mom confided, had arrived for her yearly two-weeks' visit, bringing a
pretty doll for Janet and a bookbag and ruler set for me. This
aunt, Mom's sister, was a special favorite of all of us, except
maybe Pa. He wasn't really fond of any of Mom's relatives.
How could Mom have gone off to heaven when her own sister
had just arrived? Mom just wouldn't do a thing like that.

Sister Catherine was still talking in that strange low voice
and now she said, "Your mommy's heart just stopped beating. . . ."

But why? Mom was only thirty-nine years old. . . . I wanted
to strike out, hit someone, anyone. Even God? Well, hadn't
God taken her away? But no, God was good. He wouldn't take
our Mom when we needed her so much. I looked upward,
searching for God. I couldn't see Him. Nor could I feel His
presence. Suddenly, I wanted to kick out at God.

A friend of the family had come in her car and now she was taking us home. As we took the familiar route back to our house, Doc Hopkins's words came to me again as if to taunt me: ". . . how I need You, precious Lord. . . ."

Janet, only six, knew little about death. It was only a thing people talked about in hushed voices—yet she was sobbing softly, sensing the wrongness of whatever was happening to us. The leaves had lost their autumn glory and now my eyes avoided them. Leaves falling, it occurred to me, were lives dropping in death. From then on the beginning of the fall season was always to herald an ending of life.

Aunt Concetta opened the door. She was crying bitterly. "Where's Mom?" I asked.

"She's with Our Lord. . . ."

We ran past her, Janet and I, and ran from room to room looking for her. She was not there. In her place were neighbors bringing in food, cleaning, doing neighborly things.

No one paid much attention to us. It seemed strange that, with so many people around, the house was almost as quiet as church. Women talked in whispers or low voices, the men had little or nothing to say. Everyone was wet-eyed.

One of the women said, not unkindly but purposefully, "We must go to the store and buy you girls each a dark dress. And you will wear this dress every day for the next week. In mourning. Out of respect for your mommy, who is now in heaven with Our Lord."

I felt as if I'd dried up inside. My chest was tight, my throat seemed about to close on words. But I cried deep.

And now I saw Pa. He was crying too. I couldn't believe it. In all my life I'd never seen him shed a tear, nor was I ever to see Pa cry again. Did he, now that it was too late, realize just how much she'd meant to him? Would he feel shame remembering? Regretting? What about the countless times he'd yelled at her? The times he'd struck her with his fists? The times he'd let her take the blows he intended for their kids? My anger at Pa flared fire-white. Now I'd have to fight this man alone.

By late afternoon relatives were arriving from many towns and Dom came on leave from Army duty.

Dom had loved Mom from the time she first came into his life, almost fifteen years ago. The day she married Pa. Dom's eyes were red and swollen but he did not cry publicly. Instead he squeezed my shoulder until it hurt, then took me aside and talked briefly about death.

"Mom had not been well for a very long time. And, sad as it seems, she had never told anyone. Not even Aunt Concetta. Mom wanted us to think of her as we saw her day to day. She was a good woman, the best! And she loved all of us. . . . In God's way He has rewarded her for so much goodness by removing her from this world of pain and sorrow."

As if in afterthought, he added: "Mom expects us to carry on. . . ."

I seemed destined to go through life wondering what it was like to have a mother, to envy my peers their relationships with their mothers, to idealize the state of motherhood.

In the funeral parlor Dom and Janet and I sat in the front row next to Pa. Uncles and aunts and cousins and neighbors filled the several rooms in the mortuary and now they came forward, murmuring condolences. I was empty, finding nothing to say to all the well-meaning people who came by to take my hand. My gaze was frozen to the beautiful gray coffin with its white quilted satin lining and the satin pillow under her head.

Before we left that night Pa held Janet up and then me so that we could kiss our mother in her heavenly sleep. I remember her purple dress and the white orchid placed over her heart. I could see no sign of an illness—she looked as if she were truly asleep. Yet there was a strangeness about her, as if she were one of the plaster angels we saw in pictures.

"Kiss your ma," Pa had said.

Oh, that Pa had not done this! At the moment I knew he meant to be kind but I remember thinking that I would never, never, never do such a thing to a child of mine.

I wanted to stay with Mom, not go home with the others. I wanted to remind her that I was to be confirmed the next night and to assure her I would wear the dress she had wanted me to wear. Just then someone put out the light. I screamed and blacked out and the next thing I remembered was being at home in bed, an awful loneliness inside.

Next evening I was confirmed in our church. We assembled at the back: boys in navy blazers and ties, girls in navy dresses, trimmed with white. How I hated the dress, the bra, the knee socks. And being here was being in a place I did not want to be. However, the archbishop always came at the appointed time and no one was excused, even when death took a family member.

Exactly on cue we went forward in pairs, the tallest first, fanning out at the altar and leaving the little ones in the center. The archbishop walked toward us, wearing the mighty robes and mitred hat, staff in hand. We were kneeling now, awaiting his touch on our cheeks. The touch was symbolic of a slap to denote that we, as soldiers, were willing to die for Christ. When he came to me he did a surprising thing: He leaned forward, whispered comforting words. "Your mommy is safe with Our Lord."

Now, for the first time, I accepted my mother's death. The finality of it. She would not return to us in this life.

A favorite friend of Mom's asked me to ride with them after the funeral. She was very pregnant and I lay my head in her lap, wishing her baby would be a boy, wishing I were a boy— and I fantasized about the woman I would marry, whose children I'd father. I'd be everything Pa was not: tender and warm and loving.

Pa actually tried to be both father and mother those first weeks and, looking back, I understand what a sacrifice that must have been for him. He'd somehow manage to be at home when we came from school, he'd make our meals, have our clothes washed and ironed. Gradually, I began to see Pa in a new way and almost to respect him at times. A man must be credited for trying.

Then, within less than three months, Pa brought a strange woman home and introduced her to our family. "Lenore and me—we're gonna get married. You need a ma. Lenore will be your new mother."

I froze. How could he do this to us? I'd worked so hard at trying to love this man I called Pa, I'd really begun to believe in him. And now, to bring a strange woman into our home. To live here. To sleep in Mom's bed. Use her real lace curtains— even touch the dishes Mom wouldn't let us touch.

Surely this old man, this old goat, had no intentions of sleeping in the same bed with this woman? And what about her children, especially the two who still lived with her? None of this would be happening if only Mom were here. . . . Mother of Jesus, give us our mom back again before this strange woman comes to sleep in her bed.

The tears I cried were suddenly very real, not the dried-up ones frozen inside me. They melted now and gushed and it seemed as if my heart would surely drown.

Almost three months to the day after Mom's death, Pa brought this stranger, Lenore, into our home to be our new ma. They were married in late afternoon in our living room in a civil ceremony. Not even a priest. Before our unbelieving eyes.

Lenore's father and mother had come from the Old Country, settled in a town not too far from our own, had a big family, and imbued them with the old traditions. Lenore was Italian in every way and fluent in her family's native language. She and Pa would often speak in Italian so that Janet and I would not understand.

It was a surprise then that Lenore had such modern ideas. Down came our real lace curtains and up went her flimsy white ones. Air-fresheners came in, mothballs went out. Mom's things gradually disappeared: All her photographs had been put away, the personal effects had been divided among the relatives. A special shock had to do with Mom's best dishes: Lenore took them from our china cabinet to make way for her own.

One morning at breakfast one of Mom's cups slipped out of my hand, fell to the floor, and broke its handle.

"It doesn't matter," Lenore said.

"Doesn't matter! Why, these are Mom's best dishes. She wouldn't even let us help wash and dry them. She always did them herself."

"Oh? Well, we're using them for second best now."

How could she say such a thing?

"But, Lenore, don't you realize these dishes are about all that's left around our house to remind us of Mom?"

"Your mom's in heaven now. And God's angels don't worry about worldly things."

I couldn't believe that. Even though Mom was an angel she must remember us down here, she must want us to remember her. I refused to think of such a thing as her not remembering us.

I broke into tears, abruptly left the table, grabbed my books, and ran off to school.

It was to be many years before I could appreciate Lenore's difficult position: with two children of her own trying her best to mother and understand another woman's children. It was only natural that Lenore would wish to make over a home to meet the needs of the living. But this episode seemed to be the fatal straw and, if Pa and I had been at odds before, we were at war now. It seemed to Janet and me that he always took Lenore's side. More and more he allowed her to discipline us, although she would not allow Pa to correct her children or set rules for them.

As we saw it, Lenore and Ceil and Paul had their way in everything.

Having one's own room was taken for granted at our house. Now, with Lenore's two, this was to change: Janet moved in with me, and Ceil took Janet's room. Paul took the room that had belonged to Dom.

Just out of high school, Paul was a smug, skinny kid with thick wavy hair. Ceil, a junior, was slim and quite cute. Given a different set of circumstances, she might've really shaken me up. As it was, she was just another contender for our father's meager attention.

Ceil's femininity only drew unfavorable comments on my own masculinity. Lenore berated my slacks. "Unbecoming," she'd say. "Your body is maturing at an amazing rate. It's time you begin looking more like a young lady."

My temper would flare and I'd want to shout at her. But

peace at any price. And so I smoldered.

To hell with you, I'd think. Who needs you? This is our house, not yours. What's more, we don't like you. Oh, we'll tolerate you—we have to. I'll show you, not tell you, that I don't need you, that I can take care of myself.

Mom, Mom. Why did you leave us?

Clothes would never make a lady out of me. What was a lady? Not the way she cut her hair, not the clothes she wore.

A lady walked a certain way, talked a certain way. She talked with a soft voice, warm, calm. She condoned behavior that she would not accept in herself, and she did not question the motives of others. She disliked sports, rough-and-tumble encounters. A lady did not like traveling in groups or gangs but preferred one or two good friends. Her preferences in movies were boy-meets-girls and Alice-in-Wonderland fantasies—not the action kind with cops and cowboys or Dead End kids. She was not excited by the thought of serving mass or marching in a band. Certainly she never looked at *blue bibles*, those comics considered dirty in the 1950s—and very educational for any boy who could get his hands on $2.

Many things a young lady would not understand I, Marie, could understand. Definitely, I could not be a girl. And what was I to do about it?

It was spring now and my bike was my escape. Afternoons that I could wheel away, I'd put on my favorite jeans and an old shirt of Dom's and set out on my own. Unfastening my bra, I'd yank it off and stuff it in my pocket. Oh, it was great to feel the breeze blowing through my open shirt. The farther I'd get from home the better I'd feel.

I was trying to carry on my own life. In the interim we'd been taken from the Catholic school and put in public school. No explanation. But we accepted this and, happily, found we liked it better than the other. Most of the teachers were married women and we thought of them as substitute mothers.

As my grades improved my attitudes improved. I began growing out of myself. I joined the band—and the band meant marching in pants, shirt, and tie. It was a whole new world. Mine, a new personality. I could make people laugh or bring on heated discussions simply by asking a question. I was accepted. A born noncomformist, now I was not out of step, for others too were questioning things learned in school. These were not rote lessons, taught to be taken as gospel of God, but as information to be debated. Each student was encouraged to have an open mind and to seek answers and to question the answers.

My leadership qualities were no longer suppressed and my independent thinking was reinforced. Well, I was going to be a doctor someday.

But nothing is perfect. The more I projected at school, the more I was opposed at home: Squabbles with Pa and Lenore were the usual order of any day.

Then one day I noticed blood on the bathroom tissue. *Blood?* What was it? I hadn't hurt myself, I had no pain anyplace. I quickly ran my hands over my developing body, trying to find a sore spot. None. None whatsoever. This was awful, yet it couldn't really be anything. Forget it. I did forget it—until I found blood on the tissue a second time. Could it be caused from the douche nozzle I used in secret as a false penis? No, of course not. I'd been experimenting with the nozzle for a long time now and nothing like this had ever happened.

What would Lenore say? Would she tell Pa? Would Pa somehow know I'd been acting like a male in the bathroom? Well, I couldn't tell either of them. Somehow it would work out.

But it didn't. Next morning the bed was spotted with red. Boy, was I gonna get it now! I'd have to tell Lenore—but what would I say?

I made it simple. "I'm bleeding. I don't feel any pain, I know I didn't hurt myself."

Her calm amazed me. "Don't worry."

"Don't worry? You mean you're not mad at me?"

"Of course not. You're growing into a young lady. Just as I've been telling you."

"I don't understand . . ."

"It happens every month to a woman," she said. "Wait here, I'll be right back."

She reappeared within minutes and handed me several flat

wrapped oblongs. "These are sanitary pads. Place one inside
your panties and change when it's soiled."

"But I don't want anything dirty next to my body."

"Do as I say."

"Yes, ma'am."

"I'll have Ceil pick up a belt and show you how to put it on
this evening."

No yelling about the bed. But toward evening, when Pa
came in, I heard her tell him what had happened. They both
laughed. As if it were the biggest joke in the world, a riot. How
could she tell him such a thing and how could they laugh
about it? I didn't want this messy thing happening to me every
month for the rest of my life, over and over, years on end.

Many mornings these past months I'd gone to school upset.
But nothing compared with my feelings this particular morning, and suddenly I rushed from class and into the washroom.
Miss Graham followed, and, like damned-up waters that break
with the flood, tears ran down my face and onto my blouse and
spilled onto my understanding teacher. She put her arm around
me and I cried even more.

"How can I help you, Marie?"

"I don't know, Miss Graham. It's just that my life is so
mixed up since Mom died. Pa remarried and now I have a
stepmother and I hate her. I hate my stepsister and stepbrother. I don't want to hurt them. They're not mean—it's just
that they've taken over the home that once belonged to us and
to Mom. Pa shows favoritism to them. Pa and my stepmother
insist I wear dresses most of the time. And I hate dresses, hate
dresses! I don't want to be a young lady, I want to stay the way
I am."

"Well, Marie, part of living is growing up. And growing up
isn't easy. Believe me, I remember how it was." She smiled at
me and took my hand in both of hers.

"Are you really my friend, Miss Graham?"

"Try me."

So I told her about the rivalries, the squabbles, the menses,
everything. And, as she listened, I recognized that I was begin-

ning to have a real crush on this pretty, petite teacher. She seemed to understand my needs, my obsession with jeans and shirts, my revulsion at wearing anything ladylike.

She gave me another affectionate hug. "Things will work out for you, Marie. You'll see."

Somehow things *would* work out. I'd *make* them work out.

And then I had a pretty new girl friend, Margaret Anne. She was the only child of her German-born family and lived about three blocks away. I carried her books from school every day and even taught her how to play marbles. And we'd talk about what we'd be when we grew up.

"I want to get married."

"Married?"

"Of course. Don't you want to get married, Marie?"

"No. I'm going to be a doctor."

"That's swell. Me, I want a husband and three kids."

The thought of her marrying anyone angered me. Why couldn't I tell her I wanted to marry her myself?

Things were so bad at home that toward the end of eighth grade it was decided that I would go away to a school run by nuns. Lenore took the offensive: "Maybe they can straighten you out, Marie. I've tried, but I just don't understand you."

Pa pretended it was for my own good. "Maybe they can make a lady out of you."

Shortly before going away to school I overheard Ceil and her friend talking about some boy. "He's a queer."

I didn't know what the term meant and later I asked Ceil about it.

"A queer is someone who plays with himself or loves another boy. Instead of loving a girl, which is normal."

"I didn't know."

"Well, now you do. And that's that."

That's that. I knew my feelings weren't quite right, for my girl friends were boy crazy—and here I was romanticizing about girls. Did this make me a queer in reverse? Maybe I'm like the boy—but no, I can't be because I want to be a boy.

Forget it. I'll have to, there's no one to tell.

The Christine Jorgensen story broke. How people laughed and made cruel jokes about the man who had changed into a woman. But I did not laugh. I only cried inside and started a nightly prayer that someday I, growing into a woman, could be changed into the man I knew I was meant to be.

How had Christine done it? Over and over I read the news stories I'd secreted in my room. He had been a soldier and now *he* was a *she*. Pa laughed louder than anyone. Little did he know. And his jokes seemed crueler even than the others one heard everywhere.

"Imagine going abroad and coming back a broad!" one of Pa's cronies wisecracked.

And the guffaws grew louder and more gross.

As quickly as it began, the public excitement subsided. But not within me. At last I had hope. *There were people like me.* And they were doing something about it. Now I had a plan: I must hurry through school, graduate, make a lot of money, go to Denmark. I'd not tell anyone. I'd simply leave this country as Marie, leave this girl-form in Denmark, return to the States as a man with a new name, and lead a new life.

What about my family? Well, there had to be a way. Never, never would I come back to this block, to this house, and hear the neighbors laughing, see faces peeking out from behind their real lace curtains.

Miss Graham came to dinner the night before I left for school. My family didn't approve of her, perhaps for no other reason than that she provided my safe harbor. They considered her masculine—which she was not. In fact, to me she was the essence of ladyship. However—was it because I was being banished?—my family put on their best manners and the evening passed pleasantly.

I walked my beloved teacher to her car and when we said good-bye she kissed me full on the lips. God, if I could describe the feelings that shot through me when she touched me. My response was a great physical pressure against her, and I was unwilling to let her go when she finally drew away from me. And off she went. I was not to see her again for many years, but we wrote occasionally. Someday I would make love to her!

Neighbors took us to the Greyhound bus and, unexpectedly, Pa hugged me good-bye. So did Lenore. Both of them tried to reassure me by saying I'd be happy in my new school. But I was not to be comforted. I knew I would not be happy. . . . If Mom were with us this would not be happening to me.

"You'll change your mind about a lot of things, Marie." Lenore wanted to make friends with me and perhaps she found it easier now that I was to be tucked away with the nuns.

I was sick to my stomach. The frustrations and fears, the hatreds and the angers were lumped together like so many rocks and lodged there. Why did I have to go?

I was being sent away to a boarding school where they accepted children with only one parent—or so-called displaced children. I was being punished. But why? Because I couldn't act like a lady?

"We'll make a lady out of you," the counselor at Catholic Charities had said. But I didn't want to be a lady! Accordingly, I'd packed extra jeans and my most mannish shirts to prove the point. After all, being a lady was how you felt inside, not how you dressed outside. Lots of pretty girls wore masculine clothes and it added to their femininity.

Nothing was going to change my mind about how I FELT.

The five-hour bus ride was hot and sticky, broken only by a sandwich and soft drink, which my stomach was too queasy to digest. I spent the trip wondering and looking forward to some miraculous achievements that would surely be mine. The picture was blurred, but, somehow, my future would revolve around helping other people. Furthermore, I'd never be mean or hurt anyone!

The bus pulled into the small town where I was to spend the next two years. Looking out of the narrow window, I saw a nun and a young girl waiting, staring back at me. The girl was wearing a uniform: blue skirt and white blouse.

Oh no, I groaned, not uniforms again!

Sister Julian and the girl, Lola, had come to take me to St. Michael's, and, after an exchange of greetings, we sat silently as Sister drove us to the *home*. Passing through this small town, not unlike my own, I noticed the trim lawns and clean-looking houses—a proper lead-in to the immaculate grounds surrounding the solid red brick buildings.

I broke the silence now. "Will I be allowed to help the gardener?"

Lola giggled.

Sister Julian seemed startled at the question. "Oh, no," she said quickly. "The boys do that."

Lola giggled again.

Sister indicated the two three-storied houses at the right of the administration building. "Those are the girls' cottages and you will live there."

"And what is in that building in back?"

"Father Shean has his quarters there. And, of course, our beautiful big chapel. Grade-school classrooms and the gym too —also the kitchen and dining rooms."

"It's all very neat," Lola added. "And that's the laundry in the smaller building. We have a chance to work in the laundry —and in the kitchen—even in the chapel."

She made it sound like special privileges. Big deal.

At the extreme rear we saw a few boys kicking a ball. Sister continued her explanations. Like a grand tour. "The boys play ball here and the local Catholic high school holds football practice here. Over there are the boys' quarters. Off limits to the girls, of course."

Of course? Well, rule or no rule, nothing was going to keep me from going over there at every chance—and nothing was going to keep me from playing baseball with the guys. Even though I should have to pay for it in punishment many times over.

I was proud of my independence, proud of having a mind of my own, of my inquisitive nature, and, yes, even of my inability to stay out of mischief. Competition was good for me. It spurred me to achievement.

I'd been a rebel since childhood, keen on doing the things boys do, and no one was going to change me. Become a lady? I would not! After all, I was going to Denmark just as soon as I'd earned all that money—and then folks would say, "Well, *he* was just a normal boy."

From that first glance I'd disliked the institutional look of the place, and, once inside, even the many pictures of saints did nothing to change my opinion. Not even the life-size oil painting of the bishop. This just wasn't where I wanted to be. I had the sudden impulse to bolt and run away. But to run would solve nothing. I had to graduate to make money to go to Denmark. Yes, I'd have to stick it out.

The name *St. Mary's Hall* was engraved on a small copper plaque at the right of the front door of the second cottage. The door opened without our knocking and Sister David mumbled an inaudible welcome. She was a tall stout woman, without warmth, and her pale skin showed sallow against her black habit and white headgear. She abruptly dismissed Lola and called loudly for Juanita to show me around.

St. Mary's Hall was new and the black tile floors were very shiny. "Why are you staring at the floors?" Juanita asked.

"I was wondering if they are easy to clean."

"It all depends on how you look at it." She looked resigned. "If you don't mind the acrobatics of polishing and waxing— well, who knows? One girl actually thinks it's fun."

"Well, bully for her!"

She looked at me, almost suspiciously, and then a grin of appreciation spread over her small impish face. "Careful!" she warned. But I knew she was on my side.

"How's it done?"

"Like so." She obliged by demonstrating: "You put a soft cloth under your feet, then slide back and forth. Inch by inch."

I wanted to laugh for the first time that day.

We took the stairs directly to the large dormitory on the third floor. "Fifty girls can sleep here."

"Boy!"

Juanita pointed to a bed the far side of center. "Yours."

"Mine." Two years in a room with fifty girls?

"Sh-h-h. See that door?"

"Sure. What about it?"

"It's magical."

"Come on, now."

"Well, that door leads into Sister David's room. It's magical because of what's above it: the two-way mirror."

"But who can see in a mirror way up there?"

"Sister David."

She was teasing me, of course.

"You stand there and tell me that a nun has a mirror in her room?"

"Sister David does. Don't you want to know why?"

"You're the guide, you're expected to know all, tell all."

"Well, this is the way Sister guards the dorm. She can look up and see whether we're asleep, or having a pillow fight. . . ."

Juanita led the way to the washroom. Sinks and toilets and shower stalls.

"Do we shower together—all at once?" Showering with girls was always difficult for me and not only because I did not like what I saw about my own body: I was sexually aware of my partners' nude bodies. Instinctively I'd turn my back, soap up in a hurry and rinse off in seconds, get into my clothes and out of the shower room. Looking back in my more mature years, I was to recognize this as resulting from conditioning at home: from my mother, who tried to teach me modesty, and from my father, who yelled at me to wear tops when I worked with him in yard and garden. How I longed to be a guy who could walk about without a shirt and feel not shame, but pride, in showing off his body. Had society sanctioned women's doffing their clothing, I still would not have been happy with my female equipment.

Juanita was looking at me in a strange way. Could she be reading my thoughts? My face flushed.

"No," she said. "We shower alone."

"Good."

She nodded agreement, no doubt assuming my modesty.

"One time you may be told to work over in the big laundry, another time to polish floors. Oh, there are any number of work details. You do the assignment or else."

"I envision many 'or elses.' . . ."

Again, that impish grin. "Watch it," she advised, sobering.

One thing had pleased me as we'd gone along: Lots of the kids were wearing jeans and shirts. Gosh, was I glad I'd brought mine.

Well, time would tell how it would all work out. . . .

I changed into a navy skirt and white blouse and went with

other girls down the three flights of stairs. The whistle of a bird cheered my spirits as we walked in pairs toward the chapel building that also held the dining rooms.

Accustomed to Italian cooking and its spicy, aromatic seasoning, I found the food here bland. But it was OK. At home I'd hated having only Italian food. Soon I'd have given my eyeteeth for some.

After dinner I was given my assignment for the next week: laundry work. Then I helped with the dishes before going back to the dorm to unpack and talk with the girls.

I learned that homework was not to begin until the opening of the school term and that was still two weeks away. There was ample time for playing girls' games or watching TV. Personal warmth appeared nonexistent. Some kids had brothers and sisters here, but, for the most part, we were lone individuals who came from all over the diocese. I was being regimented and I didn't like it. Still, it was better than all the fighting going on at home.

On the third day I received a letter from Lenore, in which she'd enclosed a picture of Dom's wedding. It was the first time I'd seen a picture of Barbara, the girl he'd married. She was smiling as brides do, and long brown hair curled around her small sweetheart face. Barbara was exactly the kind of girl I'd marry! So warm and kind. My ideal woman. How lucky Dom was. How lucky Dom always was.

I was on kitchen duty the second week and, accidentally, one of the kids spilled scalding milk down my legs. I was hustled off to the infirmary. My stay there kept me out of school the first three weeks of the term, and I'd have been very lonely but for Sister Timothy. She'd stop by and give me encouragement or holy pictures, bring books to read. And, almost always, she'd briefly hold my hand. Surely she could feel my mad pulse racing away, though she gave no sign, for just her touch would excite me.

Tall and slim, Sister Timothy was in charge of pastry-making in the kitchen. Her hands were slender and moved in a quiet way. Her laugh was soft and came quickly and I often wondered what her breasts were like under that big white bib. . . . (That week, on duty, I'd hurried through my kitchen chores and sneaked into the bakery room. Just to sit and watch her. Had she known my feelings, undoubtedly, she would've sent me packing. Reported me as being out-of-bounds.)

Released from the infirmary, I joined my class at Mid-City Catholic High School in town. A modern-day Christ seemed to ascend from the roof, His arms outstretched as if awaiting all who would embrace our faith.

We'd walk into town in the morning, back to the home (an orphanage, really—I knew it now!) at the day's end. Mid-City was liberal in methods of teaching, exciting in many ways. Still, the school stressed discipline, and everyone conformed as much as it is possible for freshmen to conform. I detested the uniforms with long skirts and my long hair and envied the fellows in shirts and jeans with hair cut close.

We were called to class and dismissed by a buzzer. No class started without a short prayer beforehand. And no blackboard was without the protection of a life-size crucifix hanging over it. Both boys and girls held doors for the nuns and secular teachers and stood when one of them entered the room.

The school was staffed mainly by Franciscans, Sisters of Divine Providence, Sisters of Notre Dame, and our own Sisters of the Sacred Heart from St. Michael's Home.

Every sister wore a cincture, or white cord, at her waistline, held with a slipknot. The two ends dangled down the left side. Different orders had different knots in the two ends and each knot had a special meaning. The Franciscans wore three knots on one end to remind them of their vows, first voiced by St. Francis over seven hundred years ago: *poverty, chastity, obedience.* On the other end five knots served as a constant reminder that Christ on the cross suffered five wounds.

Whether to balance the pull of gravity or from a sense of design we could only speculate, but large rosary beads hung from the cincture on the right side. Since the sisters had withdrawn from material things, surely this balance had nothing to do with ornamentation, but, fortunately for us, the beads clattered as our good sisters hurried along, very much like belled cats warning mice at mischief.

We thought of Sisters of the Sacred Heart as being a little more a part of us since we lived together. I was never able to figure out how they held their headgear in place: Was it held on by an invisible rubber band? It came out over the face and tied under the chin and stayed in place as if glued on! Did it protect them from the harassment of man and woman and all their unruly offspring? Were most of them as far removed from worldly things as they appeared to be? Could dedication to their Lord bring them true serenity?

The answers had to be *yes*. This complicated gear served a definite purpose in that it kept the nun looking purposefully ahead, warded off distractions, and helped her in keeping God foremost in mind.

Would the religious life be the life for me? I must think more about it.

But thinking about it consistently wasn't that easy.

Boys and girls went to class together in the huge gym. Here, too, we were to thrill to intramural games during the basketball season—students and teachers, parents and townspeople together. Our secular gym teacher, Miss Henderson, was a masculine type and I patterned myself after her, imitated her mannerisms. She was a great person. And rumors of her personal life fascinated me: Supposedly she lived with a lover, another woman—a teacher.

Little by little I was being caught up in the routine at St. Michael's. I had my infatuations—but not with the girls. No, I was wild about the nuns!

My second crush was on Sister Mathias, who was in charge of the boys' unit. Naturally. I'd risk anything just to spend a few minutes with her. In fact, all the kids liked her but *I*— well, truthfully, I wanted her.

My feelings were more adult now, not as innocent as the autoeroticism of my early years. I wanted to touch, fondle, kiss this sister of God. But this was not to be. Hadn't she, like all nuns, dedicated herself to God? No human was to touch them! I sublimated my feelings, happy just to be around my favored ones.

The atmosphere of the community was a wholesome one. No boy or girl dated just one person. We palled around in groups, doing things together. Our fun and excitement were in trea-

sure hunts, in pajama parties where we sang Christmas carols
in July, and in yelling our heads off after a football or basketball victory as we drove through the sports-oriented town, wav-
ing our school colors.

Although boys and girls both lived at St. Michael's and went
to school together, their quarters were quite separate. This rule
was relaxed for the occasional Sunday dances in the auditorium. Often two girls danced together. Being shy, or not wanting to be called sissies for dancing with girls, the guys would
gather at one end of the hall, leaving the girls at the other,
until the ice was broken.

Dancing was fun. I especially liked dancing with girls but,
peer pressure being what it was even at that age, I danced with
boys too. I never became an Astaire but I did bounce around the
floor to a sentimental tune or two.

It was difficult for me to keep out of trouble. I had a great
yen to play baseball and tag football, and even to run off to the
boys' cottage, where I could talk with Sister Mathias. One day
my own cottage nun, Sister David, became so angry with me
for such an infraction that she slapped my face—at the dinner
table!—in front of all the girls.

I had never liked her and now I blurted out: "You are no
nun in my eyes!"

She lashed back at me: "Suppose you tell me what, in your
eyes, is a nun. Better still, *write it!*"

When it was written, I realized I'd composed an essay that
could have been entitled "What is a Mother?" So I made a
revised copy with this new title and kept it for myself. Some
day I'd show it to the woman I was to marry, the woman who
was to mother my children.

What Is a Mother?

You were born to her physically—or, if adopted, emotionally.

A mother is a person who takes time to understand you, encourage you. She teaches you the rudiments of how to grow up. She
provides you with the ingredients of home life: stability,
warmth, bodily needs of food, spiritual needs of ideals, moral
needs of family. She displays her feelings to you in terms of
hugs and kisses.

Her discipline is strong but tempered with learning. She is not always happy with your ways and lets you know it.

She acts as buffer between you and your father and between you and the outside world.

She does her share of yelling at you but sticks up for you to outsiders, even though she may give you a whack when you get behind your own doors.

She cares what happens to you no matter how old you grow.

When you are young and growing up you put your hand in hers . . .

when she is old she puts her hand in yours.

My outburst, plus essay, did bring a sort of peace pact between us and we seemed to get on better afterward. Even so, I did not forget. I kept thinking I'd like to sock her in the mouth because of the humiliation she'd caused me. On the other hand, the very fact that I'd stood up to this woman made me something of a big shot, even among the guys.

Visits home from school were rare. Soon after the slapping incident I went to see Aunt Concetta and found her waiting, armed with a supply of verbal slaps. She must've been rehearsing since first hearing about my disgrace, and almost immediately the tirade began, ending with that terrible accusation: "You're just like your father!"

Always she'd end any scathing attack with this hated comparison, knowing well that nothing she could say would hurt me more. She'd never liked Pa and now she *hated* him almost as much as I did.

"I will not be compared with my father. He is unfeeling. He never listens."

"Well?"

"Well, I may look like him. But I'm not *like* him. I will never be mean and hurt my children or any of my family."

"But *look at yourself*, Marie. You wear pants—like your pa. You have such pretty naturally curly hair, yet you *prefer* to go to your pa's barber. What *is* this thing with you, Marie?"

"I like boys' clothes better . . ."

"You see? Like your pa."

What could I say?

If I didn't get away from her I'd explode. I made an excuse and took an early bus back to St. Michael's.

Oh, well. So much for family visits.

I had no intention then, or ever, of changing, but I began to concentrate on ways not to be labeled *like your pa*. I resolved to take a greater interest in other people's problems: help where I could, listen, keep an open door for anyone who needed comfort. I must manage to control my temper, erase my own bigotries. Expect more from myself, less from others.

I must, first of all, be in command of myself.

Four of us had been allowed to join the band. Rose played the trombone, of all things. Tim and Jack played tuba and sax, and I played the clarinet. We were called "The Foursome." We practiced long hours. Rose became sweet on Tim, but Jack and I were nothing more than pals.

Being in the band meant going to distant cities and competing in contests: place and show were exciting, winning even more so. What matter that we worked so hard to win.

We drove for about three hours for our final band competition. We'd rehearsed weeks for this appearance and were confident of winning. And win we did! Returning, we sang at the top of our voices, through small cities and towns and on country roads. Victory and applause had gone straight to our heads, leaving us quite giddy.

Back at our cottage, Tim and Jack walked Rose and me to our door and we stood there briefly, still laughing and talking. Suddenly the window above us opened and we saw Sister Steven leaning out. She was substituting for the dour Sister David and momentary fright gave way. Even so we weren't prepared for what she was about to say.

"If you boys are going to kiss those girls, then hurry up about it! It's late—and the girls have to come in." Sister withdrew.

As soon as her wimple was out of sight, Rose and Tim, skilled by practice, fell into a snug embrace and brazenly smooched right before our eyes. And before I knew what was happening, Jack leaned over and quickly kissed my lips.

It should have been a romantic moment, there by the flowering lilac bush in the tender night. But it wasn't anything at all. Neither physically nor psychologically. My first honest-to-goodness kiss on the lips by a boy should have been one of the great moments of my life, according to my peers. Girls were supposed to like this kind of stuff. *Ugh.* Yes, something was wrong: I did not belong in this female body.

Denmark. How long must I wait to change to male?

Having felt nothing from Jack's kiss, I was now more certain than ever that I belonged with that special group of individuals like Christine Jorgensen. I was a person with a *confused identity.* How could I continue living this sort of double life for all the school years ahead?

Denmark seemed a long, long way off. And God was *here.* In Mid-City Catholic High School. In St. Michael's. In all the chapels in which I'd ever prayed. Was the answer *here*? Or in Denmark? . . . .

A wonderful thing happened in my sophomore year: Kathleen Phillips took me to meet her family. The father, Jim, was a railroad man, seldom home. The mother, Martha, filled her life with husband, youngsters, church, and school. As dog-tired as Jim would be on returning home, he'd always join in whatever happenings were going on at the time. They were parents I would have picked for myself.

Kathleen, the first of four daughters, was about my age.

The house was big and the door was never locked to friends, whatever the age, who invariably descended for an hour's visit, a meal, or to sleep over. And weiners never tasted better than those roasted over bonfires we made of autumn leaves that we ourselves had raked and set to match.

Mom Phillips was always doing something for someone. When her children were at home, she was at home—once they were off to school, she was off on her benevolences. Not a Ma Kettle, exactly, but housewifely chores were low on her list of priorities. It seemed the house was always full of teenagers, pre-teens, and dirty dishes. Eventually, a routine did evolve: One set of kids would eat and wash the dishes—then another set with *their* friends.

If our adopted mom ever had a worry, we were unaware of it. But she knew how to listen to our problems. She'd try to understand, to advise. And never sit in judgment. She accepted each of us as we were.

This was home as I envisioned it, and I was to return many times through the years to talk with my second mom and ask her help in solving the insolubles. Any time, day or night, that I came to town I went straight to the Phillipses'. Her welcoming hug and kiss, her nourishing food, her listening ears—all let me know she really cared.

The Phillipses' was a home for all seasons. And this feeling of *going home* was never to leave me.

A surprising thing was happening to me: I was growing closer to the Church. Before the tabernacle I felt comfortable, and there at the altar I poured out my troubled feelings. God was surely there.

God, I'd pray, *give me the answer. Help me, Mother of Jesus. Precious Lord, You have my mom with You—I need both of You.*

My second year at St. Michael's was ending. For the most part, I'd been far happier here than I'd dared hope. I'd started a new phase in my life: making new friends, learning new things, both of which were to exert incalculable influence on my life.

Again, I was alternating between uncertainties: Which direction should I take? Should I stay here and graduate with my class? Or should I take my last two years at an aspirancy (a convent school for girls who want to become nuns)? I spent more time before the altar—I talked often with Mom Phillips —and then decided on the convent school. I sought out the social worker, who made arrangements for me to enter Mt. St. Mary's Aspirancy the following semester.

But now there was the senior prom to think about.

A mere sophomore, *I* was invited to the senior prom by a fellow who was to graduate cum laude. Virtually a hermit by peer standards, Chuck Marvin socialized almost not at all and I assumed that he was being pressured into going. What to do? I'd feel awkward and uneasy—still this was the first time anyone from St. Michael's had ever been asked to a prom. I'd been singled out for distinction, and now the nuns showed an unusual interest in me and instructed me as to what to wear and how to act.

The thought I hated most was tramping around in those high heels. What if I were to stumble and fall, embarrass the fellow and me? To fall—well, that would shatter my image back at St. Michael's. For once, *and only this once*, I'd try to act like a lady. There were weeks ahead to prepare, so I paid more attention to the infrequent Sunday dances and resolved not to fall flat on my face at this prestigious affair.

Chuck was a tall, bespectacled guy of about eighteen. Between his shyness and my reluctance we made quite a pair. Chuck looked like a young professor in his rented tux, correct white carnation in his lapel. And I, for once, slightly resembled a girl: My hair had been carefully styled and my borrowed ankle-length black dress slimmed down my appearance. The dress was sleeveless, closing at the top with tiny pearl buttons, and silver sequins decorated the lower part of the skirt. Not wanting to own a formal, I'd borrowed this from a girl who'd since gone into a convent.

Having never wanted to act like a girl, I now felt like a fool. How was I to play this new role? Well, no one was going to say I didn't try.

I almost cringed when Chuck took my elbow and escorted me to his family's car, polished and gleaming for this gala evening—and when he opened the door for me I supposed it was to keep me from soiling my long white gloves.

We arrived at the gym, now transformed into a ballroom, and then, almost before I realized what was happening, Chuck was guiding me over the dance floor. He knew just what to do! But he held me too close—was it from nervousness?—and I could feel the outline of his boyish body.

How would it feel to dance this close to a woman? I envied him for everything he was and I was not.

"You're quite light on your feet," he said, after a long pause.

"Thanks, Chuck. You're doing all right, yourself."

And so the evening passed. I had the feeling Chuck was as relieved as I was to see it end. We'd both worked at carrying this through, we'd done what was expected of us.

We small-talked on the way back to St. Michael's. "It's back to the books for me. Lots to do before college this fall."

"It's the aspirancy for me. I'm going to become a nun."

"Why, Marie—well, you'll make a good nun."

At the cottage door he lightly kissed my cheek, said thank you and good night.

I went inside and closed the door behind me. And the door became symbolic: I was closing the world behind me—I would become a nun. A good nun.

3

Secondary Education

The convent would solve all inner conflicts. I said it over and over until it became a prayer. Eventually my religious feelings would master my carnal body and convince me that I was not unlike other girls.

I wanted to become a Franciscan and pattern myself after St. Francis, founder of the order. Hadn't he scourged his body and rid it of all sexual urgings? And, in so doing, he had risen above mortal self and become a saint. I would never be a saint —but, with God's help, surely I could purify my soul and consecrate my life to Christ and the world's poor.

In the religious life there would be no thought of parenthood: This, in itself, would be a major resolution. After all, I could never be a mother and the role of father was denied me.

As I approached Mt. St. Mary, my decisions made, my emotions were far different on this hot August day from what they'd been exactly two years ago. Then I'd hated the idea of being sent to St. Michael's, today I was filled with anticipation of a school of my own choosing. Today I was happy to be met by a nun and a student, knowing that I was to be housed with other girls who aspired to the nun's life.

Sister Veronica, rotund and maternal, and the student, Maggi, introduced themselves and we happily conversed about Mt. St. Mary as we went directly there.

Everything about its environs was suggestive of a purity of heart and mind, servitude to God. A silent peace. The serenity of the two hundred acres implied a withdrawal from a tumultuous world and, more specifically, from the materialistic Midwestern city we'd left behind.

The acreage was miraculously colored: blossoms hugging the ground and climbing up onto shrub and vine, fruit trees, many already harvested, old oaks and stately maples and black walnut trees.

"We're very proud of our farm," Sister said. "We tend our garden, our flowers, our orchards. We prepare our tomatoes, potatoes, carrots, peas and beans, squash, beets, berries, and melons for the big freezers in our cellar. We make jams, jellies, and juices. Nothing is wasted. And we're almost entirely self-sufficient."

"Some day, I'm sure," Maggi added, "our sisters will find a use for skins discarded in jellying and juicing." She seemed pleased with the idea, and Sister and I laughed with her.

Sister Veronica pointed toward the small barn. "Three cows and some hundred chickens are sheltered there. We supply our own milk and cream, make our own butter and cheese. The chickens provide eggs and Sunday dinners."

Momentarily I had a flashback to Grandma Thomas, grabbing a chicken by its neck and dancing spasmodically while ringing off the head. Nausea threatened to engulf me—but no, I refused to think about it. The sisters must have perfected a more humane method.

Maggi mistook my distress. "Don't look so shocked. We girls don't work in the barn."

"Oh, no. Indeed not. Three sisters, retired from their teaching and cooking and nursing, are in charge here. They milk the cows, tend the butter- and cheese-making, care for the chickens."

I asked about the cemetery at one side of the garden.

A beatific smile brightened Sister's rosy round features. "This is the final resting place for every nun who ever lives here and serves the community. It's also a sort of private place to be alone, to pray or reflect on the ways of life."

Our circuitous route had taken us to the aspirancy. The door opened at the first ring and a tall sister welcomed me with a warm embrace. "Bless you, my child! We hope you'll be happy here."

She took me to a large waiting room. Its blinds partially drawn, with flowers in glass vases and floors sparkling with years of hand-applied wax, the room seemed cool in spite of the August humidity. Even Sister seemed cool and unaffected by soaring temperatures, though I was drenched with perspiration.

Two older students took my bags to my curtained cubicle, called a cell. One left on another errand, and Patricia quietly told me about our surroundings and her own ambitions.

At Mt. St. Mary's High School, ours was the challenge of achievement, and assistance was always available. Patricia, a senior, had taken her first three years at The Mount and was looking forward to graduation in June. Outside she indicated The Motherhouse.

"Just think. I'll have waited four years to be moving there. First, I'll be a postulant, next a novice and working toward the status of junior professed nun, eventually senior professed nun. After my first vows of poverty, chastity, and obedience—as a junior professed—it's out into the field to work as a nun." She was filled with the excitement of it.

"I have two whole years to wait before becoming a postulant," I told her.

We saw several young girls and nuns walking about the gardens, and two were coming separate ways from the cemetery. Everyone talked quietly or not at all. Mostly one heard leaves brushing together, birdsong, the whir of insect wings.

"The grounds are not always silent. We have recreation periods and all groups play volleyball, baseball, or badminton. Lots of fun and fellowship. Laughing and cheering. Sometimes we have social hours and discuss things that go on in the convent or we sew and mend."

Glass doors separated our floors from the rest of the building. Only with special permission were we to pass through these doors. Groups mixed only on rare occasions, special holy days and Christmas.

"We are never to speak to the nuns, other than those in administration or teaching. Nor can the nuns speak to us. However, from the recreation room or dining room on the first floor, we can watch as they pass by."

"And dream of the day when we can be watched."

"Yes. Life beyond the wall."

It had a nice sound. Frightening, too, in a way. . . .

Despite the regimentation, people seemed happy here and spontaneous peals of laughter and giggles were commonplace during our leisure hours. The atmosphere was conducive to an ordered coexistence.

A typical student day began at six o'clock. The morning's silence was broken only by the ringing of a bell and then resumed for another two hours. Silence was to teach self-control and encourage meditation. We were expected to be in the chapel for Mass at six forty-five, where even the seating was doled out according to rank: first, the elderly professed sisters living out their years at The Motherhouse—then the senior professed, junior professed, novices, postulants, aspirants. In that sequence. It would take years for us to work our way up to the glory of front row!

Breakfast at seven-thirty. And still the silence, which continued until we left for classes at nine o'clock. Even then, no talking in the halls or the dorms in consideration of others who might be in meditation.

We had lunch promptly at twelve, then an hour's break at twelve-thirty: to walk in the garden, go to chapel, stop at one of the outdoor grottoes, catch up on homework, or write letters. The time was ours and it was our responsibility to see that it was used to best advantage. Again, classes until four o'clock, free time until supper at five-thirty. Free, that is, if we didn't have sewing duty or work in the garden. Each was assigned her turn.

After that first month I began to feel at home. Furthermore, I was now convinced my decision to come to The Mount was the right one. Here I would surely find the fulfillment that had earlier eluded me. Maybe Dad had been right all along.

The aspirants were bent on being nice to each other, and no one worked at it more diligently than I, Marie Martino. If this was to be life's calling, then I'd be good at it, just as I'd promised Chuck that night which now seemed so long ago.

We were discouraged from attaching ourselves to any one student, yet five of us palled around and in time we became known, not without affection, as "Marie's Marauders." If ever there was the smallest trouble to get into, we did. Nothing of a serious nature. And, after gentle reprimands, the sisters smiled at our antics.

The sisters here were like St. Francis in their compassion for human frailties. Instead of rebuking me, Sister Clement complimented me: "You must remember, Marie, that leadership can be a fine thing when properly channeled. Only misdirected can it be lethal."

My main complaint at The Mount was the change in personal appearance: My hair was growing longer and curlier and I had no say in the matter, for it was cut only when Sister Clement thought it should be cut. My hemline dropped to six inches from the tops of my black Red Cross shoes. How I missed my slacks and shirts, my old loafers and barbered hair!

Nor did I like the house assignments. I'd hate to dust and clean all the days of my life. How could woman's work strengthen my desire to work with the poor? I wanted to serve God. Perhaps I wanted too much on my own terms.

Was woman's work to be one of the thorns in my crown?

"Marie, can't you put your great spirit into learning to sew?" Sister Clement recognized my reluctance to answer as an indication that I'd level with her. She tried again. "Won't you try?"

"For you, Sister, I'll try."

I did try. I worked and prayed to squelch every vestige of my rebellion. And failed.

Oh, the reprieve of dressing in the costume of St. Francis at the Halloween party and unlocking the emotions pent up in having had to conceal my masculinity. It was great to be told that I actually looked like a man. So there it was: the too mannish walk, the long stride. . . . The sadness of the morrow was in reverting to shorter, more feminine steps—with frequent lapses of memory—and to the long hemline and Red Cross shoes.

By Thanksgiving I was assimilated into the routine of The Mount. I liked my classes and was making good grades, including a midterm A in Latin.

Surely Christmas in a convent must come as close to heaven as most of us can imagine that divine state. At no other time was there such warmth and openness among us at Mt. St. Mary. As my family had done at home, we began preparations the day after Thanksgiving. Now we had entrée to the big kitchen to help with cake- and cookie-baking and corn-popping for tree decorations. We spent hours at choir practice for the midnight mass and filled leisure hours with carols and songs of Christmas. Even Marie's Marauders went into rehearsal with a special song for the great Mass.

I was growing very fond of Karen, one of my Marauders. She came from my home state and we talked about our families, former schools and teachers, and our goals. She wanted to teach nursing. And I'd finally settled on becoming a nurse, since the Franciscans did not educate their sisters as doctors. But for my new resolutions—and the circumstances under which we lived—I should have developed a crush on this slip of a girl. A crush was something I must now religiously avoid.

How tenaciously I'd clung to and lived by my resolves. I could not let them disintegrate in this holy season.

During Advent, the period between Thanksgiving and Christmas, we were expected to make little sacrifices for each other. For one week Karen polished my shoes and I made drawings for her. She said she'd never be the artist I was, and I declared my shoes had never been as shiny as they now were.

Never could any Holy Season have been more lovingly observed. In honor of His Birth, we were allowed to have recreation with the postulants, the novices, the junior and senior professed, and all the sisters who lived there. We shared with them and they with us, giving us small glimpses into their privileged lives. Our exchanged gifts were all self-made and loving.

I designed a little book of spiritual poems for Karen and made drawings for the cover and each individual page. Some of the poetry I copied from books but most of it was of my own composition. The little handmade book was my masterpiece!

Christmas Eve. The buzzer alerted us at eleven o'clock, after less than two hours' sleep. We got up in silence and dressed quickly. The glass partitions, which had separated aspirants from other groups, were open now, and, each carrying a lighted candle, we joined the procession. The chapel was radiant with more light than we'd ever seen there. The organ melodies had greater significance.

We proceeded down the aisle and approached Mother General enthroned before the altar. Kneeling, we kissed the slim gold band on the third finger of her left hand: the band that symbolized her marriage to Christ. And then we moved on to the left of the altar to genuflect and view the manger scene. Surrounded by family and lambs and angels, the Christ Child lay in his crudely hewn crib.

Mass began with all voices raised in song and praise of the Babe whose Birth we were celebrating. Communion followed. It was during this part of the service that I discovered in my prayer book the little gift from Karen: a small photograph of herself pasted onto the back of a holy picture and, with it, a note urging me to become one of the best Franciscans the Founder had ever envisioned. How I longed for this to come about, not only because Karen wanted it, but because I'd promised myself and all those who believed in me. Why, then, this conflict between spirit and body? And *here? In our chapel?*

Why must I be plagued with these thoughts? Did any of the others at The Mount feel this way? Well, I'd no way of knowing, for certainly it was not a question one asked.

I must spend more time in prayer. . . .

Snows were heavy in that part of the country and the first fall was like a gentle coverlet over our sanctuary. I felt spiritually cleansed.

Shoveling fresh snow from pathways was invigorating. I liked the crunch underfoot, I liked walking in an evening of lightly falling starry flakes with the cold air stinging. I even

liked the snowballs "marked" with my name and retaliated by
"marking" a few of my own for friendly offenders. We were all
striving for sainthood, but we hoped to be forgiven the rare
transgressions as long as they were without malice.

I'd come from a long rambling walk that cold evening and
anticipated a sound sleep. But about three o'clock I woke and
went to the bathroom—and there was Karen. We stood wash-
ing our hands and suddenly we did the unspeakable: We
spoke. We broke silence. It was only a whisper, but we were
guilty of breaking one of the strictest house rules. What
sparked such a breach I cannot recall.

Having broken one rule, the second was easy. I didn't even
care as I walked Karen back to her cubicle and went inside
with her, knowing full well such entry was strictly forbidden. I
was aroused at seeing Karen in her nightgown, and I wanted to
caress and hold her close. But I didn't go that far. Instead,
once she slipped into bed, I leaned down and kissed her cheek.

"Sleep well," I whispered and returned to my own cubicle.
For the first time since I'd come to The Mount, I masturbated.

I was not happy with what I'd done: breaking the silence,
walking Karen to her cubicle and entering it, kissing her cheek.
And, the final indignity, my own self-indulgence. Even so,
unhappy as I was and knowing my desires were sinful, I wanted to do the same things all over again.

Several days passed before I told Karen I'd meet her again. I
willed myself to stay awake that night and for many nights in
weeks to come. Our encounter never varied, ending with the
kiss on the cheek and the whispered "sleep well," return to my
own cubicle, the indulgence of sexual satisfaction.

Nothing stays the same for long. A relationship goes either
forward or back. My kisses became bolder as I held her respon-
sive body in my arms. Sometimes I thought perhaps she was
even more naïve than I imagined, perhaps she knew nothing
about sexual satisfaction.

With the fresh breath of spring I sensed a new vitality within myself but was alarmed at Karen's listlessness. It was as if
her own life was ebbing out and replenishing the earth. She
was always tired. And I grew uneasy.

Sister Clement asked me to come to her office. As kindly as was her custom, she said she knew what was happening between Karen and me. Sister too had noticed the change in Karen and had drawn from her a reluctant admission.

"Marie," Sister began, "ours is a program to train young girls who aspire to become brides of Christ. To fully dedicate ourselves we must discourage special friendships and attachments. We've no wish to force girls to become nuns, nor do we ever do so. The choice must be theirs, and theirs alone, and they must be happy in making it.

"Young women come here because they want to and they stay only after they've proven themselves to the community."

"I know this, Sister. And this was my choice."

"I'm sure of these things, Marie. However, I've discussed this friendship with Mother General and we've decided it would be better for you to seek some vocation in life other than a religious one." This must have been painful for her and she paused briefly.

"You plan to become a nurse. This would seem right for you. You're outgoing and have a true feeling for mankind. It seems to us that you could never be happy behind convent doors."

My words would not come.

"Karen has left a week early for her Easter vacation at home and you'll not see her again. If you leave next week we hope it will cause you the least heartache."

She studied me intently, then weighed her words as if not to hurt me too deeply. "Perhaps you have a problem we cannot help you with. But there is one thing you must remember: You have much to offer the world and you must accept the challenge."

My problem? Father in Heaven! Had she, in her unworldly wisdom, sensed it? Suddenly, my whole world was falling, closing in around me.

"Thank you, Sister. I'll not forget."

"Your teachers have been advised that you'll be leaving. They do not know the reason, nor will they. Only Mother General and I know. In the convent we do not ask questions. It has been arranged for you to finish your junior year at home, with lessons sent back and forth between you and your teachers. Your grades are excellent and we're sure you'll pass with flying colors. Your records will indicate that you finished the term at Mt. St. Mary's."

The conference had ended. And with it the happiest days I'd known. She took my hand now. "Marie, I'm truly sorry this has happened. I will pray for you. Pray that God will be ever good to you."

I felt guilty. I had failed in controlling my mind and body as I'd sworn to myself to do. It hurt to know that my unbridled passions had caused Karen such humiliation, yet it helped to know she would be allowed to return: She was a student of three years' standing, and this was her first serious infraction.

I could never forget Sister Clement's kindness and the masterful way in which she'd handled this awkward situation. It was characteristic of the manner in which she ordered her life and guided the lives she touched. Three weeks later she died of a heart attack.

My father must have been told why I was sent home, but at no time did he ever make reference to it. I almost loved him for this. There was less tension now, for my stepbrother had married and moved out and my stepsister had a job and active social evenings. So I settled down and worked at adjustment, continued with my classes by correspondence and finished the term with a B average.

Determined to be on my own, I took an apartment and a job in the city that summer. It was something of a surprise that Dad did not protest my plans, and this added to the pleasure of my going. I settled in just across the street from Aunt Concetta and was elated with my new independence. The small bedroom with bath and kitchen facilities was even more than I'd hoped for.

My luck held in that I found work as a nurses aide in the operating room of a large hospital. The salary was a fortune in my eyes. The extra money, plus a switch to the night shift (come September), meant I could enroll in St. Kevin's High School for Girls and finish my senior year right on schedule.

I'd already completed most of the required classes, and my extra credits entitled me to fill my schedule with elective courses. I could skip gym, study art appreciation and typing, and have time left over to earn additional money.

I taught catechism to parish children after school and on Sundays. On Saturdays, I worked with a group of nuns who managed a home for the elderly. Was this hand-washing of a sort? Well, just possibly it was a penance, but it gave me pleasure.

During the summer months I learned my new duties at the hospital and something of the doctors' routine and was elevated to the position of "circulating technician." I was properly impressed with such a high-sounding title, though actually I was little more than a glorified maid: handing gauzes and the like to the scrub nurse and hanging up the used sponges, making sure none were left inside the patient. I learned the names of surgical instruments and how to sterilize them and repack them for the next case and how to transfer patients back to their rooms.

All new and very, very exciting! Some of the doctors were world-renowned, and it was a privilege to watch their dexterity. There was only one disadvantage in changing to night shift: Had I stayed on days, I would have been allowed to scrub and hand instruments directly to the surgeons, a task that had to be postponed for now.

We worked in twos during the night hours and my co-worker was Irma Matthews, R.N. She was pleasant enough but seldom smiled. I asked why she was unhappy.

"What is there to be happy about?"

"Oh, the world is full of things. For one, we're here in this hospital, taking care of the sick, helping them to get well."

She was unimpressed. "You're very young."

The subject was closed.

Little by little Miss Matthews's disillusions came out: "Life has dealt me many bitter blows." The down lines tensed at the corners of her mouth.

There was really nothing that pleased her except infrequent visits with a faraway brother and sister-in-law and their small son. "They are my only joy," she would say, with slight change of expression.

Miss Matthews had come to this hospital fifteen years ago, had always worked the night shift, and lived in the nurses' dorm (which we flippantly referred to as "Menopause Manor"). She seemed to have no close friends. I wanted to get to know her and be a friend, but she wasn't concerned about anything except working without fuss.

She softened considerably when I said I was finishing at St. Kevin's. "Then you'd better take a break when we aren't busy. A little shut-eye never hurt the best of us."

Despite this unexpected kindness, she made no attempt to hide her displeasure when I joined the nurses who worked in the twenty-four-hour recovery room. Perhaps these bright new graduates with more modern ideas were a threat to her. They lent me their books, invited me to their dorm and out for pizza. As much as I wanted to discuss all these things with Miss Matthews, I was careful not to, dreading her sullenness. Her sulks made for a long night.

Since leaving Mt. St. Mary I no longer felt guilt because of my masculine desires, and, although I concealed these feelings, my pleasure at being with girls slightly older was increased because I regarded them in the same way as any other male would have done. Admiring them in their neat uniforms or in various stages of undress, I relished their rehash of dates: what the guy did and said, what the girl did and said and why, how they turned a guy on, how they turned him off. Their likes and dislikes. I tucked multiple observations into one corner of my mind and would one day (when I became a *man!*) reexamine them in deciding how to treat a woman. Now was a time for pigeonholing what I saw and heard. And for thinking about Denmark.

It must have been about five o'clock, for the sun was just beginning to color the morning. I went to the window and looked down into the courtyard. A man's body was sprawled there, soaked in its own blood, arms and legs awry. My God! Someone had taken this way out. A priest appeared almost miraculously, knelt down, and pushed the matted hair away from the forehead to anoint while giving last rites.

There was no concentrating in classes that day. I kept seeing the body, lifeless as an unattended puppet, and by the last period I was so unnerved I had to leave typing class. Rita, my best friend at St. Kevin's, was excused from school and took me home, put me to bed, set the alarm for me to go to work and lightly kissed me on the cheeks. And then she left.

Rita, Rita. Don't tempt me. Memories of the past year still haunted me and I'd promised myself I would not give in again, if only for the sake of the girl.

I'd quieted down by next day and took a red rose to Rita with note attached: "Thanks for the help . . . I really needed it."

Our friendship was intact. Friendship, nothing more. That was the way it was going to be.

It was because of Rita that I went to my second prom. She was full of hopes for a foursome and planned that we would ride in her boyfriend's car. I was indifferent. It was customary for each girl to invite a boy, but I could think of no one to ask.

"Marie, you're crazy. In a hospital with all kinds of young interns and residents—and you don't know anyone to ask?"

"Do you think a resident would go to a senior prom?"

"He'd love it!"

"Well . . ."

I tried to determine the least likely to turn me down and finally decided on Ernie, an anesthetist. He was here from the Philippines and sometimes joined us for coffee on weekends. A fun kind of guy, one who danced at every chance, if only to a jukebox. He was like a brother—there'd be no need to fight him off. (Tuck that in your mind, fella, I told myself: Be like Ernie with girls.)

Ernie said yes.

Aunt Concetta's pleasure was a happy bonus. Early in the school year she'd talked to me about boys: "My dear, I worry about you. It's unnatural for an attractive young girl not to date."

Anything to avoid the issue. "Please. Lots of girls aren't dating. Besides, I like to go in mixed groups."

"Well enough in the past, but now it's time you start looking around."

My aunt was all fluttery with the news as she spread it around the neighborhood. "Marie is going to the senior prom.

And you'd never guess her escort."

"Luke, that nice delivery boy from the grocery," someone offered.

"Delivery boy! My dear well-meaning friend. Luke's a lovely boy, I'm sure—but he's not for Marie. Oh no, not that choosy one. It's that nice Dr. Ernie at the hospital!"

"A doctor? Dear me. . . ."

Aunt Concetta preened.

As the preparations began, I sometimes thought she was getting more out of this than I was. Still, I was the one who'd have the evening with Rita. So, while I thought about this bewitching girl, Aunt Concetta babbled about what I'd wear.

"Of course you must have a dress made."

"Can't we borrow one?"

"I've already inquired. There isn't one for blocks around. That is, not one grand enough for a senior prom."

"As you say."

"You'll need a wrap, of course. I know you'll take care of it, so I'm lending you my white shawl with the silver threads."

"But you so seldom wear it yourself, Aunt Concetta. You always say you're saving it for something special."

"And what is more special than a senior prom?"

On the day of the prom Rita styled my hair and curled it in a becoming way and insisted I use rollers to keep in the set. How do women sleep in such damned contraptions?

Well, sleep was out of the question. After a brief rest I tugged on a borrowed girdle and crammed my feet into new silver high heels, which my aunt had forced me to buy. And then I wriggled into the tight-bodiced formal with the bouncy overskirt, a light blue-lavender. A perfect match for the three orchids Ernie had sent that afternoon.

Playfully, Rita dabbed "Evening in Paris" behind my ears and on my wrists. "It's romantic," she whispered.

The boys came early: Bob ill at ease, Ernie the dapper one. Even as he pinned the orchids on my shoulder he kept his cool, and one would've thought he'd been pinning corsages on girls for as many years as he'd been administering anesthetics before surgery. Poor Ernie—the doctor who was crazy about danc-

The rustle of chiffon over taffeta didn't delight me. I'd rather have been in a tux, taking a girl I was crazy about.

ing—and I'd neglected to tell him I'd never advanced beyond the two-step I'd learned in my sophomore year.

Aunt Concetta hovered. She arranged her white shawl around my shoulders, careful not to disarrange the orchids. She saw us to the door, kissed Rita and me, and vigorously shook hands with the two young men, cautioning them to look out for other drivers. "It's always the other car, you know."

Although I did not look back, I felt her eyes following us from behind her lace curtains until our car turned the corner and headed toward the country club.

We walked carefully inside the clubhouse, not quite sure of ourselves, and were all eyes as we tried to absorb in one evening the elegant atmosphere taken for granted by the privileged few. So this was the way of the other half.

Speculation on life-styles ended abruptly with one look at the girls. They had been transformed. Eye-poppers! Like rows of beautiful dolls. All my old feelings came back and, God, how I wished I were here with the guys, *as a guy*, in a tux. Would I give Rita something to dance about!

I dispelled these disturbing emotions and concentrated on Ernie and my friends. All generosity, I told Ernie to feel free to dance with any of the girls while Rita and I sat out a few for girl talk. Everyone looked happy—it was a night to be remembered for all the years to come. And I was doing my part.

Lucky boy, that Bob! Rita was the ultimate in feminine appeal as she lightly touched his wrist or tripped her fingers along his coat sleeve in a small flirtatious way, fluttering and lowering her sooty lashes when he whispered little sweetnesses in her ear. How I envied Bob. I didn't want to witness all this. It was a private thing, it tore me apart, yet I could not look away. Then Ernie came back and glided me out onto the dance floor.

After the prom we went to a nightclub for drinks. I was no more adept at drinking than dancing, but it was fun to prolong the evening, to talk and people-watch. Ernie was having a good time, as were Bob and Rita.

The hours passed into early morning and no one ever suspected my ambivalence. My senior prom had been a success.

Ernie was even brighter than I'd thought, for he made no attempt to kiss me good night at my apartment house. We talked for a few minutes and he thanked me for a great party.

"You're a good sport, Marie."

"Thanks. But not nearly so good a one as you."

We chuckled over nothing in particular, then Ernie went back to the waiting car.

Ah-h-h! Blessed relief to kick off the high heels and wiggle my toes again. And off with the girdle. I swiped at the lipstick, feeling almost profane from its blotch.

Why was I like I was?

Before graduation I'd applied for nurses training at a small Catholic hospital a hundred miles or so from my hometown and was accepted. The Franciscans who managed it were of a different order than those at the aspirancy and I felt certain my disgrace was unknown to the sisters at the hospital. To train as a nurse was the realization of one goal, and I was eagerly anticipating the move.

At commencement, we posed for father-daughter snapshots and, for the very first time, Dad seemed actually proud of me. That day it was easy to put aside the old angers and know a certain security in his show of affection.

During the summer I continued my work in the operating room. Nurses in the recovery room helped me in mastering blood pressures and pulses. As if to establish the fact that I was growing up, I began smoking, a habit of which my father did not approve. Nor did he condemn me. And so we had occasional homey times together, Dad with his long black cigars and I with the more ladylike cigarettes.

4

Sister Mary Dominick

It had become a pattern, going from one Catholic institution to another, being met by a nun and a student. But this time there was a difference: I was entering nurses training. Now I was going strictly on my own and being met by no one, flagging a cab at the station and arriving in what I considered style.

Sister Mary Jerome, Director of Nurses, was advised of my arrival, and I was taken to her office immediately. She welcomed me warmly and quite officially and gave me a copy of the school's rule book. One of her assistants measured me for uniforms, and another escorted me to the dormitory.

"The door is locked at ten-thirty," my escort announced. "And I mean locked. No one can sneak in—or out!—after that hour because a buzzer automatically goes off."

"Well," I said lightly, "there must be a way to get around that. I wouldn't be at all surprised but what ways have always been discovered and will continue to be."

She laughed at the idea. "Girls have tried, perhaps a very few have succeeded. But a bit of warning: One must walk past Sister Mary Jerome's room—and it's reported that she's a light sleeper."

I resolved to put it to the test. Not now, of course, but whenever. . .

Immaculata Hospital was in a quiet little town, situated in a large white middle-class residential area. A Catholic college was within walking distance. The community was distinguished by its absence of bars and honky-tonks or anything remotely sinful. The only scandal that had threatened to blight this almost impenetrable stronghold in the last ten years had to do with a nun. The rumor was that she'd run off and married.

I concluded that all institutions administered by nuns were much the same: the highly polished floors, quiet halls, cliques of giggling girls, strict discipline—and nuns who seemed to catch anyone who tampered with regulations or invented mischief.

Mary Grace Hinkenberry was my roommate. She giggled all the time, even in class, without reason. Nervousness? Well, she was making me nervous too. And her laziness in cleaning and keeping order in our shared room almost drove me up the wall: Half-eaten fruits, cookie and cracker crumbs, empty Coke bottles, what-have-you—rather, what-had-she—littered her side.

Our favorite classroom was the anatomy lab and Old Herman was our favorite subject. A human skeleton, he hung on a spring suspended from the ceiling and danced and jumped at our command, doing whatever we wanted him to do.

The only sobering thought was that once, long ago, Old Herman had been just like us—that is, he had walked and talked, laughed at improbable stories, eaten and drunk, undoubtedly loved, slept, and experienced the range of human emotions. He must have been an exceptional human being because in his last will and testament he donated himself to medical education. As the months went by we thought less and less of Old Hermie's demise and accepted these remains as the contribution of a charitable man. Perhaps he too had studied medicine or toyed with the idea of pursuing it. Very likely he'd understood the caprices of youth and somewhere, in spirit, he chuckled with us as we jiggled his bones for our own irreverent amusement.

Old Herman played a prominent role in our pranks, and one could have spelled the end of our days in nurses training.

Shortly after twelve-thirty that Friday night we deposited Old Hermie on the toilet seat in the last stall, knowing Mary G.'s habit of stumbling along half asleep to the john and knowing that she always went into that stall. And always at about one o'clock.

A nurses cap on his poor skinless head, one set of finger bones clamped over a cigarette, the other set posed as if to turn the music roll, Old Herman was ready for my unsuspecting roommate.

In darkened rooms we waited until, almost as if on cue, Mary G. made her nightly pilgrimage. And then, as we heard her unearthly shrieks, we jumped out at her from behind our doors, convulsed with laughter.

At that precise moment Sister Mary Jerome appeared and switched on the light, taking in the whole scene. Now we, the perpetrators, went into shock: Had we carried this mischief beyond the realm of innocence?

The expression on Sister's face seemed to say she knew every mischief we could possibly think of—quite possibly a few private ones, for once upon a time she too had been a student. "Now that Old Herman has accomplished all that you expected of him, don't you think it would be the considerate thing to see that he gets home safely?"

She left as abruptly as she'd come, not waiting for our excuses, and we could find nothing to say as we watched her ample six-foot frame glide with dignity down the hallway to her own door.

Still, I needed something more than pranks. An attachment. Linda, lovely and Irish, warmed my heart, and it seemed only natural that we should pair off together. She too liked to study, and she could hit as mean a baseball as I ever could—yet she was pretty and ladylike. Her femininity was the magic link.

Study hours were eight-thirty to ten o'clock and, since we were not confined to our rooms, I spent many evenings with Linda at her roommate's desk. Pam, the roommate, studied

with her special friend. It was upsetting to have Linda talk
about her engagement. Hearing the details, I suddenly desired
Linda more than anything in the world.

One evening I stayed on in her room until lights were out
and she'd crawled into bed and then we kissed each other
fondly on the cheek. If she happened to be in my room at bedtime it was Linda who tucked me in and sometimes even gave
me a backrub. Remembering my experience at The Mount, I
saw to it that our relationship did not advance beyond this
stage, and apparently it meant nothing more than a close
friendship to Linda. To me, it was almost pure heaven.

Being elected president of my class added to my self-confidence. My progress was not lost on dear Sister Scholastica,
who gave individual time to each student in her charge.

Sister seemed completely happy with her religious life and
inspired students with similar leanings to enter the convent.
She believed I fell into this pattern and, on several occasions,
she said to me: "Christ needs people like you."

It was obvious that the sisters at Mt. St. Mary had indeed
concealed my shameful secret of failure.

"But, Sister, I am not nun material. And I'm always getting
into hot water—along with Old Herman."

She twinkled at that old glint in my eye. "You are innocent
in the ways of the real world, Marie. And Christ wants the
unspoiled heart."

Oh, Sister, little do you know, I thought. I lowered my eyes
in contrition, hoping it was not mistaken for humility—and felt
like a hypocrite.

Perhaps Sister was right. Perhaps she saw things in me
which pointed toward the convent. But my confusion about
myself? Why couldn't I have opened up to her: told her what
happened at The Mount, told her that more than anything else
I wanted to be a *man*?

I concentrated more on prayer at daily Mass and asked God
for a sign. Was the religious life the answer? Could my mixed
emotional feelings be exorcised by holy rituals behind the
wall? Would I find peace?

After four months of training, we were in uniform and actu-

ally working in the hospital. I felt a renewed sense of accomplishment.

A group of us from the medical unit had voluntarily fore-
gone the usual weekend leave. We'd started in this unit only
yesterday, and I (considering myself slightly more experienced)
had made a real booboo. We were laughing about it now.

I'd goofed on one of my first assignments, a simple backrub.
The rub went fine and the male patient was relaxed from the
alcohol rub and massage and waiting for the talcum to finish
off the job. I reached into the bedside table drawer, pulled out
a can, and liberally sprinkled his back and buttocks. Something
wasn't quite right: The talc had a peculiar odor, more like pep-
permint—certainly unlike the more sterile scent of hospital
standard. Examining the can then, I discovered it was the
powder my patient used to cement in his dentures. He was a
sport and the two of us had a great howl.

Before our first postmortem, I felt confident of viewing a
cadaver with equanimity and filed with the others down to the
basement and into an off-limits room, the morgue. A large tub,
with a drain down the middle, was near a table centered in this
chilled room and behind it was a stretcher. The outline of a
body was evident under the thin white sheet.

An attendant removed the sheet from a male body. The genitals were covered. Because this autopsy did not include the
brain, a cloth was spread over the face. Otherwise the body
was nude, a yellowish color, and the nailbeds of hands and feet
were purple.

Dr. Faber, the pathologist, was meticulous. His voice was
low. "This man was eighty years old. Until little more than an
hour ago he was in almost excellent condition, recovering from
surgery for cataracts just last week. He'd had his supper, the
nurse came in to collect his tray—and found him dead."

The room itself was as silent as death. Dr. Faber was speaking again. "The family wanted to know why, and we need to
have a given number of autopsies in any hospital for teaching
purposes. In this case the family was more than willing to consent. *Family consent to an autopsy is imperative.*"

With his scalpel, Dr. Farber made a cut just under the
breastbone and continued downward to the pubic area. The

next cut extended from the right underarm all the way across to the left underarm, exposing the entire abdomen. And now we were invited to look at the organs of the body: the spleen, gallbladder, liver, common bile duct, intestines. Further dissection revealed the bladder and kidneys.

This was *death*. Before us was a dead form of what had been a man filled with life. What was it that had made this man alive up until this last hour?

What was I, myself, to achieve before I lay on such a table?

I stood transfixed, unable to turn my eyes from these revelations, oblivious to the fact that two girls were fainting and falling to the floor. The thuds brought me back to the living and *their* needs, and I found myself helping revive and carry the two from the morgue.

My life changed that day, and I made a decision: I must enter the convent.

Perhaps it had been ordained from the beginning that my destiny was to be a nun. Perhaps I would solve my personal puzzlement—and de-emphasize my sexual identity—in a life of service within convent walls. Surely others had found answers there. And solace. Serenity. But had some also faced crises of sexual identity? Was this why some women became nuns? Why some men became priests?

No! Inconceivable. Nuns and priests were selfless individuals. Their reason was far loftier than my own: Theirs was dedication to Christ, mine more self-serving.

God, help me to become a truly selfless person.

In early February I applied for entrance into the Order of St. Francis and was accepted. To provide my dowry ($300) and required wardrobe, I left school and worked at two jobs: nurses aide at two hospitals, one Catholic, one secular.

Of course I wrote Dad and Lenore about my decision, and for some reason Dad expressed neither pleasure nor displeasure. Unnatural for him. Was he afraid of a second failure?

On the first day of May I entered the novitiate, Alverno on the River. My welcome was jubilant, with excited postulants and novices, even the Mistress of Novices, Sister Caritas, crowding round me.

It was with a new kind of exhilaration that I entered the little curtained room, which was to be my cell for the next two and a half years. My new black dress covered me down to the tips of my black shoes, the sleeves stopped just short of my wrists. A stiff white collar was attached at the neck of the black cape which extended the length of the forearm. Sister Caritas now placed a black veil with white trim around my head, leaving only the front hair visible.

The elderly Franciscan Father Jamieson lived in the tiny house just off the main building, and he divided his time between Alverno and teaching at a seminary across town. The sisters treated Father with great respect: No matter what their age, the nuns opened doors for him, laundered his clothes, cooked and served his special meals in a private dining room—a safe distance from our refectory.

The laundry business was fun to see: his, hanging alongside all the hers. What would those on the outside have said to all this? Would there have been at least one I-told-you-so? Certainly, no one could ever have complained of the housekeeper —a task assigned only to an older member of our religious community.

The postulants and novices had a summer home, exclusively their own. A converted farm, the property had a lake as well as a house, and we had many happy times out at that place. We'd go in an open van, veils blowing in the breeze, and we'd sing songs from our school days—especially our favorite, ". . .ninety-nine bottles of beer on the wall." We'd be secretly delighted by the open stares of townspeople and countryfolk at the sight of a vanload of young nuns, windblown and reveling in those ". . . ninety-nine bottles . . ." Bumping along, we'd laugh all over again, recalling our antics back at the novitiate—walking near the boundary hedges and singing "There's a Tavern in the Town," aware of a sudden break in conversation and then quick laughter on the other side of the hedge.

Rank was accorded its privileges in the convent too, down to the very napkin rings. Those for the postulants were simple and bonelike, the same ring was decorated with a sprig of hand-painted flowers for the novices, and the one used by Sister Caritas was sterling silver. Only God and a select few knew the elaborateness of the one designed for Mother General, the nun who presided over the entire convent.

My favorite place was the chapel. Always quiet, with flowers on the altar, the chapel seemed to invite private prayer and meditation, spiritual reading, a few minutes of rest and solitude. In the sacristy we confessed to Father Jamieson once a week and once each month to the "extraordinary confessor," who came especially for the occasion. Not only did he hear our confessions, he counseled us individually.

In the solemn lofty library room we studied canon law, delving deep into ecclesiastical affairs of our Church. The library served another purpose, too, that for the Chapter of Faults. Once we entered the convent we were to strive for perfection, which, at our age, was far from easy. We were each given a little black book in which to record any infraction, such as speaking after nine o'clock in the evening or slamming a door. Later, we would accuse ourselves—as recorded here within our own book—before our sisters.

Our self-accusations were formalized: One by one, each in turn, we would stand, then lie face down on the floor at the feet of Sister Caritas, who sat at the front of the room, hands folded in her lap. Now she would give us a penance to say, such as three "Our Fathers" or two "Hail Marys." As humiliating as this ritual was, still it was small compared to reciting the list of misdeeds before one's peers—even though it was understood that no one ever spoke of these faults outside that room.

Still, the rituals were not without an occasional touch of humor. Will I ever forget one of the new novices who asked to be admonished for *picking her nose in chapel*? Of course nothing could have prevented the sudden outburst of laughter (which is how *not* to strive for perfection!)—whereupon we were punished as a group for the added transgression of laughter at an improper time: ordered down to say five "Our Fathers" with arms outstretched as penance.

The bread had been among the first of my failures. I'd put

the yeast in the mixture, even though every packet was outdated. To prove myself a real whiz, I decided to put the whole lot (five packets) in the dough, supposing five outdated yeasts would compensate for a fresh one. And then, just as Sister Mary Ann had instructed me, I put the bread dough to rise on the top shelf of the stove, where it was always warm.

And off to chapel.

Returning from chapel, we heard a shriek. Almost a cry of anguish. Had someone fallen down the stairs?

No. It was Sister Mary Ann from the kitchen. We all rushed in—and there, literally covering the stove, was the mushrooming dough in its slow descent. It was like a giant balloon, near the point of explosion, and I could envision it filling every crevice and circling around every knob on that monumental stove.

One disaster on kitchen duty was excusable, but a second was total humiliation. Leave it to me! Assigned to baking five pumpkin pies, I'd accidentally spilled a half pound of nutmeg into the mixture. A distraught Sister Mary Ann "doctored" the mess and said we'd add a marshmallow topping. "Just maybe no one will notice," she said, without her usual enthusiasm.

That evening, as was the custom, all eyes turned toward Sister Caritas as she lifted her fork to signal the start of dessert. With her usual composure she broke into the crust and lifted the fork-size bite to her mouth. Suddenly, her face froze as if she'd been struck by a bolt from above. She choked, was given water, swallowed hard.

In a voice that everyone could hear she demanded to know: "Who baked these pies?"

A postulant whispered to anyone who'd listen, "It looks and smells like cow pod."

Slowly I stood up at my place at table. "It was I, Sister Caritas." It was my time to swallow. "I'm sorry, Sister."

She'd known without asking. Was her question simply to gain time to compose herself? "Well," she said brightly, "not all of us are cut out to be bakers."

A friendship ripened with Sister Imelda, who was black. I asked if she found bigotry here in the convent.

"Well," she confided guardedly, "I'm not sure I'm so dearly

beloved by Sister Caritas. I may be mistaken. I must be fair—
but, at times, I'm just not sure."

Sister Imelda was well liked by the young nuns and by the
postulants. We looked up to her because of her courage: first,
in joining the order of all white nuns—second, in enduring
whatever Sister Caritas handed out.

Caritas means *charity*, but always charitable Sister was not.
One night we were told we'd be seeing a movie, *The Imitation
of Life*: a story of a black woman whose child was white. It
seemed incredible that Sister Caritas would show such a film
here at the novitiate, if only out of consideration for our black
nun. Having seen it once before, just before my mother died, I
agonized twice over: remembering Mom, dead, and empathiz-
ing with Sister Imelda, alive.

I was crying as I left the movie and, to comfort me, Sister
Imelda took me in her arms. "Don't cry, Marie," she whis-
pered. "I've had deeper hurts than seeing this movie tonight.
In time, hurts lessen."

"I know. Still, time does not correct the wrong done."

Sister Caritas saw this little tableau and seemed to sense
what was being said. Wanting to avoid an issue, I hurried on to
prayers and began to cry again as I poured out my troubled
thoughts for only God to hear.

This episode marked the beginning of dialogue between
Sister Imelda and me on discrimination in the convent. The
film gave me a sudden awareness of angry feelings toward
Sister Caritas and others who shared her biased philosophies. I
had lost a few of my illusions. In compensation, some of my
own philosophies took definite shape and solidified: Always,
for all time to come, I would respect the achiever—the greater
the problems, real or metaphysical, the greater my respect.

At the end of a six-month probationary period we were each
evaluated by Mother General and her council. Without exception, and despite our countless imperfections, all were accepted
to receive habits and become novices. Thus, we'd taken the
first step and were being elevated to the second on the long
climb to becoming full-fledged nuns.

I was caught up in my religious life, with no time to think about my sexual confusion or, for that matter, the need to satisfy the desires that had led to my dedication to this new life as ordered by St. Francis. I was mastering my baser feelings. My past conflicts faded and gave promise of leaving the page cleansed and readied for a second beginning.

According to tradition, we had to have an eight-day retreat of silence and meditation at The Motherhouse before we became brides. But, about a week before retreat, the bishop came to interview and question each one of us, separately, and to stamp his approval or disapproval. His word was final.

One would expect his questions to be more or less routine, almost ritualized, and it came as something of a shock when he asked me: "Have you ever experienced intercourse, serious petting?"

"I have never had intercourse or serious petting with a boy."

Undoubtedly he was asking each of us the same question and I wondered if anyone here even understood what he meant by "intercourse."

"And what are your feelings toward boys and men?"

"I have no sexual feelings toward men." I was sure I never would have. "I feel all males are my brothers."

I began to perspire. What would I say if he asked my feelings toward women? There could be no lying, for he was a man of God. Yet he would send me home If he even suspected my real reason for having come here. Had I betrayed myself by not volunteering this information?

The bishop continued. "Do you truly wish to become a bride of Christ?"

"With my full heart I want to work with and for Christ. Yes, I wish to become a bride of Christ."

Even as I made this affirmation, the word *bride* irritated my newly sensitized feelings. Well, Christ knew of my struggle, He knew I was trying with full heart, He accepted my less than perfect state. If I had not been entirely open with the bishop, at least I had not lied.

We were to leave on Saturday for the eight days at The

Motherhouse. The junior professed, the professed nuns, and elderly members of the community lived there, and we could count on a warm welcome.

Since Franciscans do not eat meat on Wednesday, Friday, or Saturday, we were served a full steak dinner on Thursday. That night the tables were covered with white cloths and we were invited to sit with Sister Caritas. Placed next to each of our chairs was the inevitable pair of secular white shoes with high heels, which we were to practice wearing before dressing for our wedding.

After the dinner hour and return to our cells, we found a roll of toilet tissue on each bed. This roll of tissue was a symbol of status in the convent: an acknowledgment that the one who slept there had earned a headpiece! The roll's function was to hold the headpiece, when removed, so that the sister need not take it apart each night.

I wished Mom could have been there to see me receive this great honor. I felt her presence and could not dismiss thoughts of her, even in my dream that last Friday night:

> Mom lay in her coffin.
> Dressed as a man from hat to shoes, I was on a treadmill, running toward the coffin. But every time I seemed near enough to reach out and touch her, the moving step of the wheel turned me away from my mother.
> In her coffin she looked as I remembered her in those years before I was twelve. She'd gone beyond my reach then, she was beyond touching now. Why did she have to go?
> And why was I not in such a state of perfection as to find God blameless?

Pondering these things in my dream, I awoke, my pillow wet with tears.

My loneliness passed and I was happy again. Saturday was here at last, and we loaded our suitcases into the waiting station wagons for the fifty-mile drive to The Motherhouse and a new way of life. Congratulations mingled with the good-byes and affectionate hugs and cheek-kissing and then we drove off.

This time no fun songs. The past weeks had been ones of momentous decision, and we were continuing our pursuit of perfection with meditation and prayer and minimal chatter.

Upon arrival, we went immediately to meet with Mother General. Though she was well into her seventies, her clarity of mind compensated for the infirmity of her stout body. She greeted us with a kiss on each cheek and praise for our decision to continue in the community. She invited us to tour the House and personally showed us to our rooms. We were to be two in a room, here to spend the next eight days: praying, meditating, sleeping, eating—all in silence.

Silent for eight days? Could I conform?

Actually, there was no time for talking. That would come at the end of the eighth day with the great celebration.

The rising bell sounded at five o'clock and by eight we had heard Mass, said the *Little Office of the Virgin Mary*, and were off to hear the retreat master's words of wisdom. Truly, they were just that. Our master was a Jesuit who delighted in mixing dogma with humor: His was the rare gift of making us laugh and think at the same time.

That particular day he talked about the mansions of holiness. Later I went to confession.

"And which mansion do you believe yourself to be in, Marie?"

After a flash of self-evaluation, I admitted: "Reflecting over my life up to this point, especially the last six months as postulant, I fear I'm still out in the garage."

The good man chuckled behind the curtain. "At least, Marie, you're in out of the cold."

My feelings exactly.

The eight days winged away as I searched my soul and still found time to learn to balance myself on those white heels. It seemed hopeless, and once I almost fell during our practice session. Fine time to fall and break my neck, just before my own wedding. . . .

The eight days' silence had taken its toll on most of us and we were glad to see its end, happy in knowing that the next day we were to receive our habits. In the meantime a letter had come from Dad, saying he was coming with my sister Jan and my aunts and cousins. This would be the second time he'd come to witness any real accomplishment of mine. I wanted him to be proud.

Following dinner, we were to go before Mother General's head table, where she sat with her council, drop to the floor, lie face downward, and ask to be received into the Order of St. Francis. I was the last to get down on my knees, and that's when it happened: My old black Sunday shoes (those heavy Red Cross models) caught in the hem of my long black dress. Mortified, and losing all sense of composure, I began to laugh because I couldn't lie down, I couldn't get up. And how could I recite the words of the ceremony not yet flat on my face?

An older sister hurried forward and managed the disentanglement. "Sh-h-h. Contain yourself."

But too late. The postulants were tittering, very likely as much from the relief of breaking the long silence as from the humor of the situation. The humor was appreciated by none of the others, unfortunately, and now the day was to end with most of us saying penitential prayers with arms outstretched in front of the entire community before saying our nightly prayers.

My unrehearsed comic relief had dispelled many tensions.

I dreamed of my mother in her coffin again that night. Understandable, since I longed to reach out to her at this crucial turning in my life. Not understandable was my second dream: that I was making love to one of the postulants. I woke in a cold sweat, long before the rising bell.

Of course I was fond of this girl but thoughts of lovemaking were out of my life now. It was terrifying, and I prayed to God to remove this sinful thorn.

An eternity seemed to pass before the bell tolled the hour of five and our mistress promptly knocked three times and entered with these words: "Arise, bride of Christ!"

For the first and last time in convent life we were served breakfast in bed. A special treat for a new bride-to-be, a beautiful memory to cherish. Strange to have breakfast *before* Mass.

After Mass we could talk freely, and now all the sisters gathered round, embracing us, saluting us with the traditional cheek kiss. Promptly at nine o'clock we would dress in our wedding gowns in readiness for the investiture.

Mixed feelings whirred in my head, leaving me with a disturbing giddiness. Was becoming a bride of Christ my hope of salvation? And what about that frightening dream of making love? Was my past always to sneak up on me, could I live my entire life with women and not become emotionally involved with them?

Could I become a perfect bride within hours of this torment?

And what about that incident at home on my two-week vacation almost at the end of postulancy?

It had been fun going home dressed like no one else. After a short stay with Dad and Lenore, I'd gone to see my aunts and old classmates from my senior year at St. Kevin's High. Many of my school chums had gone into the convent and their coming home on holiday always meant partying, including a pajama party. My homecoming was greeted with hoopla, and I was thrilled to be back again. After the last piece of pizza and the last soda, we staggered up the stairs and into the bedroom large enough to accommodate three beds: a set of bunks and a single. It was my lot to share a bed with Rita, that old girl friend who'd held such a spell over me.

There's no explaining why I did what I did: Suddenly I had my arms around Rita, was kissing and holding her close. It was as if all my striving had been too much and I'd missed the warmth of human touch. I'd wanted to touch this lovely girl lying here beside me, yet wanted to restrain impulses forbidden my state. I'd not wanted this to happen, yet it was happening and there was no stopping me. It was like an evil force I could not escape.

For a brief moment my hand lay loosely on her breast and she did nothing to stop me. And, as suddenly as it began, I was freed of this mortal need.

"I'm truly sorry, Rita . . ." I whispered.

Her answer was barely audible. "It's quite all right, dear friend. Sometimes I long for someone to hold me. Innocently hold me."

How innocent had been our encounter? For her, a friendly gesture—for me a sin.

On my departure the following day Rita gave me a lovely note. She wrote in part:

> Do not upset yourself about last night.
> It was only momentary and in all innocence
> and I'll always cherish it as a memory of you,
> Marie, my very dear friend.

Before leaving home for what was to be my last time as *Marie*, I called on Miss Graham, my grade-school teacher. I had to confess to someone what I could not confess at the convent.

"Why should you think it a sin to kiss a woman?"

"In the religious life we must refrain from showing signs of affection. Open embracing and a kiss on the cheek are reserved for special occasions. But I am impulsive by nature—and I have this almost desperate need to touch another human being. A warm human who will respond to me in kind."

"Every person on God's earth needs love, some in one way, some in another. Could we truly survive without love?"

"With a nun, love must be a spiritual state."

"I consider myself a good Catholic. In my eyes you are innocent of sin."

"Oh, I wish *I* could believe I am innocent of sin! But my need to touch another human being is one thorn I can't seem to pull out of my mortal flesh." I longed to reach out to Miss Graham but instead thanked her for listening to me. "You've been a kind of mother confessor—and I'll never forget you."

I turned at the door and she smiled reassuringly.

Our hair had been cropped short in preparation for this day when we were to become brides of Christ. Yet we were not as bald as we'd expected. We found this amusing as we dressed in our more intimate garments and put on the long novice underskirts. By nine-thirty we were in our long bridal gowns. Each was gathered at the waistline with many little puckers, and I felt I looked something like one of my aunts' pincushions. A long white veil covered my head. Most of all I was conscious of my white heels and asked God to forgive my worldly prayer that I'd not encounter some mishap and disgrace the assemblage.

My sister Jan and Kathleen Phillips were my two bridesmaids. They were beyond description, beautiful in their pastel gowns, and I could not quite snuff out my worldly pride in them as they escorted me down the aisle to the accompaniment of organ music and up to the bishop enthroned on red velvet. The hymn was *Veni Sponse Christi* ("Come, Bride of Christ"). This moment was one of rededication and a strengthening of my finest resolves.

At the altar rail the brides, each carrying a lighted taper, and their maids fanned out. All the brides knelt before the bishop, and now he put the question: "What do you ask, my children?"

The answers were the same and in unison: "To be accepted into the community of the Sisters of St. Francis."

"Will you strive for perfection and, in time, ask to make the holy vows of poverty, chastity, and obedience?"

"We will, Your Excellency."

The bishop requested removal of the veils, and now the front bridesmaid (Janet was mine) lifted the veil from the face of the bride she was escorting, and the one in back took the candle.

Making the sign of the cross, the bishop cut a few strands of hair from each of our heads, saying as he did this: "Be prepared to cover all your womanly beauty for Christ, who has died for you, prepare to make Him your groom and the Church a mother to be served as any child would serve her mother."

Not only do I have a groom but I have a mother-in-law too, I thought, and as quickly stifled this imperfect, worldly idea.

Now he spoke to us individually, the words identical, save for the name taken from one of the three each girl had chosen for herself. To me, the bishop said: "From this day until such time as you either decide to take your perpetual vows or leave the community, you will be known as Sister Mary Dominick."

My first choice: Dom's name! It was like a new bond between my brother and me, almost placing me on par with him.

Janet replaced the veil on my head, and Sister Theresa Ann stepped forward and placed the pile of folded garments in the bishop's lap. He blessed each piece and handed me my nun's habit.

When the rituals ended, we filed out of the chapel and were greeted by family and friends, kisses and tears and flashing bulbs. Even Dad had a mist in his eye as he came up and kissed me, his rough whiskers pressing against my cheek.

"You look nice, you look nice . . ." he repeated several times.

My aunts crowded around, with gifts and embraces and congratulations. "Your mother would be proud of you!" one said. They were saying what I was thinking, and my happiness dimmed with thoughts of her absence.

The torment of all the years was over, done with. I was happy. I'd overcome my sensual needs and was directing my energies into channels of perfection.

After today we were not to see families or these other sisters at The Motherhouse until we had completed one year of novitiate. This was the canonical year, and letters to and from home were confined to holy days and Christmas. Not until our second year could we receive visitors and write regular letters.

We returned to Alverno the following day, and greetings were more or less like those of the day before, though less effusive with no proud parents and family around. We found the tissue roll on each bed and laughed a great deal—but it did symbolize our first step upward. It would be a long time, however, before we'd slip our new headgear into place with much haste.

The first year of novitiate was an eye-opener for several of us. Now on the inside of the community circle, I did not like many of the things I was seeing. With this new perspective I began to understand Sister Imelda better and more deeply sympathize with her problems. My suspicions became fact as, little by little, I detected ways that Sister Caritas, rules notwithstanding, could bend things. It was apparent that she favored two novices, Sister Martha and Sister Stella, in that they would laugh and talk in her private office well after lights were out and Grand Silence observed. These two nuns were allowed to

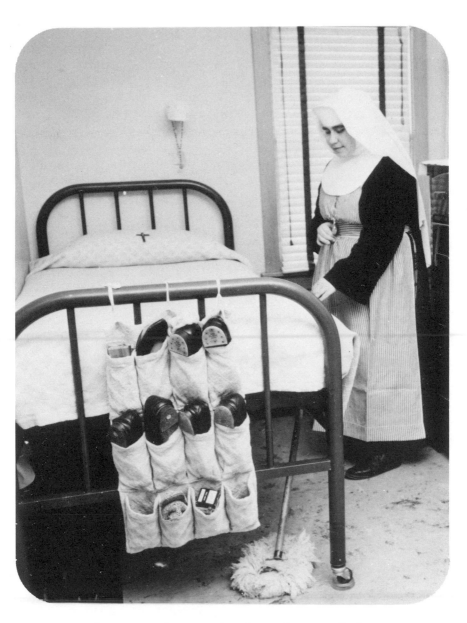

In the convent: housework and sexual urges still plague me.

have visitors from their school of nursing and from former instructors, even their mothers and fathers, who just happened to
bring a group of nuns to visit Sister Caritas. This favoritism
was a disruptive force among all of us who were aware of it.

As our learning of canon law and our duties became more
involved, we were upset by the contradiction between the
preaching and practice of Sister Caritas. Tensions began to
build.

As I approached the second year of novitiate, the old feelings of sexual frustration returned. Debates, art, gardening,
summer picnics and cookouts, hours of silence and meditation
—all these could not use up the energies building within me.
These involvements could not smother my need for self, my
need to touch another human being. Hours of hitting at a golf
ball, playing volleyball and tennis, practice at archery—none
of these physical exercises dispelled my need for the touch of a
woman. Little things began bothering me, and my frustrations
mounted. All this uneasiness was further aggravated by Sister
Caritas's partiality for the two novices and her harassment of a
few of the new postulants.

Sister Caritas went away to study advanced nursing for six
weeks and was temporarily replaced by Sister Margaret Mary.
Her inner beauty equaled her outer appearance, and we welcomed the change. She seemed to sense the undercurrents here
at Alverno and tried to pull everything back in focus, but, for
some of us, the damage was irreparable.

We'd talked in Sister Margaret Mary's office on several occasions, and now, today, I skirted my sexual feelings and
blamed my unrest on the generalities. "Why does everyone expect nuns to be different in every way?" I asked.

"I'm having a difficult time myself," she said, forgetting my
question. "Looking back, it seems that life in the hospital was
more important to me than the ringing bell that calls me to my
religious life."

Sister paused, waiting for me to absorb this startling revelation, then continued: "Dom, I must talk with someone. Since
we have rapport, perhaps you'll listen?"

"Our talking about your problems may help me with mine."

"Good. My superiors sent me to the novitiate to be with the

younger nuns, hoping I'd be revitalized by their youthful enthusiasm. They hoped that with this transfer would come the
spark within me that has somehow dimmed."

"And it hasn't?"

"No. I say this in all sadness, knowing that one day soon I
will leave the community."

Sudden pounding in my heart and head.

Sister Margaret Mary talked on: "I don't want to marry. But
I want to nurse—on my own terms. I want to reach out and
touch people physically."

My God! She wants to touch people too. Did she want to be
touched? In this respect she was no different than I. For the
moment I wanted only to hold this beautiful creature in my
arms.

Fingering my brown habit, as if to reassure myself of control, I said only that I felt the same way. "And there seems no
way out."

The day before Sister Caritas returned to her post, we had
a farewell party for Sister Margaret Mary, and I was given permission to see her before returning to my cell. Our talk was a
lengthy one and centered on what was ahead for each of us.

"Give the religious life a chance, Dom. Don't sell it short
just because of the bad example you see here. One day Sister
Caritas will get her due—but *you*? You are young and should
be able to bend."

"I am not as flexible as I might be."

"Work at it. One must be flexible to grow. Not all of us
belong in the religious life and I am happy to have discovered
this truth while young enough to adjust outside the community."

"I almost envy you."

Sister took my hand and held onto it.

"Don't. Pray for me instead."

"I promise. And, Sister, *you* have revitalized *my life* these
past six weeks. Your counseling has given me new insight on
the way things are here and within myself. I shall work at seeing things your way."

"I'll always remember you, Dom, and our good talks together."

We embraced with much warmth and I kissed her lightly on each cheek.

Soon after Sister Caritas's return I asked to leave the convent. She stiffened at my request. "Why do you want to leave the religious life?"

"I no longer feel I belong here."

"You haven't been here long enough to arrive at such a conclusion."

"It is too confining here. I feel the need to be out doing more as I please."

"Sister Dominick, you are being tempted by the Devil. Pray. And I will pray with you and for you."

"I'll try to pray myself onward."

"Yes, Sister Dominick. Pray. Cast out your private devils."

Why suddenly this holy-holy? How was I to know that I was but one of four who were requesting leave? Just as Sister Caritas took credit for the good in us, she must also assume blame for our shortcomings, and for half of all the novices to leave Alverno would be a black reflection on its Mistress of Novices. No wonder she blamed the devil.

I, for one, didn't care how black the picture was. I'd lost my respect for Sister Caritas because she preached one thing, practiced another. And I had strong suspicions that she could be bought off, which meant she was disloyal to her own vows.

The old sexual urges returned more and more frequently, and each time I'd hurry to the chapel to pray and meditate. But the magical powers of spirit seemed to diminish with each return of sexuality. Because it was not always possible to go to the bathroom at a given time, my bladder was often full, and it was at such times that I began to realize a full bladder heightens sexual feelings. And so I'd purposely postpone this need just to indulge in the pleasure of my newly discovered means of sensual satisfaction. Indulging these feelings, I began to long again for the feel of trousers and a man's shirt on my body, at the same time hating myself for wanting to trade away my nun's habit.

By spring I knew the identity of the other three novices who wished to leave, and we would get together during recreation and discuss reasons for our unhappiness here. Sister Paulette, who liked traveling, found convent life too restricting. Sister Martin was the motherly type and felt she could be just as close to God as wife and mother. Sister Ellen Marie, oldest of the four, had a Ph.D. in nursing and was unaccustomed to taking orders. "In the convent," she said, "I must hold my tongue to the point where I am ready to burst!"

Bolstered with the knowledge that I was not alone in my wish to leave, I again approached Sister, this time almost disrespectfully. "I want to leave, Sister Caritas. The religious life is not for me and—without being a nun—I can offer myself to the world as a good person, educated, a good Catholic."

Her disapproving appraisal said more than words.

"I have prayed over this a long time, Sister Caritas, and feel in my heart that I do not belong here. Feeling as I do, no one can stop me." And now the blow: "I demand to see Mother General."

She blanched slightly. "Mother General is away visiting other houses in the community. When she returns I will convey your feeling to her and her council."

"Thank you, Sister Caritas."

"Consider well these things: It is difficult for the woman who leaves the convent. As such, she will be shunned by family and friends, for the religious life is the highest goal any Catholic girl can hope to achieve."

She was right, I knew. The nun rumored to have run away from Immaculata to get married was, in the public eye, as guilty as if she'd committed murder.

I'd been forewarned. Yet this was the chance I had to take. God knew how I felt and I must be true to Him and to myself.

Sister Caritas waited out the months under obvious strain. She was edgy and cross most of the time, no doubt fearful as to eventual revelations when the four of us would meet with Mother General. One question kept turning in my mind, one to which I was never to find a satisfactory answer: Why did she try to keep us in a life that we did not want to inhabit? And then I'd think of the kind sisters at Mt. St. Mary who'd said they had no desire to keep a girl who did not wish to stay.

As much as I disliked the inscrutable Sister Caritas, I hated myself even more for no longer holding myself in control: succumbing when temptation became too great by masturbating —no easy feat when sleeping in a nun's cell.

Sister Paulette disappeared during the second month. No explanations. No questions asked. She just was no longer there: Her place was removed from table and from chapel, her name omitted from house duty lists. We never knew when she left or where she went.

Early one morning of the third month I was called from the flower garden to Sister Caritas's office. Her toneless voice recited the words: "Sister Dominick, tonight, during evening prayers, you will leave the convent."

I didn't understand. It was customary to be interviewed by Mother General before any release from the convent.

"Mother General . . . ?"

"Mother is too busy to see you, but, after deliberation and discussion with her council, she feels you will be better off in the world. She agrees that the convent is not for you."

I'd used almost the same words in requesting permission to leave. But now, coming from Sister Caritas, they were harsh, ugly.

She handed me $50 in cash. Where, I wondered, was the other $250 of the $300 dowry I'd brought to the convent, to be refunded if ever I were to leave? Had she turned in only $50?

"This cash will pay your train fare home, plus taxi, which will be at our door at seven o'clock. You will go to the attic for your suitcase while the others are at morning prayers, pack during supper. You are to be waiting downstairs for the taxi promptly at seven."

"Sister Caritas, may I say good-bye to the others?"

"No. This would not be good for the spirit of the group."

What spirit?

I was just to leave. Without fanfare. I knew a sudden sadness. Not only was I leaving friends, but worse still I was leaving illusions.

My secular clothes felt strange and uncomfortable. I waited in my cell until a few minutes before departure. The sun was still shining and its last rays fell on my discarded habit on the narrow bed and touched the tissue roll hanging on its hook in my cell.

This was not the way I would have chosen to leave the convent. Without good-byes. Well, there is one thing a convent is not: It is not a place for warm farewells.

Living at the convent had been a marvelous learning experience, most of which was positive. I'd miss the security here, the comradeship, laughter, the mutual strivings. Yet I could not have continued living in a habit I could not spiritually measure up to, taking orders from a superior I considered disloyal to her vows. In my most un-Christian moments I wondered about the "one bad apple" and hoped someday someone would have guts enough to tell Mother General of the dissatisfactions at the convent. It was to be another five years before she made the discovery and, subsequently, I was told, Sister Caritas was stripped of her habit and made to live as a "secular" on three-year probation, working as housekeeper in a convent far removed from Alverno. In my more charitable moments I know this was a heartbreak for her, since she had already celebrated her silver anniversary as a nun.

Twenty-five years is a long time to live with one's mistakes.

But I had no wish to be judgmental. Each experience is but a piece of the pattern of life, and I was eager to get on with new experiences.

5

Louise · Tina · Helga

Sister Caritas's words drummed in my ears like a refrain: ". . . the woman who leaves the convent . . . will be shunned by family and friends. . . ."

My leaving had been too abrupt for forewarning, and now I prepared myself for the worst when I walked into my family's home.

"Marie," my father almost shouted. "What happened?"

Lenore carefully propped her cleaning mop against the kitchen table. She spoke with resignation. "Yes, Marie, what did happen?"

"I just left the convent. That's all. I felt the convent was not the place for me."

"Just like that! And where *is* the place for you?" He was full of contempt for this latest breach.

"I've been wondering that for years, Dad. And, frankly, I don't know where I belong. But it's not in the convent."

"In-fi-del!" he flung at me, slamming the door as he ran from the room.

Since I had made him something of a celebrity by entering the convent, my leaving was not only robbing him of this brief fame but also degrading him in the eyes of his cronies.

This was not the time to tell Dad of my true feelings: wanting a wife, one like Dom's, and children, with a home in the suburbs.

My peers were less prejudicial. They did not condemn my leaving the religious life, and in time, a few of these friends became as important to me as family.

But lack of family acceptance continued to rankle. Now I suffered greater guilt than at any time in my life. Mine had been an honest decision—so why all this guilt? Was I punishing myself in some way? Well, not on a conscious level. And certainly I did not wish to hurt my family.

Life at home was far from satisfactory, and so, after a few weeks, I went to see my several aunts. They cried openly on our meeting, but soon we turned to the more practical side of the picture: Did I have enough money? Where was I going? What did I plan to do with my life? Would I go back into nursing?

Irma Matthews was next on my list of people to see. She was still at the same hospital, still at Menopause Manor. She seemed a little kinder. Or perhaps we'd both matured in these past three years. For the most part she'd been good to me, and now I decided that she, an R.N., was the one person I might be able to talk to about my sexual confusion.

When the moment came, I began by saying I felt different.

"How different from anyone else do you feel, Marie?"

"I've had sexual feelings toward women for as long as I remember. As a little girl I was sure I should've been a boy."

She got up and circled my chair. "You look like a normal female to me, Marie. I'd say you're a lesbian."

This was a new word. "Is lesbian the same as homosexual?"

"Yes," she said, not really knowing. "Maybe a psychiatrist could help. Why don't you find a shrink?"

"You don't understand, Irma. I don't want to change my feelings—I want to change my body. And I want understanding."

Such frank talk was not for Irma Matthews. She grew flustered. Perhaps she'd never permitted herself to talk about sex and all this was too much for her. I sensed that she had no wish to get involved with my problems, that she was upset even by the prospect of attempting to understand them.

Now I wanted to see and talk with Mom Phillips more than anyone. The Phillipses lived in a predominantly Catholic community, where almost every family boasted a priest or a nun as one of its members. Were Mom's views broad enough to welcome this defector? My meeting with her would prove the real test of rejection versus acceptance.

Her arms opened and held me and she smothered me with the affection I so desperately needed. No one in the family questioned my reasons for being there, and then, when I was ready to talk, the whole family was a warm audience.

"You can stay right here until you find a place to live," Mom said. "Your being here will liven up our usual madness even more."

The papers advertised a small room with kitchenette for a weekly rent of $20. Mrs. Hall, widow, owner of the three-storied house, quickly ran through the ground rules.

"No loud music, mind you. And absolutely no cavorting with men in the rooms. All gentlemen callers are entertained on the porch. We've lots of attractive chairs and a big swing."

"Don't worry about gentlemen callers, Mrs. Hall. I've just returned from a convent."

This sealed her approval.

Mrs. Hall was soft and pretty and indeed a very nice person. It developed, though, that she tippled on occasion, at which times her manner tended toward a gentle rowdiness—but never to the point of losing control.

At her house I learned about life and people. One tenant was retired and crippled, but her shuffled gait was forgotten when she smiled and her charm soon won me. Sometimes I picked up her groceries or carried out her garbage, and afterward she would invite me for tea. I felt a personal loss when she was found one morning in her chair: dead, a smile touching her face at something she must have seen in the *Evening News* that lay in her lap.

Another tenant, Louise, was about my age and height, her hair brown and curly, and, for some reason, she was slow to smile. Too bad. When she smiled she was cuter than a button. She worked at the local fiberglass factory, nine to five, and within two weeks she invited me for supper.

That first Monday I went to see the nuns at St. Michael's and asked if they could help me get a position at the local Catholic hospital in an adjoining suburb. They could and did.

Early in our interview, the director of nurses had put the question to me bluntly: "Having left the convent, how will you feel about working in a Catholic hospital?"

"I feel there would be many advantages because I understand the bells and penance and the Chapter and many of the rituals."

"Yes. But the important thing will be the sisters' attitudes about your having left their way of life. How will you react to all this?"

"I can only say, Sister, that I will try to understand their feelings, try not to be overly sensitive."

"It will take courage. And you have courage."

Working under this new set of circumstances was not as easy as I'd supposed. I'd lived a protected life until now, always around women but too young to know the real meaning of organizational politics. Here, as a nurses aide in the operating room, I heard jokes, some of them not always complimentary to our own religion. I relished choice pieces of gossip as much as the next one—yet not the story circulating that one of the nuns was being intimate with the chief of staff. That simply couldn't be. But never had I known a nun so blatant about her vows! I refused to believe it. Still, I'd get that uneasy feeling when I saw the two of them laughing together as they walked to her office and closed the door behind them. Somehow, all this must have seemed even worse as viewed by our Protestant co-workers.

Work here was exciting, and my many friends surpassed my expectations. I was doubly fortunate to be placed on call at the end of my working shift, which meant I was available for emergency surgeries and time-and-a-half pay. I liked the challenge of getting up in the night and on holidays, assisting in such life-saving measures.

In addition, this extra money meant curtains and a few

things for my apartment. Eventually I bought a record player and records and a small desk table. Because I favor dark woods, my apartment began to take on the appearance of a monk's cell, and I was happy with it.

Life was pleasant at our rooming house. Mrs. Hall kept out of our personal lives, contenting herself with lavishing her affections on her cat and canary. I made friends with the two men who lived on the third floor: one quite elderly, the other in his middle years. Bart, the younger, was always puttering around, working like a handyman to keep everything in shape.

Nothing ever seemed to bother Bart—he was a man apparently at peace with himself and the world. He had great respect for the woman who had divorced him, and this attitude was new to me. Bart treated me like a buddy: no sexual advances, no mention of the word. We got along fine.

My contemporary, Louise, usually went to her family home on Friday afternoon and returned on Monday, going directly to her work at the factory. But more and more we began to spend other evenings together—and often now she'd complain about time I was spending with Bart.

"Why do you have to see the guy so often? Because he takes you for a spin, or because he makes you laugh?"

"Both. We're buddies."

"What do you find to talk about?"

"Life. Married life. About how much fun he and his wife once had together. We laugh at silly jokes."

Louise was annoyed with anyone who laughed easily. Was it because she was living alone, too much wrapped up in herself? Whatever she wanted she bought for cash, whether a TV or new wardrobe or even a car. She seemed to handle her life well, but where was she going?

"Are you going to live out your life working, going home weekends, buying for cash?"

"And what's wrong with that?"

"What about fun?"

"Well, I have friends who bowl and golf with me. Days pass quickly."

"How do you feel sexually?"

"What do you mean 'sexually'?" She snarled out the words.

"Have you ever been with a man?"

"God, no!"

Could it be that she felt that she, too, should have been male instead of female? No, impossible. She was far too feminine in her walk, her quiet manner, her desire for the latest fashions. But was she capable of real emotion?

I was determined to find out for myself. I wanted to touch her breasts, caress and kiss her. I wanted to fulfill her sexual needs, wanted her to fulfill mine. I wanted Louise as my first sex partner—but just as desperately I wanted her regard and her acceptance of me as a male lover.

My only inadequacies were physical, and so I set about fashioning an artificial phallus. Bart looked a little startled when I asked, but he gave me a condom. I inserted a large test tube inside this protective sheath, filled both with water, and secured them with string and a rubber band. Placing this device between my labia, I maneuvered it back and forth and achieved orgasm. It worked! This is the way it would be. Now, I believed, it was all a matter of timing.

Louise and I went to a park one evening and sat in the car, watching the play of colored lights on the waters of the fountain. There in the soft semidarkness I felt a great need to grab and hold her close to me, to smother her with kisses. With a control I had not suspected of myself, I suppressed these longings, but our conversation became idle and labored.

On returning home, I lost that control. Grabbing her, I held her in a viselike embrace. The passion of youth is quick, and, scarcely aware of it, I was undressing her and pushing her over onto the sofa. She was no longer resisting, but was making soft little sounds of pleasure.

Her pleasure turned instantly to displeasure when I touched her breasts. "No, please! Not that."

A momentary setback, but, in lovemaking, I was not to be discouraged. I waited. Then I lightly brushed her nipples with my lips, felt them harden under my tongue. . . . She begged me not to stop.

I was proud of the artificial phallus I'd constructed and was wearing it now. After foreplay I could no longer wait to penetrate her vagina.

She froze. "*No!* Only your fingers. *Outside. Not in.* Just play —"

We finished the evening with a shared cigarette.

"Has this ever happened to you before?" I had to know.

She talked in whispers. "A few years ago I lived in a place where there was this beautiful girl. I wanted her so much that once I seduced her."

"And what was her response to you?"

"She didn't like my actions and told me so. But we've managed to remain friends and I travel East every year to see her and her husband and their three children."

"And you'd never had sex but that one time?"

"Absolutely not."

"Well," I confessed, "believe it or not, you are the first woman I've ever gone all the way with."

She looked at me suspiciously. "That seems unlikely."

"Honest, it's true."

She was not convinced. But I was excited, for this must mean she found me knowledgeable, and, from her response at her highest pitch, I knew she was satisfied.

Our relationship abruptly did a turnabout. Louise became standoffish. She seldom spoke. She was angered if Bart invited me for ice cream or a ride. It was beyond comprehension: I had pleased her and now she was avoiding me.

Within the week she asked me in again, and this time she made the first advance and we both lay back exhausted on the bed. Her guard was down and it seemed the right moment to tell her I was falling in love with her.

"I think I am a lesbian," she said.

"Well, I am *not* a lesbian."

"You wear men's clothing and short hair, you tell me that you're falling in love with me—yet say you're not a lesbian."

"I don't feel like a woman, especially in the kip."

"What's a kip?"

"It's a bed, you innocent. At least, bed is one definition."

"Oh."

"I feel I should have been a man. And I look forward to the day when I can have a home and wife and children."

"You don't know what you're saying. . . ." Louise quickly changed the subject.

Louise's way of showing affection was gifts bought with her

ready cash. She showered me with books, records, men's shirts. Sexually, she wanted nothing beyond her own satisfaction, without concern for mine. After the act was over, she wanted nothing more from me. What matter to her if my own sexual feelings were still at high tide? She never bothered to ask if I were content.

Her lack of consideration for my sexual fulfillment began to disturb me, and I grew angry and hostile.

Early in our friendship I took Louise for visits with the Phillipses. She was never overly friendly, but here she would withdraw and sit in a corner chair. Without warning she'd pop up and announce she was leaving, and to me she would say something like this: "You can come if you want to, but if not, stay and someone else will bring you home."

The Phillips family and their friends went out of their way to bring her into the general conversation, asking about her work with fiberglass, her hobbies and special interests. Louise simply had no wish to make small talk—or perhaps she was punishing me. Why else would she run away before the evenings ended with pizza or cake and coffee?

I wondered if her rejection by the one girl she'd seduced had embittered her and if this had to poison her for a lifetime.

In fact, Louise was cool to all my friends. When the invitation came for Terry's violin recital, I invited Louise to go as my guest. Terry, a friend of long standing, was both talented and beautiful, and to please her I wore a dress and heels. My wanting to please Terry displeased Louise.

Seeing me at the recital hall, Terry ran over and kissed my cheek, and Louise literally froze. She scarcely acknowledged the introduction, and her mood did not change throughout the performance or on the way home. But, inside the house, she ran to me, held me close and begged me to make love to her.

Lovemaking was a more or less spontaneous thing for Louise, and once it was over, she went back to her brooding. When we were alone or at the Phillipses or riding together in the car, she was often unhappy and uncommunicative. She was in the porch swing, and in such a mood, that late afternoon when Bart and I pulled up after shopping for fishing tackle.

What in the hell was wrong with her? Did she think her material gifts satisfied my need for acceptance, especially from the woman I believed I loved?

Impulsively, or in desperation perhaps, I turned to Bart. "Old Buddy, I want to have intercourse with you."

The motor was still running and now the car lurched to a stop. He turned and looked at me as if seeing me for the first time.

"Marie, I know you've been in a convent—and I doubt you've ever had a man."

"No, I never have."

"Think about it for a while, Marie. Then if you still want the experience, I'll provide you with it."

"This is a strange request, Bart, but I *wonder* what it's like. Frankly, I wonder how a man goes about it. I've read a good deal but reading isn't experience."

"No, I guess not."

"Bart, there are no sexual feelings between us. We're just very close friends and that's why I can ask *you.*"

"I'm complimented, Marie." Bart reached over, and his big hand covered mine for a brief moment.

Louise was cool to both of us as we came up the walk. Bart and I said so long, and Louise went with me to my apartment. Scarcely was the door closed than she began.

"You say you don't go to bed with him—so why do you have to go out with Bart all the time?"

"Because we're buddies."

"Buddies? Ha. You don't fool me. He tried dating me and I flatly told him *no.* But you? He asks, you go. What's up?"

"Oh, for Pete's sake, Louise. Bart is a nice guy. He's taught me a lot about fishing, painting, and mending broken fences. Can't you get jealousy out of your system?"

"Jealous! Me, jealous of that guy?"

"Then let's cut it."

"OK. Let's concentrate on improving your mind with the books I buy you, spending a little more time with your record player."

For the moment I pitied her: She thinks she can buy my affections—and now she's throwing it up to me.

Similar scenes were becoming commonplace. They tainted

the hazy days of autumn and threatened our relationship. I longed for our earlier, less turbulent times. Eventually we found a measure of comfort in sharing the food budget, and Louise proved herself rather adept at cooking simple meals. Our evenings slipped into a pleasurable routine as the icy fingers of winter closed about us.

She invited me to go home with her to meet her people. They were especially nice to me, not minding that I spent time with the men of the house, watching football on TV, while the women busied themselves with cooking and baking and kitchen-cleaning. Louise's brother-in-law smoked a pipe, and I was fascinated with his ease and obvious pride in it. That settled it for me: I'd buy myself a pipe as soon as I returned home.

This visit crystallized the picture I'd been constructing of the *man of the house*: a man satisfied with himself and his homelife, wanting to provide his wife with everything within his means to make hers a good life, one she would miss if he were not around. And he smoked a pipe, of course.

A rather great picture of *man*, I thought, but Louise did not share my opinion.

"You're crazy!" she all but screamed at me.

By spring I'd had a salary increase and my car was almost paid for. My life was no longer subject to attack by Dad or Lenore. My only unhappiness was right here with Louise. During a ride in Bart's car, I said I'd thought about the favor I'd asked of him last fall and that, clinical as it sounded, I was now ready for the experience. If he was surprised he gave no sign but did remark on my growing relationship with Louise.

"You and Louise are good friends. I know she has a lot of strange feelings and no doubt she gets all hepped up when she sees us together."

"You're right, she does. And I don't know why."

"Well—what I'm trying to say is that perhaps we should wait until she goes home this weekend."

"Good idea. No sense causing unnecessary friction."

Early Friday evening I went to Bart's room and said that I was ready.

"I'll be down to your apartment in a minute—after I get my protectors."

"I'd like to see your ———" I couldn't say the word. But Bart knew what I meant and quickly slipped out of his trousers.

God, what I wouldn't give for such a set of organs! I had no enthusiasm at seeing this set on Bart. I could only envision having my own and displaying it for Louise.

With Bart, it was like being back in biology class with some-one showing a model and slides of the human male genitalia. I was too absorbed to notice gradual engorgement until sudden-ly the phallus turned into an erect tool.

"Well, it's now or never," I announced with what I hoped was nonchalance as I removed my own clothes.

How strange it was, altering my position to suit that of a partner kneeling in front of me. Why had I undertaken such an experiment?

I had no guilt feelings. I was inquisitive, young enough to feel this was life or at least a part that I knew nothing about.

With a short grasping at my ample breasts, Bart had come to full measurement and was now thrusting, trying to penetrate my very tight vagina.

"God, you are a virgin!" Perspiration was coating his body, and he was struggling.

Why had there been no foreplay? It seemed funny now that I'd thought he could teach me a trick or two—why, I could teach him.

No matter how high he elevated my lower torso he could not penetrate and finally gave up. "Marie, you're a virgin and I don't want to hurt you. So I'll take care of 'my friend' here while you get dressed."

He went over to a corner and finished the job my entire body refused to do, and I couldn't help thinking what a real friend he was. As he reached his climax, his body swayed in the semidarkness, and I could hear his groans of satisfaction. He pulled on his clothes and I turned on the lights. Afterward we smoked and had soft drinks, and then he went back to his room.

That experience sealed my fate. I knew I could never live as a female, that I should never have been born one. It was all some horrendous mistake.

By our second spring together, Louise and I were finding rough times. She intimated that her parents had remarked on my mannish ways and it seemed wise not to take me for another weekend.

What was the cause of this girl's discontent? Was it my other friends and our outings—or her visits at home and wanting the normalcy she found within her own family circle?

Louise knew how much family life meant to me, and she knew my conviction that my female form was a mistake of nature. Was she indeed a woman's woman, afraid of anything male, even a masculine female? Were my mannish ways offensive to her? Then why her mannish gifts to me?

With these differences, questions, paradoxes all unresolved, it was inevitable that we should reach an impasse. Care for her as I did, I could no longer tolerate things as they were.

Leafing through a professional magazine at coffee break, I noted an ad by a medical school just over the border of one of our neighboring states. The opening was for a lab technician to work with a research team on lipid or fat content of the blood, and one of the prerequisites was knowledge of anatomy. (Bless Old Herman!)

I went for an interview with Dr. Janet Wise, who, with her associate, had researched and published on the adrenals. Sparing of words, she was a good listener, and, when I filled out a lengthy application, she gave it a look and said I'd be hearing from her.

Her acceptance letter came within two weeks. My feelings were both glad and sad at leaving this town, now my home, and all my friends, especially Louise.

Louise's reaction was predictable. "You see! I knew I shouldn't get close to you, that some day you'd leave me."

"I'm leaving, Louise, to save my sanity."

"Your only interest is sex!"

"Not true. We seldom have sex. I want a woman to share my life, a life that is as close to a male-female relationship as is possible. You know this—yet you keep reminding me I'm female. And that, dear heart, is not what I feel."

"But you like sex."

"Yes, I like sex! So do you, admit it. But I'm not horny all the time and you know it."

"You'd like to be. . . ."

"All right, let's talk about sex. Sex is a great and beautiful experience. But you just lie there, waiting for it to be given to you, making no attempt to give what you take. You never reach out to me—not physically, not emotionally. You are not concerned with my satisfaction. You leave me with only my fantasies of fulfillment.

"As for self, you're a taker, not a giver! You don't give out with the laugh, you don't give out with the joys of living, you don't give of yourself. You'd like to live like a hermit. And I'm not like that. I like being with friends, many friends, the more the better. I like to go to fairs, weddings, graduations, recitals."

"Have you finished your tirade?"

"No. One thing more: I enjoy sharing."

Sometimes Louise came up with the unexpected, and now she offered to help me move by taking some of my stuff in her own car. The town was over an hour's drive from here, the day was hot and muggy, and heat waves bounced off the highway and up, hitting us squarely in the face.

Dr. Wise had suggested a room just three blocks from the university, and Louise helped carry in the two carloads. Words between us were awkward, but we chatted about inconsequentials and she wished me luck and we both cried. I'd always cried easily, but it hurt me to see a woman cry. And seeing Louise crying—well, I wanted to throw all this junk back into the two cars and go back to the old rooming house.

The researchers—Nat, Paul, and Ed—were great to work with. To them I was just one of the fellas, and, in spite of younger years, they included me in their jokes and stories of their personal love life.

I especially liked working with Nat. He'd just returned from a six-month study of marine life in foreign waters. The rigors of his exploration had weathered his young face and his features resembled those of a monkey. Nat was so homely it became

him, and in time he seemed actually good-looking in an individual way.

One morning soon after his return, I discovered him with his
head on the table, crying. We were both early, and neither of
us had expected this encounter.

"What's wrong, fella?"

Nat was at a point where he had to confide in someone and
he'd trusted me before, so he grabbed my hand and blurted
out his latest grievance against his frigid wife: "How do you
explain having to rape your wife after you've been away for six
months?"

"I can't even imagine. . . ."

"Before I went away I told her jokingly: 'Wear your oldest
clothes to meet my return ship 'cause I'm gonna rip 'em off!' "

I took a firm grip on his shoulder and muttered I was sorry. I
tried to picture his wife as Nat had explained her to me: that
she never really participated in their lovemaking, that he was
filled with elation if she even so much as moved.

His wife must have been very much like Louise. But Nat? A
genetic male, yet having problems not unlike my own. Not
that she objected to his maleness, he had assured me; unre-
sponsiveness was just her way. I was sorry for both of them.

I missed Louise. I began calling her, just to hear her voice,
and (partially to cover the cost of long-distance calls) I took a
second job to work evenings in the admitting office of a Catholic hospital.

It was in that office that I met Tina. A girl from a small
town in the Midwest, she had a come-hither smile and all the
right measurements and was my idea of sophistication. As our
friendship grew, Tina confided she was still a virgin at the advanced age of twenty-three. No, she was not a lesbian, she was
frightened. I told her about Louise.

"I've heard about a gay club in the downtown district. I'd
be uncomfortable, but if you'd like to go, Marie, I'll go with
you."

"Great! I want more information about myself, Tina. I'd like
to find out if others in this part of my world feel as I do: that
I've been cast in the wrong body mold."

We decided to go the next evening after leaving work at eleven o'clock.

We were greeted at the Sandal Bar by cheers and halloos and forced camaraderie. Three or four gals were huddled together at the bar and others sat at small tables. Males packed the house.

Freddy Milton, owner of the bar, came forward and introduced himself. "You're new here," he began, "so let me tell you a little about house rules: If you need anything, or anyone bothers you, let me know. This is a nice place—and we mean to keep it so, and the gals don't go for anyone horning in on their properties."

He was warning us but could have spared himself the trouble. Both Tina and I felt out of place here and did not stay long. Quiet, tastefully restrained in decor, it seemed to be a meeting place for gays from the university and local business community. Its affluent clientele frowned on the occasional "lower types," as they were termed, who came in. We returned a few times, but, finding little in common with anyone there, became bored with it.

But I had learned one thing: I was definitely *not* a lesbian!

Not long after, Tina met a guy from the local Air Force base and lost no time in forsaking her virginity.

I turned my attention to a blonde registered nurse on the second floor. Her name was Helga and she reminded me of Louise. I invited her for pizza one night after work, we continued to see each other, and then the inevitable: Not love, it was plain old sex. I had something emotional to offer, but, after Louise, I wanted someone to offer to me in return. I asked Helga to stay the night and, surprisingly, she said yes.

She assured me she was not a lesbian, she was straight. Exactly what I wanted to hear. I had never wanted—nor was I ever to want—anything other than a straight woman. I'd seen too many hassles at Sandal Bar even to feel comfortable with a lesbian.

Helga was virginal as far as women were concerned and gave every indication of knowing even less about men. We sat on the edge of the bed talking, and I was growing impatient to turn out the lights. But any romantic notions I entertained were abruptly shattered with her announcement: "I'm pregnant."

I couldn't speak for the moment. And then I felt a great compassion for this unhappy girl.

"I know you'll keep my secret, Marie."

"You can depend on me." And then the idea came to me: How wonderful if I could live with Helga and she would have the baby and we could be a family. "Don't worry about a thing, Helga. I'll take care of you and the baby."

"Arrangements are already made: I'm to go to another city and have the baby. I'll live in a Catholic home for unwed mothers and give the baby up for adoption."

"What about the father?"

"That was a mistake. On graduation night I drank too much and went to a motel with one of the guys I knew—but not well enough. A month later, when I told him about my pregnancy, he told me he was married. He immediately dropped out of sight." She began to cry. "I've made a mess out of my life."

"Don't say such a thing. Let me look after you. And now that you've been so honest with me, I'll tell you about myself."

I spared nothing. Helga knew about Christine Jorgensen but wondered if I could solve my own problems by sex change. "Where will you get the money for such surgery? And where will you go? Europe?"

"I'll cross that bridge. But first, let me help you, and when the baby is born we can make our decisions."

In the lab we were analyzing our own urine. The test, *17-ketosteroids*, is a measurement of the hormones normally found in a twenty-four-hour specimen of urine—and greater or lesser amount of normal excretion is indicative of certain endocrine disorders.

"We don't understand this, Marie. Yours is abnormal: You have the 17-ketosteroids of a seventeen-year-old male!"

"I knew it: *I'm a guy!*"

Everyone laughed at the idea. And I laughed louder and longer than anyone. This was just one more proof of my maleness. Something very definite to hang onto.

The next step was to find someone to help me.

Sometimes I wondered if it was only to repay me for the support I had promised and was giving her that Helga and I entered into a sexual relationship. She was the complete opposite of Louise. Helga was a giver: She was warm and loving and reached out emotionally. We shared, laughed, and cried together. She would listen to my grumbles about goings-on at the hospital, make suggestions, help resolve problems. She respected me, accepted my maleness, and encouraged my plans for sex change, all of which was sexually stimulating to me. Perhaps it even added to my tender feelings about the baby she was carrying.

A ready-made family! I was elated at the thought. I liked the responsibility. Helga needed me, I needed her. I felt complete with her. The painful memory of Louise dimmed and eventually faded.

Helga and I were happy, considering this peculiar set of circumstances: knowing that Helga would follow through on the initial arrangements—and I would too, in spite of my wanting to keep the baby and continue as a family. Our resignations were in before Helga's pregnancy was discernible, and we were showered with parties before our leave-taking in that faithful old Dodge.

This had been the proper time for me to change jobs. In the all-new Village Hospital I'd be working in the delivery room, a different experience for me. The pay was good and this meant we could afford a nice apartment in the suburbs, where shopkeepers remembered anyone who returned more than three times. This whole life-style was as I wanted it—if only I could be a husband and father.

Helga was not to be dissuaded, and in less than three months she'd be moving to the Catholic home.

In obstetrics I scrubbed for Caesarean sections and sometimes assisted at birth. Seeing a child being born continued to be a miracle. If only I could help create a child—if only I had the sperm—if only a great many things. . . .

Because of my short hair, rumpled from the surgeon's cap, and my masculine face, women coming out of anesthesia sometimes mistook me for their husbands and would pull me down to the stretcher and kiss me with a most beautiful tenderness. And, for the moment, I could imagine myself being that husband, the father of this new life.

My work in OB gave me the itch to get back to nurses training. Even though my salary was good, it would be far better with a nurses license. I also wanted to get on with plans for my sex change.

Early in her last month Helga moved into the Home of the Sisters of Divine Guidance. Again, that awful void. My life was empty. I visited her as often as I could, and twice she came home with me. I'd put my ear to her enlarged abdomen and listen to the baby's heartbeat. He (it had to be *he*—we'd even named him *Marlin*) would move and give me a kick in the ear. Did he feel I was intruding?

It was a bittersweet sort of happiness.

Mine was a strong affection in our present relationship. Whether my feelings were from compassion or from fulfillment of my own needs I was never to know. But if Helga could truly learn to love me, and I her, then we could have our own family unit—and when my surgeries were complete, we'd legally marry and I'd adopt little Marlin.

A few problems were coming up in my work at Village. I was working as a scrub, not as a registered nurse, and some of the surgeons resented this. Especially one resident, Dr. Mellon. Bright, gifted and dedicated, admired by his colleagues, he had another two years before taking his boards. In spite of all these attributes our doctor was a grouch. He had no hesitation in yelling orders. He was well within his rights in demanding that we wear our surgical scrub caps even in cleaning the delivery room after a birth. All right. But it was the way he yelled. Most of the others in the unit cowered before him, but I was not that subservient and was sometimes bold enough to talk back to him. It was three in the morning the first time I scrubbed with Dr. Mellon on a Caesarean section. He looked at me over horn-rimmed glasses and asked: "What's the matter? Don't I rate an R.N.?"

"I'm sure Miss Martino will prove satisfactory," the ranking nurse on duty said. "Please give her a chance."

The best Christmas gift was the lab test which showed I had the hormones of a seventeen-year-old male.

Considering the hour, there was little else our Dr. Mellon could do other than carry on.

The reason was never explained, but I worked again with Dr. Mellon, and that second night passed without incident. The next time he was up for Caesarean section I was not on call, and later the R.N. reported to me that our good doctor was upset that I was not there that night.

"You should have seen him!" She giggled. "His first words were: 'Where's Martino when I need her?' "

Things were easier between us from that time on.

One September Saturday I drove to the Catholic home to see Helga. One of the sisters met me in the waiting room.

"Are you a member of her family?" she asked quietly.

Something was wrong. "Where is Helga?"

Sister put her hand gently on my arm and began vague explanations about *placenta previa*, which I knew as a condition producing serious hemorrhage during labor. "There was a still-born baby girl."

"My God! And Helga—what about Helga?"

Sister named the hospital and I was out and away, rushing to Helga's side. She lay on the bed, her abdomen no longer heavy, her skin as pale as linens on the bed. She was being given blood.

I took her cold white hand. "Helga, it's me, Marie. Open your eyes and look at me."

But her eyes did not open.

I couldn't imagine why this had happened. Helga was an R.N. and should have recognized signs of any problems. Why didn't she tell anyone? Tell me? Or did she want to die?

Helga did not die that day, nor the next. Although her heart continued its weakened beat, she never responded even so much as to squeezing my hand. Did she know I was there?

On the fifth day the heartbeat stopped. I wish I could say I was there when it happened. . . .

Death is a threshold we must cross alone.

I could only remember her self-depreciation because of one indiscretion. She did not blame the partner, she blamed only herself. I'd begged her to make an effort to locate the father and her answer was always no.

Once I had resolved my own identity, I vowed I would establish a halfway home for unhappy persons: perhaps for other Helgas, perhaps for those with confused identities. I must prove to these tormented individuals that there are responsible persons who sincerely want to understand their problems, the social stigma, the pain they suffer.

Living in the apartment I'd once shared with Helga became intolerable and I began asking about rentals near Village Hospital. Dr. Mellon learned of this and asked me to come see him.

"Marie, why don't you move in with me and my family?"

"What would your wife say about having a boarder? Shouldn't you discuss it with her?"

"Naturally. I'll discuss it with her tonight and you can drop by tomorrow and talk with her."

The family lived in a quiet neighborhood just six blocks from the hospital. Mrs. Mellon was soft-spoken in contrast to her husband's abrasiveness. The children were amusing themselves in what appeared to be a well-governed household, sparkling clean. Mrs. Mellon showed me the room just off the playroom in the basement.

"You'll have your own shower and washroom, and you can use our washer and dryer. And, of course, you'll eat with our family."

The price she asked was such a modest one I was almost embarrassed. "I'd be happy to baby-sit for you," I offered.

"With Dr. Steve's schedule—home only two nights one week, three the next—we seldom go out. But, on occasion—and if you really want the experience—the job is yours."

I liked Joan Mellon the minute I saw her. She was the other side of the family coin: the person who watched over the family while her doctor husband worked for their bread and butter. Theirs was a good firm family unit and I liked living in this atmosphere. And they never pried into my private life.

Because of being on night call I was out most evenings but participated, as work permitted, in the cookouts and card games with family and friends. Baby Jenny was about four months old when I moved in. The first time I changed her diapers I forgot the plastic pants. Learning to make Jenny's Pablum, I must've used half of the box before getting the proper consistency. Between one thing and another I knew I would not—could not—be a mother. I was not psychologically equipped for motherhood—I lacked the fortitude.

About a year later I decided to return to nurses training and mailed applications to three schools.

Something strange was taking place: In each instance, just before I was to go for my physical, a letter of rejection would arrive. Why did the school authorities bring me as far along as an appointment for the exam if they had no intention of accepting me?

A letter came from a longtime friend, who was director of nursing at another school to which I'd very recently mailed an application. In writing me she had acted against all rules.

My dear Marie,

This letter leaves me with a heavy heart but it must be written. I have not submitted your application to the board of directors because of a critical letter of reference from a professional person. I know she has your interest at heart, for she recommends your ability and integrity in the field of medicine as the highest we could hope for. But she believes you are a lesbian (though she does not state why).

She goes on to say that your moral integrity was never questioned—still she believes it would be difficult for you to live around young girls.

Fondly,
Annabella

So this solved the riddle of my rejection by the nursing schools. Well, my old buddy, in whom I'd confided, in her stilted little life, was playing God. Why had she done this? I'd never been in trouble, never hurt anyone. And now this condemnation.

This breach of faith was a riddle I'd never understand.

I couldn't wait to get a letter off to this contemptible woman, a former supervisor.

Dear Irma Matthews,

For several months now I've been wondering just why I've been all but accepted in schools of nursing and then dropped like a hot potato. Now I know the reason.

Why do you so condemn me? You were taken into confidence about things I felt I could discuss with you. Accordingly, you've made your own decision as to my moral integrity.

I do not consider myself a lesbian. As you recall, the term was unfamiliar to me when I heard it from you for the first time.

Yours was a character assassination of the first order. Why? Do you envy my potential? Or do you attempt to assassinate me because you are not a star achiever?

I am sorry for you because you are so embittered. My wish is that I shall never become so.

I asked your professional opinion, nothing more. Yet now you would destroy me.

I sense an echo in you—but am unsure as to whether you are punishing *me* or *yourself*. . . . Whichever, I am very, very sorry for you.

Your one-time friend,
Marie Martino

I had an answer.

Marie,

Do not blame me if you don't get into nurses training. You are bright and have great will—so if you don't achieve, it's not my fault.

You did not ask my permission to use my name as reference. Please stop.

Irma Matthews

Time dulled the heartache, the blow to my ego, my anger. I could not bring myself to give the real reason to the Mellons for my rejections and fabricated one of my own: I could not meet the chemistry requirements. Truth was too painful at this turbulent time in my life, but sometime, I promised myself, I'd tell them the whole story.

Steve came down to my room one night and suggested I make application for a very special school that had practical nursing in its curriculum.

"But, Steve, I want to be a registered nurse, not a practical."

"I'm well aware of that. But I'm thinking of this school where you can get an excellent training that will serve as your steppingstone. And you'll have many cultural advantages too." Almost as an afterthought, he added: "Furthermore, they give scholarships."

"Scholarships? Hm-m-m. A scholarship would be an incentive."

"Here's a dime, Marie. Invest it in a phone call—it could change your life."

"Thanks. OK. I'll call tomorrow."

Next morning I made the call to Renner's School for Women. The administrator verified all that Steve had told me and more: Every woman accepted was given a scholarship to cover the entire cost of the year's course, board and room, the cost of the bus to and from the training hospital. In exchange, each student was expected to help with chores around the school.

Steve's encouragement, and Joan's, plus the pleasant voice of the administrator, all gave a miraculous boost to my morale. Within a very short time I took the entrance exam and was formally accepted.

Never would I have a fonder memory than that of my farewell party, given by the entire staff at Village Hospital. My supervisor had asked me to go with her to one of the nurses houses to pick up some tires for her car, and I dressed comfortably in slacks and shirt. When we arrived at the house, she said we must go to the basement.

A sudden burst of flashbulbs and cheers greeted us and everyone began to sing: ". . . for *he's* a jolly good fellow. . . ." (News of my 17-ketosteroids had circulated throughout!) And, before I realized exactly what was happening, I was being passed from friend to friend, kissed and hugged as I'd never been buzzed over before. Physician staff and wives, OB staff, administration, personnel, dietary, maintenance, supervisors, researchers, lab technicians—every department in that hospital was represented.

The buffet table was loaded. Foods I couldn't even name. Par excellence.

"The booze is flowing," the barkeeper announced. "Drink up!" A nondrinker, I did have a small one to celebrate my own celebration.

Our hilarity had one disquieting interruption: Police officers arrived because, it seemed, special permission from the county seat was necessary for our black orderly and his wife to attend our festivities. I felt a great shame for the cops and the insensitive lawmakers, who ought to have felt shame too. Only the orderly and his wife seemed to accept this incident with outward unflappability.

The celebrators were clamoring for me to open my going-away gifts.

Under its extravagant disguise I found a box marked "Sanitary Pads" and I couldn't resist calling out: "Hey, everybody! You mean there's someone here who hasn't heard the results of my 17-ketosteroids?"

"We've skeptics in our midst!"

"Pity!"

Opening the box I had the surprise of my life: The thing was wadded with money! Every person on the payroll (I was to learn later) had contributed to this jackpot. I felt like a millionaire!

And here were cigarettes by the carton and a shoulder bag which would hold my special books.

Someone put on the recording "Climb Every Mountain." The tensions, bottled up these last three years, broke, and I cried. And then abruptly stopped. How good God was to give me these exceptional friends.

6

Becky

A New Dream Begins,
an Old One Ends . . .

From the very first day I met her I knew my destiny was with Rebecca. Love at first sight? I'd swear it. Romanticist? Of course.

Her face was as delicate as a cameo, her eyes were like the changing colors in her light brown hair. Her figure was lithe and poised, petite. Rebecca was my opposite: quiet, reserved. Every inch a lady.

I knew that first day I wanted to marry Becky. And now that I'd found *The Woman*, I resolved to do everything to make her want me—and I couldn't wait for the day that sex-change surgery was to alter my anatomy to that of a man.

But when would that day be? At times, it seemed almost a fantasy, clouded by the unknown. How much did I really know about sex-change surgery? Well, from female to male, it meant a mastectomy (removal of the breasts), a hysterectomy (removal of the uterus), a phalloplasty (creation of an artificial phallus or penis). And prior to surgery, it meant a series of tests to be taken, certain hormones to be prescribed.

What an obstacle course! So what? I'd meet the challenges head on. Then, *as a man*, I could face that bright new world in which I'd live and love—and meet new professional challenges too.

For now, I must concentrate on the courtship. I would be the initiator. Anything to draw Becky into conversation, or to pair off with her when we went after classes as a group to the nearby shopping center. Little kindnesses, a single flower, a note under her door.

In Becky I recognized those womanly virtues for which I'd been searching, and now that I'd found her I wanted her with all my being.

The school was a charitable institution, endowed by a wealthy recluse as a memorial to his mother, Mrs. Wallace Renner. Designed as a private finishing school for girls and women without financial means, it was a place to improve socially and at the same time prepare for professional or business careers. Cultivating the social graces at Renner's meant occasional teas at wealthy homes, tours of monuments and landmarks. The curriculum offered a choice of bookkeeping and related commercial subjects, or housekeeping, or practical nursing.

Miss Hendrix, our director, was a tall stately woman with exquisitely coiffed auburn hair. World-traveled, well-versed, she radiated a warmth and humaneness and a special affection for the whole student body. She understood and loved youth and knew no generation gap. We could go to her about anything, tell her our problems. Miss Hendrix had a keen awareness of human frailties and wanted us, as nurses and as human beings, to empathize with our patients and with one another.

To illustrate her point, Miss Hendrix often told us pathetic stories of how *not* to act in given circumstances. How could we ever forget this one? A patient was scheduled for a laryngectomy (removal of the voice box) the following morning. That last evening he begged that his wife be permitted to stay beyond visiting hours.

"This is the last time I shall be able to speak to my wife."

"Sorry. No." The nurse said, "Rules are rules."

Miss Hendrix concluded her story with these words: "It's very important to listen with your heart. . . ."

The second month I broached the subject of dating to Becky. She wasn't dating at school, she said, but there was this boy back home. Richard, she finally told me.

"Are you engaged to this Richard?"

She looked me straight in the eye, but the pause before her answer shook me up. "No-o-o. That is, not exactly."

"What do you mean 'not exactly'? Either you are or you aren't. Which?"

Was she hedging? Again that infuriating pause. "Well," she said, "you might say we're sort of—well, engaged to be engaged."

Hell. That was saying nothing—and everything. "Let's drop it."

Becky carried pictures of the guy and the letters he continued to write. Not to be outdone, I began writing little notes and pushing them under her door across the hall. Innocuous little nothings, such as "How was your day?" Anything at all just to get a note back under my own door. I was filled with jealousy every time I saw her slip into her room with that secret look she always wore when a letter came from Richard.

Inside I was steaming. This guy Richard was unfair competition. I was just as much a man—but without the body to prove it. Well, I was not to be defeated: The day *would* come and we would become man and wife. *I felt it in my guts.*

Knowing she was just across the hall, desiring her, I worked at keeping my emotions under control. She was such an innocent and I was fearful of making some false or impetuous move and losing her forever.

To Becky, I was just "a very nice person." She'd always been interested in meeting new people and making new friends, she said casually. Under questioning she confessed she admired my ingenuity, respected me as an intelligent person. . . . All nicely said—but damn noncommittal. Oh, yes, she liked my personality.

No relationship stands still: Either it goes forward or it goes back. I was determined there'd be no going back.

The advance began in early November with my gently kissing her on the neck at bedtime. Becky became confused, thinking this rather strange behavior between girl friends. But, liking me more than a little, she accepted this expression of friendship and in time seemed actually to enjoy it. And once, when I would have kissed her squarely on the mouth, she pushed me gently away and laughingly reminded me, "My lips are for Richard."

Damn. Damn Richard.

For the moment I wanted to rant and rage and punch Richard in the kisser. Wanting to hide my hurt, I hurried back to my room. Cooling off, I knew that to punch Richard—if we ever met—would only alienate Becky for all time.

I planned strategy as carefully as a Don Juan—though with one certain woman in mind.

I'd learned Becky's history piecemeal. And I liked what I'd learned. Becky's family were farm people, and the two boys and three girls worked along with their parents in trying to earn a living on their less than adequate land. They loved God, based their lives on the Ten Commandments, and went to church on Sundays.

"It's early to bed, early to rise," Becky said. "When the weather is warm, our whole family sits outside and listens to the night sounds. No one ever talks very much, especially about those things closest to us. Even as kids, we played quietly. Winters are longer than summer and we huddle around the old potbellied stove, munching apples from our own trees. But inside in winter, or outside in summer, Dad always reads to us from the big Bible before he and Mom listen to our prayers. Our bedrooms are unheated and we sleep under high mounds of homemade quilts.

"We've always loved each other and are close. I guess you'd say we're a typical American family."

Two civic-minded members of their Protestant church took an active interest in Becky's religious education and were, in fact, largely responsible for her enrollment at Renner's. Aware of her obligation, she wrote them regularly and kept them advised of her progress.

As our talks deepened, I searched her thoughts. What about love? And marriage?

"My family is traditional. We believe a woman's place is in the home. Like my friends I hope to marry one day and have children of my own. It's God's way."

"And how do you feel about me, Becky?"

"I'm attracted to you because you're very kind to me."

"Is that all?"

"No. Perhaps, most of all, it's your true interest in me as a person—your respect for me."

"No more?"

"I love you as a very dear friend."

"And Richard? Do you love Richard?"

"Richard? Let's just say 'taboo' for now."

Bit by bit she learned to confide in me—except on the subject of Richard. As to Richard? Well, she just wasn't talking.

Friendship with Becky took on new meaning when she shortened my uniforms. I could scarcely thread a needle—how could I sew a hemline? Except for her touch (which stimulated me!), I felt like a damn fool: like a man trying on his wife's dress so she can hem it evenly.

Several students went home for the Thanksgiving holidays. The others were downtown and Becky and I were the only two left on our floor. Actually, we'd planned it that way. Of course, Becky's thoughts were for the pleasure we found in being with each other, but mine were far bolder. She came smiling to my door and my heart all but flipped. I gave her the usual embrace and nuzzled her neck and she teased: "You're tickling."

It was too much. My pent-up emotions erupted. I pushed her against the door, reached down and turned the key.

Becky literally froze. And then I was kissing her: her neck, her face, her mouth. The feel of her lips was overpowering. I had this great need to touch her, caress her, show her the power of my emotions. Not recognizing her state of trauma, I thought only of her nonresistance—and this, to me, was acceptance.

Voices in the hallway abruptly ended our dramatic encounter. The kids were back from shopping, wanting to share their meager purchases and the excitement of their downtown excursion. Hell! We sprang apart and quickly and silently unlocked the door and, faking enthusiasm we did not feel, invited them in. They stayed with us until dinnertime and regaled us with chitchat, none of which we really heard, for we were reliving in our own thoughts the unfulfilled episode. Again, I realized my maleness—and how completely out of place I was in this room filled with girls.

And so I agonized through the hours until bedtime. Occasionally I'd glance at Becky, but she still seemed to be in that trancelike state. Her face was pale, almost expressionless, and she talked almost not at all. Alone with me again, would she be as submissive as she had been at that moment of capitulation? Or would she rally her thoughts and come up with a gentle but unyielding *no*?

When we were at last alone, I silently turned the key in the lock and put my hands on her shoulders. Becky looked at me thoughtfully—and rather sadly, I thought.

"What do you feel, my love?"

"I—I don't know. . . ."

I gathered her up and carried her tenderly to the bed. We consummated our love then, knew its fulfillment and its afterglow. In a very small uncertain voice, Becky admitted that she had never felt like this about anyone, man or woman, that she was drawn to me in some inexplicable way.

"It's some force I cannot understand. It's all so strange."

It came to me in a flash that this must be her sexual awakening, and she herself confirmed my belief by asking: "Is this the way it would be with a man?"

Becky was a virgin. God, how I loved this woman!

"I've never had a sexual experience," she said in a barely audible whisper. "I would never have imagined myself capable of such arousal."

Words choked in my throat.

"Can our love transcend our genetic anatomies?" Her voice seemed to come from far, far away.

"Becky, those are beautiful words. You are the quiet one, yet, when you look deep within yourself—well, you come up with the words of a poet."

"I feel like a poet: searching for a whole new set of words."

"You mean new words for this new experience?"

"Yes." She paused briefly. "I feel suspended—in midair."

Life changed for us that Thanksgiving Saturday. Becky was confused by our relationship. It had never occurred to her that she would ever experience anything like this, and the very thought of such intimacy between two women was contrary to all the things she believed in. She wavered between elation and the weight of guilt and often wandered off to pray alone or just to try to straighten things out in her mind.

Her confusion was, for now, our biggest insoluble. It seemed to me that Becky was a long time in evolving from her trance-like state, and this, in turn, aroused my own feelings of guilt. And then, quite suddenly, she talked. "Religion has played such an important part in my life. And you know I've often thought of dedicating myself to the foreign missions: It would please my church, it's what my sponsors keep urging me to do."

"What about me, Becky? Can't you make *me*, Marie—who has this great need to find myself as a man—*your mission* in life?"

"Oh, Marie! If only I could believe that you *are* my mission. . . . Would to God that the answer were that simple. . . ."

"All my life I've been trying to explain that I should have been born a male. I've acted like one, thought like one, loved like one." I knew this was still confusing to her. "Give me a chance, Becky! And tell me how to get through to you—how to set your mind at rest."

She did not answer.

After a long pause, she spoke brokenly.

"The questions keep hammering away: What would my church think? What would Mom think? Oh, God, what have I done to her? And to Dad? And what have I done to myself? How could I have changed so from the innocent to—to—whatever it is I have become?"

"Becky! Dear Becky. You've suddenly become a woman."

"Then why do I have this sensation of falling? Falling in the eyes of God, falling into nothingness?"

"It's this new awakening in your life. Think of the bright side. Of this love we share. Of how we can work together, building useful lives, helping others."

"Creating our own missions, so to speak?"

"Exactly."

I bought *The Well of Loneliness* for Becky to read. About the love relationship between two women, it was so honestly and beautifully written that Becky felt she could accept *their* liaison. But, since neither of the heroines wanted to change sex, there was a difference: Psychologically, I could never fit the mold of *woman*. Would that I could have found a book describing a relationship such as ours, but, insofar as I knew, there were none. All I'd read about sex change were the news stories about Christine.

A few evenings later, Becky visited a longtime friend and eventually they talked about this book.

"Disgusting!" the girl had said. "All about two lesbians."

Such a comment from her valued friend had a traumatic effect on Becky, she told me later. "Does everyone feel this way, Marie?"

"Heavens, no! Besides, Becky, *you and I are not lesbians*. We relate as man to woman, woman to man. I'm not sure of all the differences now—*but there are differences*. And, some day, we shall know."

"Perhaps, as you say, Marie, I suddenly became a woman—without knowing what to expect. I hadn't realized the power of love between two people. This love transcends anything I could ever imagine."

Words in black and white make their indelible impression, and I decided to write a long letter to Becky, declaring my love and asking her to let me prove that such love between two women can be as deep and enduring as that between man and woman.

> *Dear One,*
>
> I know you will find all this difficult to understand, but I ask you to hear me out. The first time I saw you I felt a great physical attraction for you. As I got to know you, your kindness toward me and others, your true caring for people—which you show in many ways—and your loyalty have made me also realize an emotional attraction for you. This goes deeper than mere physical want.
>
> Becky, since a child, I have felt that I should have been a

boy. I know you can't understand how this could be, so I'll be realistic and say I don't know why I feel physically attracted to women, but I do. It's been this way all my life and, while it has made me very happy, it has also hurt me in many ways. What I'm trying to say is that I have grown to love you and want to share my love—and the physical part of that love also. I want to share life with you: everything from family life, with its joys and sorrows, to what life may have in store for both of us.

Some day I may see my feelings of manhood realized, but, for now, I will settle for what we can grasp of life as two women. By now you realize two women can share a sexual feeling for each other. These things do exist. It matters only that we are able to relate in a love union. It can last forever.

I hope, one day, you will feel the same way. I cannot say it will not cause problems—it will!—but I will stand beside you, whatever they are.

My love,
Marie

My letter seemed to confuse Becky even more.

Our stolen moments of lovemaking were not as frequent as we would have liked, but they had to suffice. Our love ripened and matured and, in time, Becky accepted ours as a man-to-woman involvement.

"I've always reacted to women as a man," I would remind her. "I've never had any feelings about a man other than that of boy to boy, man to man."

"When we're alone I will always call you Mario. Not Marie."

Mario. *Mario?* I liked that. Becky had given me a man's name. Now she saw me more clearly as I saw myself: a man.

I reexamined Becky's feelings for me as she had expressed them: "Mario, no one else has ever been so truly interested in me as a person. You would do anything in the world for me, give me anything. Now, it's not the gift itself that's important to me—what is important is that you want to care and provide for me."

And piecing together the cherished tidbits she'd let fall from time to time, I recalled that she found me ". . . vibrant, loving, robust, mischievous, kind, caring, understanding—a sharer of self, a good and gentle lover—a strong person who keeps everything moving, pushing, going."

All of which brought more clearly into focus my image of myself. Weren't her feelings for me similar to any woman's for her man?

Any resemblance to lesbianism on our part was due to my lack of the proper organs. Never did I use my vagina during lovemaking—always I attached and wore my false penis. Wanting only to be a man, I went to all imaginable lengths to be one: affecting male attire, male mannerisms and figures of speech, having my hair clipped at the men's barbershop, roughing up my bushy brows.

But no matter what I did, the picture remained imperfect. Becky, my faithful soulmate, would do her best to comfort me. "Mario, you look just fine."

"*Almost* male?"

"Well—almost."

My spirits would fall. No amount of masquerading could ever hide a forty-four-inch bustline. Automatically, I'd draw in my breath.

"The day will come!"

We'd laugh then, rather sadly, and tighten our hold on the dream of change.

We were young. And excitable. Our moments of lovemaking were cherished.

But sex did not dominate our lives.

We had goals to meet in training, in achievements. Sex was —and would continue to be—a wondrous part of our lives, but the exigencies of living thrust us into a fast-moving world far removed from the bedroom. Ours was a warm, sometimes difficult, but loving relationship, tender, protective, satisfying to both of us. Our mutual bond was by far the most important thing in our life. Sexual intercourse was the end product of our sharing: It was the frosting on our cake.

A heavy snow had fallen during the night before our Christmas vacation began. Now it was snowing again as Becky and I said our farewell. Her bus left before mine. Watching her from the back, all alone, I thought of a little orphan turned out into the world. She was wearing a black and white coat and black boots and I can see her still—with the rainbow colors of her silk scarf fluttering in the wind, as if she were beckoning me. Before turning the corner, she stopped and looked back—and smiled at me. I wanted to run after her, hold her close, watch over her for the rest of our lives. I didn't want to let her go— also, I knew she'd be seeing Richard. Which of us would she choose? She tells me I am the one she loves—yet how will she feel when she sees Richard again?

After Christmas, it was difficult to hold my impatience in check: I wanted to get Becky alone and ask about Richard. Was the old feeling for him still there? Had she made her choice?

At last. Alone. "Well, did you see him?"

"Yes."

"What happened?"

"Oh, nothing much . . ."

God, you had to use tweezers to pull anything from this woman. I tried again. "Did—did anything happen?"

"No."

Frustration. I wanted to believe her. But she was such a gentle person, maybe she was protecting me—or thinking she was —by not telling me. All the pictures I'd envisioned of a joyful evening now vanished. I was angry and hurt that she had been with him. *Him*. Richard. I kissed her lightly on the cheek, said good night, and closed my door.

Was it possible I could have lost her? I refused to face such a possibility. I suffered through the next few days, and then it was New Year's Eve. We planned some time together to watch the New Year in. I'd make one more try. . . .

We kissed lightly on the last stroke of midnight. And then it was all passion and lovemaking and reassurance. Resting in the curve of my arm, she said softly, "It's over with Richard. . . ."

His name was never mentioned again.

During these months we'd been most discreet. Inseparable, yes, but always discreet. We were ever mindful of the fact that discovery meant nothing less than expulsion. Evenings were for study. We had no intentions of being exceptions. First and foremost, both Becky and I were there to learn a profession, to improve our cultural backgrounds, to excel in grades. The year did prove the happiest and most satisfying one of my education.

Still we had one, and only one, experience which was almost our undoing. (From that day on we were to shudder when we remembered it, and could only say that Providence had been on our side.) Having begged off from the St. Patrick's party—because we were not good dancers—we had an evening of love together. Cramped in the twin bed, bodies still relaxed from our union, suddenly we froze at the sound of voices calling our names: "Marie! Becky! Where are you two?"

Knuckles were rapping on my door, knuckles were rapping on Becky's. We heard running back and forth. Now they were banging both locked doors. Locked? Why? The rules were that no one ever locked doors unless they were to be away—and they knew we were here. Why didn't we answer?

"Wake up!" They were shouting now. "You've missed out on the fun of a lifetime."

We recognized the voices. But the voices were strange, not quite familiar. Slurred. And their laughter was becoming boisterous. They'd wake our whole second floor, maybe even the third. It was evident they'd had something out of the ordinary to drink at that dancing party. In fact, they were sloshed!

Sloshed? Their being out of control was our one chance.

They retreated and scrambled out onto the patio, upsetting chairs, loudly cautioning one another to be quiet. Next, they tried climbing into my window, only to find it locked. Becky's window they found unlocked and pushed it open with a clatter. I jumped out of Becky's bed, ran into the hall and toward my own room, only to be caught by these young rowdies—students, acting like a bunch of kids. In all stages of inebriation. And strictly against all regulations.

My worst instincts—or were they for survival?—came out and I did not hesitate to blackmail them. "If you kids tell anyone I was in Becky's room after hours I'll tell that you were drunk." This was meant to knock some sense into them but the partygoers were uncomprehending.

I hardened the defense: "What the hell do you think you're

doing? Upsetting chairs? Crawling in bedroom windows? Breaking rules by waking people on two floors?"

Intoxicated, these happy kids were almost totally oblivious to what had been going on, and so, rather shamefacedly, they shuffled off to their rooms.

The next few days were anxious ones for Becky and me. How much had these kids seen? What were they thinking?

The transgressions on both sides were never talked about, and, it seems, the celebrators had little or no memory.

The bond strengthened between Becky and me, and by Easter we were making plans for our future. Where to live? To work? We formulated short- and long-term goals. In my mind, a top priority was the surgical procedure for sex change.

God, how I wished I could marry this woman tomorrow. Stealing words from the poet, to know her was to love her. But marriage would have to wait until the day I legally became a male. . . .

Becky's family expected her home for Easter and I begged her to stay at school. But she'd promised and couldn't disappoint them. Why didn't I go with her? On second thought that didn't seem wise.

I came from the hospital just as her taxi was leaving the grounds, and, seeing me, she asked the driver to stop so we could say good-bye again. I held her close and kissed her and said how much I'd be missing her. The driver grew impatient and insisted that they leave for the station.

By evening I couldn't take this aloneness, so I phoned Becky and said I was taking the bus next morning to their farm.

Whatever our anxieties, it was wonderful being there. Just as Becky had said, her family talked very little but they had a way of lighting up at my exuberance, and the weekend was filled with more than the usual seasonal joys.

I slipped away from the family long enough to buy two corsages: tiny rosebuds for Becky to match the pink skirt she was wearing to the sunrise service, white carnations for her mom.

We went for an interview with the representative of a large medical center, famed for its research. The acceptance letters

arrived in early August. Rebecca wrote to her family and, du-
tifully, to the two civic-minded sponsors who had arranged for
her scholarship here at this school.

Time went by too quickly that last month: National League
of Nursing exams, the school's final exams, instructors' parties
for the student body, arranging for our new positions—our first
as nurses.

Cramming took precedence those last weeks. Final talks
with close classmates we might never see again were brief and
bittersweet. Parents of many students were coming for our
graduation, Becky's mother was coming—and suddenly I knew
again that great emptiness, a void, because no one of my family would be there to witness my personal triumph. Perhaps
because of these anxieties, my tensions mounted. And with the
tensions The Dream returned—now for the fifth time: the
same dream of being on the treadmill and trying to reach my
mother as I had remembered her in the coffin—only to have
the wheel turn me away and out of reach of her. . . .

Maybe because of the year's training—I don't know—suddenly I understood the significance of my recurring dream: a
projection of my frustrations, and the emotional loss of not
having her here to share my joy in accomplishment. But now, I
had successfully completed the first step toward my life goal
and I had a secure relationship with the woman I loved above
all else. Wherever my mother was, she somehow knew I had
succeeded in what I had undertaken. There was no need to
prove anything more to her.

Having satisfied myself with this explanation, I knew The
Dream would never again return to sadden me.

Finding Rebecca had fulfilled my life.

Those last days were frenzied days, with plans for graduation and launching careers. We were near nervous exhaustion
when we were proclaimed first and second in class standing.

Graduation over, Becky's brother took the two of us and their
mother back home. We had a restful week before taking up
residence in the city and beginning a new way of life.

When I managed to find her alone I had talked with Becky's
mom. She was even more reticent than her daughter, but,

looking me directly in the eye, she said, "Of all my children I think Becky has made the right choice in deciding to be with you."

Few things anyone had ever said had given me greater satisfaction. I had the distinct feeling that she was telling me she approved of me.

Yet I wondered: Exactly *why* did she believe Becky had made the right choice? Living by her Bible, literally word for word, did this mother believe I was trustworthy as a solid friend who bolstered her daughter's self-confidence? Or, could it be that she sensed something within me that she herself could not quite define? Was she, unknowingly, as perceptive as Sister Clement had been at Mt. St. Mary?

Whatever her reasons, I needed the comfort of her words for the turbulent years ahead.

7

R.N.: A Time of Decision

Eager to get on with our plans Becky and I left on schedule for Medical Center. We wanted the experience that comes only in a teaching institution.

Our first two weeks at the Center were taken up with orientation. Buildings were monumental, the rules seemingly inexhaustible. In the third week I was shunted off to the neurological ward. A major disappointment, since I'd specifically asked to be in obstetrics. No vacancies.

At first we had to live in a hotel, which, on our meager budget, meant carrying our lunches, Becky's handing me a dime for a carton of milk, no desserts. After three months we were out of the hotel and in the dormitory for employees (other than R.N.s), along with women from the kitchen, laundry, and auxiliary staff. Becky and I shared a room with twin steel beds, a dresser, and desk. The washroom was communal and we found ourselves again subjected to institutional living: I'd been sharing some part of my privacy for almost as long as I could remember. Well, come spring, we'd look for our first apartment.

But for now we were anxious about our state boards. Books, with all their meaning, needed the added experience of actually nursing here at Medical Center, but we kept at our boning and in November we went to City Hall for fingerprinting and a full day of testing. The morning exams were difficult and the whole group cheered the lunch break: a relief, which was to turn into a sort of postmortem. We kicked around a few questions and could come to no agreement on answers. The exams ended in late afternoon, and Becky and I wished the others luck, then boarded the bus back to the hospital dorm. Like everyone else who has ever taken the boards, we were downright glum about passing grades.

Becky was happy to be on a medical unit. She liked the work and had a good rapport with the gals. It was rather a jolt to see a worried little frown marring her usual calm at the end of one working day.

No amount of questioning could draw her out until bedtime when lights were dimmed. She turned to me and asked: "Mario, what is a butch?"

I could actually feel my skin bristle. "Where did you hear that word?"

"My head nurse asked about my 'butch.' . . ."

My masculinity had not escaped anyone. Yet how could a head nurse be so insensitive? Becky had no idea what the word implied, and I was glad lights were low when I told her. "A butch is the masculine member of a lesbian team. That would make you the feminine member. But, Becky, honest-to-God, I don't feel that we're lesbians. I still maintain I should have been a male."

She was so quiet there beside me.

"Well, Becky, I guess this is what I have to offer you: nothing but heartache."

No answer.

"God! But for a damn twig I'd be a man. And no one could ever make these hurtful remarks to you, Becky. But some day . . ."

"Yes, Mario." Her voice was soft, soothing. "It *will* work it-self out some day. I know—because you say so—and what you believe in always seems to happen."

"It will, Becky, it will! With God's help and yours."

No sleep for me that night. The word *butch* magnified itself before my eyes. *Butch* implied female—and I had never thought of myself as such. Would the word be as persistent, as stingingly painful as the word *nasty* my mom, had used when she found me touching my privates?

The incident was a deeply disturbing thing for us. It com-pounded my frustration in the neurological unit. The patients, because of their general nonresponsiveness, began to get to me. It was all but impossible to make them comfortable, other than to change their beds when they lost control and feed them through tubes inserted through noses and pushed down into stomachs.

In February, a full three months later, the letters came about our state boards. Holding my own in my hand, I broke into a cold sweat standing there in the mail alcove of our building. Half afraid of reading the results, I opened mine slowly. . . . I read. . . . I'd passed! Another time 'round! I grabbed Becky and squeezed her tight. A broad smile crossed her face when she opened hers. No need to say the words. We hugged again and looked at our reports still another time. Not until later were we to learn that Becky was second in our class, and I was first.

Six months passed and I begged to be taken off the neurolog-ical unit. Still no vacancies in obstetrics. And then I was of-fered a place on the *postpartum* (following childbirth) unit—if I wanted it. Did I want it!

The change to another unit, for the most part a happy one, was like changing worlds. This was the floor where mothers stayed after their babies came, smiling and proud to show off their newborns to one another and to anyone who'd look. They discussed their pregnancies and deliveries, their plans, their choice of names, colors, the nurseries waiting at home. Or, in times of sorrow, they'd try to console the mother whose infant was stillborn or died soon after birth. The mood in postpartum affected the whole floor.

How easy here in postpartum for me secretly to fantasize being the proud husband helping his wife through a most intimate and happy time of life: delivering our fine baby into its mother's—*my wife's!*—arms. Everything's just great, I could imagine myself saying as I passed the cigars. . . .

We found an air-conditioned studio apartment. We combined our checks and bought new furniture at a warehouse sale for our three rooms. It was paradise! Our first real home. A place to come to after work and be ourselves. I could wear slacks and shirts and smoke my pipe with just the two of us here. (The pipe was hidden when guests appeared.) House chores were divided according to traditional roles: I polished the shoes while Becky washed the nylons. She cooked the food, I washed the dishes. We worked and shared together. I was always Mario, the name she'd given me.

We continued on the evening shift, four to twelve. We'd have our times together then: talking, hi-fi turned low, a light supper, bed about three in the morning. It was the best life either of us had ever known.

Sometimes we'd go out with friends, sometimes they'd come here. One of our favorites was Miss Anderson, my head nurse. She was striking in appearance, proud of her blackness, proud of her ability at running her floor.

"I can run a floor from the seat of my pants," she'd say. True, she could. She never seemed to move from her chair yet knew everything that went on. She demanded excellence in nursing care, demanded we prove whatever point we were making. If we couldn't answer a question she'd send us to the medical library to discover for ourselves and to learn the answer sufficiently well to elaborate on the subject during our patient conferences.

To say we were fond of Miss Anderson was an understatement.

She was hell-bent on getting me out of my slacks and into dresses.

"How do you ever expect to get a man, Marie, dressed like that?"

"Come on, Miss Anderson," I'd banter. "Not everyone is out to get a man, you know."

This was always in the privacy of our home, never referred to at any other time. And, it's worth noting, she was the only one at this hospital who ever spoke directly to me about my mannish ways. Others were less honest, resorting to innuendos, or remarks behind our backs.

Through underground papers I located a *dildo*. Shaped like the male phallus, it is a venerable instrument used for intercourse. I was unhappy resorting to this device, it seemed demeaning to me. Strapping such a part to my body was playacting in a way. Hell, I was no actor. I *should* have been born with male anatomy.

So the dildo was a compromise. For now. It assuaged that inner urge that compelled me to accentuate my maleness; it was a step toward matching my body to my gender. Furthermore, *it deepened my determination that my own destiny was not to be set by biological patterns.* I refused to accept such a biological dictum.

Becky and I were happy together. "I love you as you are, Mario," she would say. "But, whatever makes you happy. . . ."

On one occasion I'd mentioned to Miss Anderson that my periods stopped when I left the convent. She was fearful that something had gone wrong and suggested I have a *culdoscopy*, a surgical procedure for visual examination of the uterus, tubes, and ovaries. During this procedure the surgeon puts a slim tube up through the vagina and looks at the ovaries. He may or may not take a specimen, depending on what he finds.

Miss Anderson kept at me for the next year, insisting I investigate this rather strange circumstance. The examination was scheduled.

I was hospitalized for only three days, but now, unexpectedly, our neighboring merchants came bearing gifts and free deliveries and special privileges. And one merchant toted a bouquet of flowers, which he himself had chosen at the florist's and brought directly to my bedside.

The surgeon found cystic ovaries: The ovaries were encapsulated in a fluid-filled sac. The condition did not warrant removal, but the required medication would start the ovaries functioning again—and, as my doctor put it, I'd become more womanly. I accepted the prescribed pills but never took even one.

Certainly, I had no desire to be *womanly*. I'd been working *against* that state for a lifetime.

Saving money on our combined salaries was slow, and we decided on a student loan so I could return to college. Our next goal was for me to become an R.N.

The thing that bothered me most was that Becky would be working to support both of us and to keep me in school. For Becky to have demurred would have been totally out of character. Yet her total acquiescence made me wonder sometimes, too.

"Becky, you're too good," I'd say. "Are you for real?"

Her laugh would lift my spirits and banish my self-doubts. "Mario, you'll be working toward that R.N. Why wait?"

"I make you a promise: As soon as I finish college I'll work while you earn your R.N."

"Agreed." She kissed me and the pact was made.

Going back to school full time would also mean my giving up, for most of the time, the apartment we thought of as home. Here was the life we'd carved out for ourselves. Living in the nurses dorm I'd be away from Becky (except for weekends) for three years. I was also sorry to leave our mutual friends, even sorrier to go back to the regimented life of textbooks.

The bank advised there would be a three-week wait on the student loan, so I went to the Werners, who for twenty-three years had owned the laundromat across the street from the hospital. I was not timid in my approach to Jacob. I simply told him about the three-week wait on the loan.

"Don't tell me what you need it for—just tell me how much. And don't think of paying it back until you graduate."

"Oh, but I will. I need $200 and will repay your loan as soon as mine comes through the bank. In three weeks."

Jacob insisted that we discuss it no further. This was his way of saying he trusted me implicitly.

Three weeks later I returned, as promised, with the $200. Jacob began his sermonizing all over again. "No hurry, Marie.

Just wait until you graduate."

I pressed the check into his hand and closed his fingers over it. "Just to prove to you that I am as good as my word."

"I know!"

I was sorry to leave Medical Center. By now I'd acquired greater confidence in myself as a nurse. I'd seen many types of cases before ever going to the postpartum floor and, once there, had been given charge of the floor. (Practical nurses were not usually promoted to this exalted position.) Too, I'd been elected president of the Licensed Practical Nurse group at the hospital and one of my duties was to attend meetings of all department heads. I was never reluctant to express my views and often did, and, in many instances, my suggestions were employed.

I registered for three subjects at Community College, all of which would be credited as requirements when I eventually became a regular student. And now the thought occurred to me that I'd be competing with people several years my junior.

A friend drove Becky and me to the dorm, and I wore a skirt and blouse on this very special day. Not by choice, to be sure. Too soon it was time for farewells, and my heart was heavy as Becky turned at the car to wave at me.

I joined a line of new students and filed into the auditorium, where instructors and the school's director were onstage. Miss Sapley, Director of Students, gave a curt welcome and the tone of her voice implied that we'd better not unpack if we'd no intentions of serious study.

Included in the rules were those for dress: street clothes to class, dresses to the cafeteria. Certainly I was not looking forward to living by a rule book. Still, if it meant my R.N. . . .

The seniors cautioned us to tread lightly.

"If you've been a practical nurse," one of them said, "don't do anything that shows you know anything. Act dumb."

Such advice required explanation. "Some of the instructors have come directly from a college program for nursing to a master's program—without having had actual experience."

"But there must be exceptions," I said hopefully.

"We know of only a few. Unfortunately, some of these inexperienced instructors made up the study and class plan and the lectures for the entire staff of instructors!"

One thing I liked: Each student had her own room. The girls on my floor were nice enough, but I had no wish to know too much about their personal lives. Infrequently I'd join them as several crammed into one room after a date or on a night before exams. I'd listen to their chatter about boyfriends, the latest movies, price of Wedgwood china, or a diamond engagement ring.

I just didn't fit in with this group. . . .

Weekends with Becky were anything but satisfactory, for she was often at work and my lessons were always in progress. A hell of a lot of work! But Becky's work was just as confining. I was short on patience, partly from a guilt-sense, of course.

In time the students started coming to me, and this was rather complimentary, I thought, considering the difference in our ages. Or maybe it was because of this very difference that they felt free to come to me with their problems, knowing I did not carry gossip. I began to feel like a father confessor.

It was a good feeling.

It was now clear to me exactly what the seniors had meant by saying the instructors did not take well to any student who knew too much. In class one day we were discussing steroids. Weight gain is an adverse reaction brought on by one, but my instructor insisted no, it was weight loss, *not* gain. I pointed out that that was in error, according to the pharmacology textbook.

I gained in students' eyes that day. And lost grace with almost every instructor in school. One does not make a fool out of an instructor and get away with it.

I longed for the day I could return to the hospital atmosphere. Life as a student was not for me. Accustomed to working with a staff that *knew* medicine, I was being taught by people without actual practice, people who had learned to teach by rote.

One of the gals on our floor and a pal went on a binge and

they returned drunk to the dorm. They were in deep depression. There was a scream. Running out into the hall, I saw girls crowding into one room.

"Marie! Quick. Millie and Alice are going to jump out the window."

I shoved my way into the room just in time to grab Millie, who was wailing incoherently, one leg over the sill. She fought me with an unbelievable strength and once she almost slipped away, but I managed to get her off that sill. Alice, protesting as vehemently, was restrained by the others. It took a half hour to get the would-be suicides quieted down, and three girls assigned themselves to Millie, three to Alice, promising to stay with them for the night.

Everyone was visibly shaken as we assembled in the recreation room to decide what to do about this mess.

A senior suggested that someone go to an instructor who could be trusted to give advice and keep the confidence. And I found myself appointed to seek help for Millie and Alice.

Alice I liked. Millie was a little on the strange side.

"All right," I said. "Tomorrow morning I'll see Mrs. Arenstein. She seems pro-student. Maybe she can help."

The incident recalled the figure sprawled on the courtyard that early morning back at my first hospital. Should the girls succeed at a second attempt, the whole affair would be forever on my conscience. Still, I'd feel like a fink, revealing the behavior of the two.

Why had I accepted this responsibility?

I was actually scared. I'd never gone to anyone with such a problem. And what if the girls were expelled? Well, I'd been persuaded to undertake this mission and must face up to it.

I was waiting for Mrs. Arenstein as she came through the door and, wanting to get the words out, I lost no time in asking her: "May I have a quick conference with you? It's a matter that cannot wait."

"Of course, Marie. Come with me and we'll talk in my office."

She listened patiently and her answer was a disconcerting one. "I'm sorry you came to me, Marie. Now that the incident has been brought to my attention, I shall have to report it to

Miss Sapley, our director. Attempted suicide is one of two problems we must report—the other is overt lesbianism."

"These kids must not be expelled, Mrs. Arenstein. They're good kids. *You must give them another chance.*"

"They'll not be expelled, I promise you. But we must report to Miss Sapley and she, in turn, will see that the two girls get professional help."

"And what if they don't want professional help? What then?"

"Once reported, it must be followed through."

"Please! Can't you make an exception this once? Can't you and I handle it together?"

I hadn't wanted this responsibility—why was I now so desperate to add to it?

"Marie, from our psych classes you know that attempted suicide is a call for help. These young women need help, they're crying for it."

"You're right. I know that only too well, Mrs. Arenstein. But grant me this one favor: Let me go with you to talk with Miss Sapley."

"Favor granted. You may plead their cases."

Miss Sapley promised genuine help: Millie and Alice were not to be expelled—they would be permitted to continue classes—with the stipulation that they see the psychiatrist three times each week for as long as the psychiatrist deemed the sessions necessary.

News of my meeting with the director raced along the grapevine, and by lunchtime I was avoided as if I had the plague. By evening voices coming from the recreation room were loud and angry.

Who had betrayed the confidence?

I stepped inside the room and was confronted by several girls trying to subdue Millie, who was clawing at them. Seeing me, she shrieked: "What the hell did you do to me?"

"I've only tried to help. . . ."

And Alice was screaming, "I know I'm going to be expelled. And all this will kill my parents!"

"See," someone was calling above the din, "I knew we should never have sent Marie."

It was twenty minutes before my small audience was calm enough that I could make myself heard. "Now that you've piped down I'll give you the play-by-play report."

Just then Millie lunged at me with a pair of scissors and I grabbed her wrist. Passing Millie over to the girl nearest her, I excused myself and left the room.

Only five people spoke to me during the next three weeks. But the conclusion was far from a fiasco: Miss Sapley kept her promise, and the girls had the sessions with the shrink. Millie left school later of her own accord—Alice, because of failing grades, was held back for one semester. I knew I could have done nothing differently. The silent treatment was hard to take, but perhaps it was a small price for two human lives. And I won a few friends who were to endure through all the years.

Donna, who lived across the hall from me, was a gifted student. Throughout the year she'd been rather withdrawn, but now, after this crisis with Millie and Alice, she was one of the five who came to tell me how courageously I'd acted, that I'd handled the situation as it should have been done. And on this first visit to my room she openly confessed that, prior to now, she'd thought I was lesbian.

"But what made you think that?"

"Your short hair, your masculine manners, your clothes. And, well—I'm sorry for having ever thought that of you, Marie."

"Set your mind at rest, Donna. It's not true."

I'd earned her respect. I wanted her friendship. I was not about to jeopardize all this by revealing my true feelings regarding my sexual confusion. Not for now. . . .

God, how I missed Becky. I'd feel that little prick of conscience, remembering that she was working to put me through school—and remembering the too little time we actually had together on the weekends.

Educational relationships were more relaxed my second year. Those of us who had been practical nurses prior to coming here were now given more responsibility in helping those who hadn't had this experience. It went against my grain, however, to be teaching peers: It made us appear as if we knew more than we actually did and led to dissension. When classes took us to OB we were assigned to work as a team of two in the labor room, and I was told to stay with my student the entire day. Our patient complained of burning during urination, and I told my student to ask our instructor, Miss White, if we could pour warm water over the genital area when the patient (who'd been shaved for delivery) used the bedpan. Miss White agreed with the suggestion, but, at the end of the day, she gave my student an A and me a C.

When I stormed into her office to complain, Miss White reprimanded me. "But your teammate asked a very intelligent question and I saw her listening for the fetal heartbeat—and I didn't see you doing a thing."

An argument followed. "Damn it, Miss White! I'm not here to teach, you are—and you're doing a miserable job of it."

I tore up my day's grade and threw it to the floor next to her desk.

Having learned of my run-in with Miss White, Valerie Brooks, my favorite instructor, called me aside. "Marie, you must realize you've turned almost all the instructors against you. What really happened between White and you?"

I was only too happy to tell her my version and when I'd finished she asked. "What do you want to do when you graduate, Marie?"

"I have long-term goals. But first I must work and get back on my feet financially."

It was too much to tell her that Becky was working and financing my education. I felt degraded, just thinking about it. A man worked for his wife—not the other way round—and, although Becky was not legally my wife, she was my wife in my way of thinking.

"I'm thinking of a halfway house of some kind," I added. "Right now, I'm thinking of unwed mothers."

"I hear the students come to you with their problems. Now, don't you suppose the faculty just might feel they're being circumvented?"

"Who cares!" I could be myself with Mrs. Brooks. "I don't ask the gals to come banging on my door at all hours to discuss possible pregnancies and low grades."

"I believe you, Marie. But it's not what I believe that

counts. Don't you see, Marie, *you must care*. Some of these instructors are not too secure in their positions and you are un-
dermining their authority. They will retaliate. In fact, Marie, if
you don't change your ways you're likely to find yourself failing."

"Impossible. I have a B average."

"Try to stay out of trouble, Marie. If you need to blow off
steam, then try my door. It's always open."

By the third (senior) year I resolved to stick by the advice
Mrs. Brooks had given me. Furthermore, I wouldn't ask questions in class and wouldn't volunteer information.

We went to the psychiatric unit for our four-month rotation.
Our instructor, Miss Hilary, was mannish in her tailored suits
and shirts, with which she wore a long soft tie. It was rumored
she had a liaison with an instructor who had said she'd ruin
me. So, with all this hearsay, what could I expect from Miss
Hilary but absolute hell?

On each visit to a psychiatric hospital Miss Hilary would assign me to a patient who was withdrawn, uncommunicative.
On our written reports we were to express our feelings about
each patient, but, whatever I reported, it was never to her satisfaction. Her manner toward me was condescending, and I
said as little as I could and still get a passing mark.

One day she called me to her office. "Miss Martino," she
said, "I'm giving you an F for every day you are in the hospital."

"I don't understand, Miss Hilary. Why?"

Inside I was steaming. She knew it.

"You don't participate in class discussions as you used to,
and your reports do not reflect any interaction with your patients."

"I am as honest as I know how to be in my reports. And how
much can I say about a withdrawn patient? As for class—well,
I get tired of hearing myself always talking—especially since
my contributions seem to be unappreciated. . . ."

"Miss Martino, why do you misuse your great leadership
abilities? Why not use them in positive ways?" She hesitated,
as if reluctant to give me the only compliment she was ever to

give me: "In case you haven't noticed, other students are following your lead."

Either way, I thought, I'm damned.

"Well, Miss Martino, you'd better resume talking in class—otherwise you'll fail in nursing this semester."

Not trusting myself to say anything more, I told her I'd try to follow her wishes and left the room. Definitely, Miss Hilary had the upper hand.

I couldn't face the prospect of failing the last three months of my final semester. But how could that be, since I had a B average?

Becky was not to know of my deep depression. Nothing was to upset her before she left soon on her yearly vacation. I'd have to work this out alone.

At about this time, all hospital personnel were invited to submit paintings, drawings, and other artworks for an exhibition. I had a few drawings I'd made with a black felt pen, one of which was a piece of lettering: *PLEASURE*. Representing Freud's Pleasure Principle, I had titled the piece *Freud*.

All my drawings were returned with this note: "Miss Hilary was consulted about your submitted artwork and feels it is too sexually oriented to be acceptable."

What a bitch!

And what could I do about it? Not a damn thing.

Becky left for her vacation that Thursday—and, alone, I wallowed in self-pity.

How could I get to that bitch Hilary and beat her at her own game? What had I done to her personally to make her so thoroughly dislike me? Did I make her feel threatened? Did she envy my living in the nurses dorm with all those young girls? (But, as she couldn't know, these gals meant nothing to me—I loved Becky.)

I'd hate to confess just how murderous my thoughts were the day my art was returned and, recognizing my negativism, I switched to the positive and thought of the beautiful Mrs. Brooks and her sound advice. Acting on that, I'd ask for a conference with Mrs. Lazier, student adviser, right after my last class tomorrow. Mrs. Lazier was liked and trusted so completely by the student body that she was actually distrusted by her own peers. She was in full command of her position and of herself and said exactly what she thought. Her time was our time whenever the need presented itself.

Mrs. Lazier had other plans this Friday afternoon, and her husband was outside waiting in the car when I went to her office. But she said yes, come in, we'd talk briefly.

Actually, we talked for more than two hours, and I gave her a full recitation of the talk with Miss Hilary.

"She filed her report this morning so I am aware of the problem. I don't believe I'm breaking confidence when I say she considers your attire much too masculine. Personally, I can't see her talking about masculine attire—those suits and shirts and ties she wears don't make her into the most feminine woman I've ever met. Be that as it may, Miss Hilary does seem to have the knack of getting her own way."

Mrs. Lazier asked for more details as to my work in the mental hospital and seemed satisfied with what I said.

"Mrs. Lazier, I'd rather quit and appear a fool than to fail as a dimwit."

"You won't quit, Marie, and you won't fail," she assured me. "But I believe this would help you: In Miss Hilary's class wear a little makeup, perhaps a pair of earrings. Look a little more feminine. This would be one of your small compromises. It's not too much to ask, considering all that is at stake.

"Go even further. See her privately and tell her about the suicides, tell her you find it difficult to be around patients who exhibit the same latent characteristics. She'll get the feeling that you're coming to her with a problem that she, Miss Hilary, can solve. Your confessing this one uncertainty about yourself will give her the superior feeling that you are privately exposing your soul for her scrutiny—and she'll obligate you by helping solve this one problem. Also, she'll consider she's doing you a favor just by listening. . . ."

"I'll try, Mrs. Lazier. That I do promise. But every time I see her, I want to punch her in the mouth. Too bad we aren't both men—then I could meet her in an alley and take care of her."

My conference with Miss Hilary took place the following Tuesday. If she mistook my solemn countenance and downcast eyes for contrition she was mistaken. Quite the contrary: I hated this woman so violently that just looking at her would surely betray me. I avoided eye contact. To me she was a bitter, hostile woman in a position to cause harm.

Miss Hilary patiently heard me through: the truth, with a few theatrical embellishments for the sake of telling a good story. And, just as Mrs. Lazier had predicted, Miss Hilary thanked me for coming.

"Return to class tomorrow," she concluded. "I'm glad you've come to me with all that's been on your mind during this four-month period in psychiatry."

I couldn't get back to Mrs. Lazier quickly enough and tell her how right she'd been. We embraced over our combined success and she said: "Don't worry, Marie. You're going to graduate—and I'll be the first one in the audience to yell."

Sure enough: The day came, I went forward for my diploma —and I heard a familiar "hurray!" from the audience.

Two days after graduation, Becky and I went away for a restful weekend, the first time we'd really had to ourselves in three rough years. Nothing waiting to be done on schedule. Unimaginable contentment. Now I would be taking care of Becky. And the next day, even though her birthday was not for a couple of months, I bought her a color TV as a surprise. It was solid proof I was home to stay.

I reaffiliated with my hospital and, in addition, took a summer position as nurses aide teacher. My students were mostly older men and women, and they adapted easily with my encouragement. I was proud that I could reverse the negative procedures of my former teachers.

That summer I was one of thousands who traveled to the state capital for R.N. state board examinations. The two-day exams were grueling and the general feeling among the examinees was one of having flunked the whole thing. And ahead was that intolerable wait while the papers were processed.

One day it came: the official envelope from the Nursing Examining Board. As I had with those exams for L.P.N., today I made the smallest slit—just enough to see the word *Passed*. One rip, the envelope was opened, its contents spilled out. Tears streamed down my face, and for one instant I saw my mother's face and she was smiling.

I kept saying, "Thank God, thank God." Grades 85 to 95 in all subjects and, shock of shocks, the psychiatry mark was one of the highest. If old Hilary could see this, I thought suddenly, she'd have a fit!

Now, with all the requisites completed, I could earn enough to plan the sex change I dreamed about. This little slip of paper would help me achieve my goals, *thank God*.

I took a position at North Oaks Hospital and stayed there for more than a year, putting in time in the medical unit, taking the special course in coronary care and then working in that unit. I liked the challenges and I liked the staff. The staff was exceptional: young, enthusiastic, and eager to learn. We worked hard and under terrific pressures and often, at the end of this late shift, we'd relax together. Becky and I were happier than we'd ever been, with good friends and professional satisfactions.

In the fall of my second year I was offered a position I felt ready for, that of nursing supervisor at another hospital. This one step up the ladder meant a larger paycheck, more to save toward sex surgery. Equally important was the experience I could gain.

Becky and I decided that I should go home for my two weeks' vacation and talk seriously with my family about my plans, even though we had yet to find a reputable medical doctor associated with a sex-change program. I'd talk with Jan and Jim, Dad and Lenore, before Becky came at the end of the first week.

Janet and Jim and family had just settled in a comfortable suburban home. Exactly what I'd hope for some day when Becky and I could legally marry.

The dinner hour was over, dishes washed, kitchen tidied,

kids safely tucked in. And now the three of us, Janet and Jim and I, talked about the drastic changes I was determined to make in my life.

"I'd say you have some tough going ahead. Have you thought this thing through, Marie?"

"I've been thinking about it for what seems forever, Jim."

"And what about Becky?" Janet asked.

"Well, we know that Becky is the silent type. She doesn't say much. Mostly, she just looks at me with those marvelous eyes and I do most of the talking. She does say one thing, though: 'Let's not do anything that would change things between us. I can be happy as we are. And that's for always.' "

"I can just see her and hear her." Janet was lost to us for the moment, as if she were feeling the very things that Becky had said.

Five hours passed while we tossed questions and answers back and forth. How would I begin? What would it cost? How long must I work to get the money? Was a loan ever made for such a program? Was surgery reversible? What would we tell our families, the kids in our families? Our friends? How could I change without going out of circulation for a year? How many others were there in the world with problems like mine? Was it easier for a man to be transformed into a woman than a woman into a man? How would this affect sex life?

I didn't know all the answers but promised to keep them advised. I had no definite idea where to start, perhaps at Johns Hopkins: Hopkins was the first to admit publicly it helped individuals who might benefit by such changes.

"Don't you realize all your interrelations with both sexes will change?" Jim asked.

"I don't see that. I'll still be sticking to all the old family traditions, simply playing a reversal of roles."

"How will the husbands feel when you drop by to see their wives?"

"Jan, that's one thing I hadn't considered. You're right, of course."

"And don't forget, pal," Jim reminded me, "the psychological games that go on between the sexes."

"I'll have to play by ear."

"Once the change is made will you and Becky marry legally?"

"God, I hope so! I don't ask too much of life: just to live quietly with my wife, perhaps with children—like any other family on the block."

"Will you tell Mom's family?"

"I don't see so much of them since Aunt Concetta died, and I've decided not to visit them this trip. I want to talk to Dad and Lenore, of course, and, for the life of me, I don't know what to say. Maybe we should sleep on it."

"Yes. But let me say this, Marie: I admire your courage and anything I can do for you, well, whistle."

"I'm whistling now, Jim. Tomorrow you can teach me to tie a Windsor knot tie."

Greeting me in the morning, Janet whispered tearfully in my ear: "I want you to be happy and I'm behind you a thousand percent."

She and I left in time to arrive at Dad's apartment by ten o'clock. After the familial embraces I excused myself long enough to go to Dad's bedroom (a custom I'd acquired with my more adult years) and changed to one of his old shirts, took one of his hats from the shelf. In a way it was like dressing for the guillotine: wondering how I'd react when the edge of Dad's verbal ax touched that vital part of me.

Dad had grown old in a comparatively short time. Some of the family said he'd mellowed, others that he was too crippled with Parkinson's disease and diabetes to dominate any longer the lives of his children. Maybe he had mellowed under the patient care of Lenore, who loved him as Mom had once loved him.

How would this shuffling old man, once so vigorous, react to what I was about to tell him?

As a child I'd known this man's strength both physically and emotionally. Now his facial muscles were partially paralyzed and he could scarcely smile at all.

I put his hat on my head, tilted it at a rakish angle, and moved to the door. "Well, Dad, how does it look?"

"Ma-ria, Ma-ria. Are you always going to wear those clothes?"

"Dad, this is exactly what I've come to talk to you about."

His face brightened for the briefest moment, then dimmed, and the light died out.

"All these years I've worn these clothes. You've yelled and carried on about them but now you won't have to worry about my wearing the wrong kind of clothes."

A brief brightened look. "No, Ma-ria?"

"No. Next year I'm having sex-change surgery and will become the man I've always thought myself to be."

"My, God, Ma-ria!" He clutched at his chair. "Go! Take that hat off. Behave yourself."

The subject was closed.

We turned to the inconsequentials, and Lenore tried to lessen the chill with coffee and her homemade pastries. Jan and I returned home in time for lunch.

A door had been slammed shut.

Later that day I took Jim aside for some man-to-man talk.

"I'm terrified to go into a men's store and buy pants. What will I do when I'm measured for an inseam?"

"Well—gee, I've never thought about it. Maybe you'd just shape a sock and put it inside the flap of your jocks. The tailor will be none the wiser."

"Do all men use the urinal every time they go to the john?"

"Of course not. Most of the guys at my office use the stalls. You have a lot to learn."

"One other thing: I don't normally use curse words. Most of the guys I've known don't curse but maybe it's only when I'm around."

"You're worrying too much, Marie. When the time comes and you feel like it, then cuss a streak. If the time comes you'll know it. For the record, most of the men I know swear very little."

"And what about all this sex business? Do other guys have sex on their minds most of the time?"

"Most guys outgrow the locker room stage as they mature, and, at your age, there's nothing more than an occasional joke or a wolf whistle at the centerfold of *Playboy*."

"Then I can just be myself?"

"Of course. You'll fit into whatever circle you feel you'd like to be a part of. You've managed your gender feelings all these years and now, in a new way, you'll have even more freedom to be yourself."

"Blessed words!"

"From what you've told me about your friends, I'd guess they'll help you in minimizing your problems."

"Well, I'd bet my life on that."

"I say you'll fit in just fine."

Our talkathons continued and we were happy to have Becky fly in late Friday to complete our foursome. Becky's way of communicating was quiet listening, saying little, her inner thoughts buried deep. Were they troubled thoughts? We loved her because of her concern for me, we loved her for herself.

"Do you think you'll ever come home again after you've made the change?" Janet asked almost every day.

"I can't say right now. I don't want to cause Dad any more unhappiness. I've grown up in many ways and am beginning to understand something of his feelings, his loyalties to old family traditions. Not that I've blanked out my childhood. I remember it distinctly, painfully. But now that my life gives promise of being reshaped, I no longer hold the old hatreds."

At other times we'd discuss Dad's state of health. Perhaps seeing him reduced to an aging simple man touched some responsibility toward him that had lain dormant. Maybe it was nothing more than pity. Whatever my emotions were today, much of the hurt of all the yesterdays had blurred.

Before going home I'd made certain decisions: I'd give up my family rather than cause any ill feelings or wounds. But I'd waited too long and wanted too intensely to find my identity to let anything or anybody deter me now. Not my family, not even Becky!

My mind was now at rest. Janet and Jim were fully supportive. And Becky? Well, I could always count on her. . . .

Rewarding, and surprising, was my change in attitude toward those I'd disliked so vehemently in my school of nursing.

I realized now that my own accomplishments were more than satisfactory. I hadn't asked for negative learning but I'd had it and had put it to constructive use. I was finding I could rise above my own frustrations in imparting knowledge to those seeking it. Even the enmity I'd once held for Miss Hilary had turned to compassion.

I was realigning my life. The pieces were falling into place, my questing was ending, answers were coming.

After what seemed eons, I was emerging from this labyrinth of erroneous human anatomy.

8

Neo-Gender

The Christine Jorgensen story had surfaced in newspapers when I was fifteen. When her book came out in 1967 I was undoubtedly the very first buyer at our local bookstore, for the salesperson raised an eyebrow, looked at me a second time, and, embarrassed, handed me the copy.

I was saddened at the public scorn and ridicule inflicted on Christine and saw that she had been able to endure such rejection because she had the support of her family. Would I have that? Christine's father had told the press: "She is ours—and we love her!"

(To even imagine my father's reaction to my coming sex change was to panic. "Butchery!" he'd called the Jorgensen surgery.)

In her book, Ms. Jorgensen defines her own case: ". . . an individual belonging to the 'highest degree of intersexuality; male organs in a female body.' "

Christine Jorgensen fit Dr. Harry Benjamin's definition of a transsexual. Her book established the term and its meaning in the public's mind. Now, if I must label myself, I could hope for some degree of recognition, perhaps even for understanding.

I toyed with the thought that I was an individual belonging to the highest degree of intersexuality, only my case was the reverse of Christine's, since she had begun life as a boy. Then I was *not* too different! And there were tens of thousands all over the world with varying degrees of this same intersexuality.

1967: The year of the Christine Jorgensen book would be my year too!

To have *my* body reflect my image of myself as a male I would pay any price, do anything within honor, to restructure my life. Rejection would be overcome. As to the thousands of dollars needed for complete surgical sex change? Well, I'd never been afraid of work, I looked forward to working at a career, and I knew the value of my savings account. Money would be a problem, yes, but only one of many.

I would take the bull by the horns right now!

And *scared* was the word. No other word adequately described my feeling as I picked up the phone and put in a long-distance call to the man I wanted most in the world to see, Dr. Harry Benjamin. His amiable secretary explained that the doctor was away. She would, however, refer me to a most reputable physician in the city where I was working. "He can advise you," she said, "and make recommendations."

I thanked her and placed the call. That secretary said the doctor had just left on vacation and she had no recommendations to offer. I phoned the county Medical Society and was given three names, among them that of Dr. Patterson. My fourth call was to his office.

Dr. Patterson's voice came over the wire: professional, impersonal, neither friendly nor unfriendly. I was still scared and now the words tumbled out: how I'd felt all my life I should have been a male, I was sure I was a male—and when could I see him regarding treatment?

His answer was surprising. "Well, jump into a cab and come right over. I'm leaving the office early today and will be gone for at least a week."

So it was arranged. *My day had come.*

My heart seemed to have taken a high dive and lodged in my throat. After a quick scrub and change into slacks and tailored shirt I was on my way.

As I waited to see him, I wondered how I could convince Dr. Patterson that I was a good candidate for sex change. I thought of Becky. Of late she had withdrawn. How could she be so indifferent to my elated mood? What was wrong? For eight years we'd talked about a sex change, and she knew I wanted to be a male more than I wanted anything in this world. Why couldn't she share my joy? My black thoughts were cut short by the secretary, who came to say the doctor would see me now.

In his paneled office, Dr. Patterson stood to greet me and shake my hand. Here, I hoped, was a man who understood my confusion. A man I could talk to. A man, a doctor, who could and would help me.

Dr. Patterson explained the criteria for the patient who wishes to change his or her anatomical structure to fit the psychological gender the patient believes himself or herself to be. He discussed at length the problems of living successfully in that gender role for a period of readjustment.

"The patient's stability must be supported by a psychiatrist's letter, stating that said patient has no psychosis or neurosis. With such a letter or report at hand, I will expect you to come in for periodic injections.

"You understand, of course, you must undergo a complete physical examination. We would want a twenty-four-hour urine specimen brought to our lab for a study of a test known as 17-ketosteroids. As a nurse you must know this is a measurement of the hormones normally found in urine: greater or lesser amount than normal excretion is indicative of certain endocrine disorders."

I couldn't help boasting. "I've had the test. A few years back. Mine proved to be that of a seventeen-year-old male."

"Well now. It sounds as if we're off to a good start."

As I undressed in the small examining room, my mind was reeling from the intensive personal probing into my life patterns which the doctor had done. He had questioned me on my feelings as I was growing up, my relationships with parents, siblings, peers—relationships with both sexes and at all ages. And sitting there naked on the examining table, I wanted this physical part of the workup over. I tried to hide my bulbous breasts by folding my arms atop them and my lower portion by drawing my legs up in a bending fashion.

The doctor ignored my embarrassment—if, indeed, he was even aware of it. He asked me to stand and be weighed and have my height taken. He measured my shoulders, bust, waist, and hips.

We talked about hormones. "They sometimes cause water retention," he said, "and add weight."

"I'm aware of that, Dr. Patterson."

Suddenly I felt a new surge of excitement. The doctor was talking as if I were already accepted.

Taking my blood pressure was routine—but how I dreaded the internal examination. This had been done once before and was extremely painful because my vagina was abnormally small. But now, since it must be done, I tried every technique I'd ever learned to relax. Deep breathing didn't work. Suddenly a searing burning pain, and I almost jumped off the table.

"What the hell did you do?"

"I simply inserted this tiny cotton-tipped applicator to get secretions. We must see the smear under the microscope to determine the hormonal effects manifested here."

But why did he have to push that damn applicator in with such a thrust? I was suddenly apprehensive. Was this doctor as professional as he first appeared? Was he just impersonal? Or did he enjoy inflicting pain?

The physical was over, and I dressed quickly. Back in his office he gave the name and address of the lab and that of Dr. Harris, the psychiatrist I was to see. He, it happened, was just across the hall from Dr. Patterson. I was given a future appointment and, on the way out, stopped in and arranged to see Dr. Harris on the afternoon of my next visit.

In spite of the nagging little upset during the internal exam, I was exuberant. I hailed a cab, talked animatedly with the driver, as if this would hasten my trip home. I wanted to tell Becky the wonderful news.

I was very sure of acceptance for the Gender Identity Program. As I understood the program, it was a prescribed course for all transsexuals who wanted sex-change surgery and were willing to go on a strictly disciplined routine of role-playing for one year prior to surgery.

I kept thinking how happy Becky would be for me, and began counting the blocks home. There at last! But no Becky at the door. Where was she?

Inside. Knitting. Not a word.

"Becky, I'm home. And I think I've been accepted for reassignment!"

"Oh." She did not look up from her knitting. "You'll find your mail on the desk."

This was not the time to talk about it. . . .

The psychiatric evaluation by Dr. Harris went about as I had expected: terse questions about my life from the time I first felt I was a male child, my formative years, my loves. He turned over old memories long dormant. After all this delving he validated that I was a legitimate patient: not a homosexual, transvestite, schizoid, psychopath, or exhibitionist. Approved for reorientation!

But wait—approval on the *first visit*? Was I being taken in? Believing what I wanted to hear? No, not I. I was too sure of what I was. And I believed in Dr. Patterson.

I would not look for trouble: I would accept the "approval" and proceed.

I took my psychiatric evaluation directly to Dr. Patterson and we discussed it freely and at length. Without hesitation, he said, "I shall be happy to take you on as a patient. But one thing you must always remember: Transsexual patients remain patients until they die—they are on hormones as long as they live."

"I can accept that."

"Good. We can proceed."

Dr. Patterson's outline of the program came as words recited in a litany: inspiring, awesome. For one year I was to be masculinized with hormone therapy, which would decrease menstruation for the average female (but my periods had stopped, as I've said, when I left the religious life), increase facial and body hair, increase the libido, and deepen the voice. During this time I was to play that role of the man I wanted above all else to be: dressing the part, learning new speech patterns and inflections, mannerisms, carriage, and gait. If, at the end of the year, I was unhappy, the therapy would be reversed and I would be refeminized. If, however, I was content as a male, we would take the second of three procedures, a mastectomy.

I scarcely felt the prick of the hormone injection, heard little of what Dr. Patterson was saying. The years of frustration would surely end. How little do we know!

In my spirit of high elation, again I couldn't wait to get home to Becky, wanting to share with her this all-engulfing happiness. When I came through the door she was setting her hair, but I grabbed her anyway and held her tight.

"I've been accepted!"

Silence. Stony silence.

What was wrong? She knew how I felt, she had given me a male name, and our roles in the home were those of husband and wife.

"Becky, what's wrong? I don't understand."

The silence. Her face frozen.

I was hurt at her lack of appreciation of the fact that after all these years I was going to be what I should always have been: *male*.

For the first time in eight years Becky refused to talk. Could she not face the prospects ahead, the possible loss of friends, rejection by parents and peers? What other reasons could there be?

Yes, I was hurt. We had such a good life together. And now it would be even better in countless ways—even if we did have to move and make new friends. Couldn't she see this?

Her silence continued and the days passed. I fell into deep depression, almost to the point of illness. And, just as suddenly as she froze, she broke silence.

"I cannot accept the idea, Mario." She was devoid of emotion.

"Are you afraid of a *man*? Are you afraid of being *close* to a man?"

"No."

"Has ours been a sham of a relationship?"

"No."

"What then?"

"I accept the change intellectually—I just can't accept it ethically."

"Ethically?"

"You're interfering with one of God's divine principles in mutilating your God-given body!"

"But if God gives man the talents . . . ?"

"Can man reverse divine principles to please a whim and not pay a penalty?"

"You're ignoring the God-given talents, dammit! If it weren't that He wanted to help me out of this mess, He wouldn't make it possible for me now to achieve this goal of finally becoming the man I was meant to be!"

"For the moment, let's leave ethics out of it. Let's think of family attitudes: There's your father, for instance—and my mother. Would he accept it? No. And Mom would never accept it. In our small community almost everything new is considered a sin."

"We don't need ever to tell your family, they need never know. I will simply look and act more masculine than I already do."

She was unmoved. I tried another tack. "We could say I am my cousin."

"No! I will not lie."

In the darkness of night she said, "I'm leaving you."

The room seemed to whirl and the world crash around me. My dreams and aspirations were rubble. Chaos. Heartache replaced the dreamed-of glories.

"Becky, you are my right arm, my right leg. You are my heart. You are my all, the woman I love. I don't know how to make it any stronger than this. But, Becky, I have to live with *me*—and if I have only this one chance to achieve my lifetime ambition, I have to take it."

Gloom set in. Automatically we slept, got up, and went to work, came home to sleep and to get up still another morning and go again to work. I was scarcely aware of the hours. I didn't know how to contend with this impasse. Where once we had discussed everything, now there was nothing. No communication between us for three months—and now I knew what it must be like to suffer the death separation from a beloved mate. I was dead inside.

During my periodic visits to Dr. Patterson I told him of this problem at home but he seemed not to understand the enormity of it.

Dr. Patterson had left his plush offices at a prestigious address in the metropolis and moved to the ghetto. Crumbling paint revealed an earlier grandeur, but the building was old and just to walk up those thirty-three rickety steps was to wonder if one would reach the top. He held monthly meetings here for his patients, and occasionally other doctors came to talk and listen. None of us minded too much this change of environs, for we came to meet and to educate each other. Since each of us was in some stage of sex reassignment, we exchanged experiences, ideas on male attire, how and where to have clothes made to order, the feelings and facts of our new anatomy.

It was at one of these Sunday group sessions that I met Nick, who had just gone through two major surgeries: the bilateral mastectomy and complete hysterectomy. Having been on hormones for a longer period than I, he had the beginnings of a dark beard.

A stranger to the city, in fact an alien from a Communist country, he was ready to start his new life, but first he must find a job. This was going to be difficult because he could not change his legal papers. Resigned to working as a laborer, he'd torn up his college degrees and changed his name, wanting to destroy all trace of origin. Impulsively, I invited him home with me for the holidays.

If Becky had rejected *me*, how then could I expect her to accept Nick, unknown, who had already accomplished what I was working toward?

Her reception was cool. She did absolutely nothing for Nick. Not the smallest courtesy, not a flicker of a smile.

Nick was a highly perceptive person. To avoid embarrassing us, he suggested our quarters were too small for three people and that it would be better for him to stick to his original plan.

"Nick, you're just out of the hospital. In a cheap rooming house you'll be a target for muggers and thieves."

"Don't worry about that. My worldly goods are all here inside these two suitcases—nothing worth much anyhow. As for money, well, it's pinned to my underwear. Anyone who wants it will have to kill me to get it." But his laugh was without mirth. (I was to learn later that he had $3,000 pinned next to his new body.)

Nick left after an hour or so and moved into a cheap room in a rather run-down part of town. On Christmas Eve he called from a pay phone to greet us, but I was in the shower and Becky answered. Their talk was brief—and she did not invite him to join our festivities the next day. I knew of no way to reach him.

This was a side of Becky I'd never seen: distant, cold. Unfeeling. So I built up my defenses, wanting to hurt her in the same way she was hurting me.

Considering the break between us, I was touched and surprised on Christmas morning when we opened gifts under the tree. Becky was her generous self in the number of presents she'd so carefully chosen for me, and I was beginning to feel twinges of guilt even before opening the box she'd held until last. And when I saw it—this man's ring of perfect black onyx! —I reached out to her. But she remained motionless, as cool as the feel of the onyx, and answered only with her sad smile.

The moment had passed.

I pleaded with Dr. Patterson to advise me on my home situation. He was far less comprehending than Becky ever was: "Dump the broad!"

I wanted to punch him in the mouth. Didn't he understand what I was going through, couldn't he advise me on how to handle this so neither Rebecca nor I would lose what we had treasured?

The doctor was evidently incapable of counseling on anything as sensitive as a threatened relationship between man and woman. From that day on he took no real personal interest in me as a patient with innumerable needs—nor in any one of his patients. He could offer only a so-called clear-cut path to a new life. Dr. Patterson simply refused to recognize obstacles in that path and so, one by one, his patients began to mistrust him. Our doctor was like a stuck needle on a record player, repeating until it ran in our ears like a refrain: "All the surgeries will be easy to obtain . . . easy to obtain . . . easy. . . ."

Not so, Doctor! Nick had waited the designated time and was now eager for the phalloplasty, or construction of a penis. Dr. Patterson kept putting him off: "A phalloplasty will be easy to obtain. Easy."

Beyond this assurance, and reassurance, nothing.

We were learning more about other physicians, and, in early January, Nick and I consulted another doctor involved with treatment of transsexuals. "No one is doing the phalloplasty at this time," he said.

Patterson had been lying to us all along! Nick gritted his teeth and said at that moment he'd gladly kill the SOB. "But let's be realistic. Sometime, perhaps soon, someone will help."

A day or so later Becky said bluntly that she didn't like having Nick around. "He's too great an influence on you, Mario. He spurs you on toward a goal I cannot accept."

Certainly this could not be denied. "Indeed he is—and he does. And I thank him for it! Not that I need motivation. I started all this before Nick ever came into the picture."

Becky did not answer.

"Hell, Becky. Can't you understand?"

Deadlock.

I couldn't wait out the full year programmed before surgery. Masculinization had begun and escalated with the hormones: My voice was deepening, my stubbly beard had to be shaved daily. Hair on my chin seemed to grow faster than that on the sides of my face. I was uncomfortable in my white nurse's uniform and wanted desperately to be rid of these breasts that advertised my female body.

When I asked Dr. Patterson for the name of a surgeon, he suggested I ask Nick. What was wrong with this doctor that he must refer one patient to another? I'd been paying him a great deal of money regularly every two weeks—for what? The hormone injection? Was I patronizing a quack? Was I ever going to be helped? Hadn't he eyes to see that I could never tie down my oversized breasts and pass for a male—just to prove I could get a job in that role and withstand its pressures?

And I had another barrier: How was I supposed to get a job as a male when my nursing license bore a female name?

I did turn to Nick and he gave me the name of his surgeon for the mastectomy. But, we were to discover, the man who did hysterectomies was being stopped because the University Hospital (where he was on staff) opposed him. Their claim was that the uteri in such patients were not diseased. Therefore their removal was without reason. All the hospitals in this great city were holding to the same view, thus refusing this type of surgery. In addition, insurance companies would not reimburse the patient for such an operation.

Eventually I arranged an appointment with Dr. Lake, the plastic surgeon associated with a hospital in the suburbs about fifty miles from the city proper. Planning the trip, the trip itself, the several hours' wait in the reception room all added to the strain in meeting still another medical man. Once there, however, I was struck by the fact that many waiting patients were in my boat. Some were obviously male, but the maleness of several was marked only by deep voices in what appeared to be feminine bodies. It seemed to me that the males-to-females had one common characteristic: Their voices were not masculine, nor were they feminine—more a blend of both.

Sylvia, the secretary, smiled and beckoned me to her desk. "Sit down, Mr. Martino."

It was the first time anyone, other than the doctors, had ever addressed me as Mister. It gave me a sensation of pleasure, even power—and a devotion to Sylvia that was to last forever. She had a way of putting the patient immediately at ease, plus a bright sense of humor. She quickly took down all necessary information before ushering me in to see Dr. Lake.

The paneled walls were richly decorated with many diplomas. Against a side wall, the large black leather couch reminded me of the old familiar one in psychiatrists' offices around the country. The black leather was repeated in the easy chairs. All this simple elegance made its favorable impression, but not nearly so great an impression as the graciousness of the man who stood before me. About five feet eight and of slim build, he had an easy smile and a firm handshake.

Dr. Lake invited me to sit down. "I know the purpose of your visit," he said without preamble. "Now, tell me about yourself."

He gave my story his full attention. "Yes," he said, "surgery can be performed at a hospital in this city. In fact, I'll make arrangements at once."

Accordingly, Dr. Lake made notations in a small appointment book. I was surprised he did not do a physical. Instead he asked further questions about my background.

"My fee is $1,000." He was matter-of-fact. "Payable in advance. The anesthetist's fee of $200 must also be paid beforehand. You make your own arrangements for payment of hospital costs."

The fees were staggering! But I quickly recovered and, though my head was going round and round, made the arrangements.

Where would I get the money? Never mind, *I would!*

The date was set. The realization of it gave me a tremendous emotional uplift, but, already, new problems and new challenges were posing themselves.

On the long ride back to the city I was happier than I'd been for months: My life's greatest goal was about to be achieved. The problems I would put aside for these few hours. Tomorrow would be time enough. Tomorrow I would go to the bank for a loan. Having paid off my student loan within six months after graduation, surely I'd have no problem borrowing $1,200—I hoped.

I asked for a personal loan for medical expenses. No matter how good one's credit still there's always that bit of doubt that nags during a routine investigation. . . . Hallelujahs! The check arrived three days later and I returned to the bank and made the deposit: the deposit on a dream that promised fulfillment.

That evening I told Becky about the meeting with Dr. Lake and the arrangements. I told her about the loan and showed her the deposit slip.

She was noncommittal.

As the new year began I felt that we must face up to the un-thinkable consequences of what was happening to Becky and me: the possibility of splitting up. And, if such a thing *was* to happen, *how* and *when*. *We had to talk about it!* Becky could take Jo-Jo, our dog, and she could have our apartment and its furnishings we'd so happily chosen together, share it if she wished—or she could take everything out and move to a place without memories. . . . I wanted only my personal belong-ings.

Becky said nothing. What did she feel? What was going on inside her? Did she feel as dead as I felt?

She gave no indication. One way or the other. She made no attempt to enter the discussion I'd labored at organizing. Did she approve? Disapprove? She might have been an exquisite piece of statuary placed there.

Well, if she wouldn't talk about it I'd have to write her about it. I wrote with my heart:

> *My dearest,*
>
> First, let me say that you are and always will be the most beautiful person I have ever met. We have had a wonderful, warm relationship filled with much love. But, as you know, I have always told you I wanted a home and family. You have opposed me on both counts. I want to live the most normal life possible and it can't be done living as two women. I want to achieve something with my life and have a child and happy home before I die. I want roots.
>
> You hurt me when you say our friends disapprove of my dress and intentions. If so, let them say it to me. As far as your parents are concerned—I see no reason to tell them.
>
> You give me the impression it's useless to go on, so I guess it is—but I want you to know I'm going to have my mastectomy on March 3. I don't expect you to be there but I'll call you when I wake up. I'm drawing up a will and you will be given everything I have.
>
> When you leave you must take Jo-Jo, for he needs mothering. I never did think a father could take care of a child, even a little dog that thinks it's human. You may take from the apartment whatever you wish.
>
> You may think mine is an easy decision. Well, it's the worst thing I have ever had to do in my life. I have, however, always

wanted to be a man (as I've told you how many times?). Although I can't see why a penis should make a difference in my case as far as we are concerned, it apparently does.

I still owe you your education, so if you want me to move out and still pay for our apartment I will. This way the ties will be cut and you won't have to worry about anything. Whatever you decide is OK with me. I will never change in regard to my feelings toward you—and it will be a lucky person who does get you.

As for Nick, you don't know it, but he has cautioned me to really weigh this whole thing before making the ultimate decision. I won't ask him up again.

I want our parting to be on good standing. I think your family is the greatest. They have had a lot to put up with these days and I wouldn't want to add to their ever-growing distress.

> My love always,
> *ME*

Not really expecting an answer, I waited. . . . Nothing.

My sister Janet still lived in the Midwest, and to see a letter from Jan, addressed only to Becky, came as something of a surprise. She opened it and read stoically through until its end. Laying the letter aside, she said, "This is an answer to the letter I wrote Janet, telling her that I'm leaving you."

"How could you!"

Then, as if wanting to hide nothing further, she withdrew a copy of a letter in her own handwriting from the pages of a magazine. "Perhaps you'd like to read this first."

Dear Jan,

This is a difficult letter for me to write, but it is necessary to tell you how I feel.

I love Marie very much and, as you must know, I hurt because of what's happening between us. I know that this change is something she wants to be truly happy and I will not stand in her way.

I'm sorry but I can't accept what she is about to do. I just feel that it is not right. So, because I cannot accept this interference with the Plan of Things, I will be leaving Marie and returning to my hometown.

I have enjoyed being part of your family and visiting with you, Jim, and the children. I shall miss you all very much and want to thank you again for the good times and for allowing me to become part of your family over the past years.

I hope Marie will be happy and will find someone to share her life. She has much to offer.

With love,
Becky

Suddenly I understood. "Becky, I'm sorry. You, too, need to turn to someone who just might understand this crisis we're facing."

"Yes."

"I would like to read my sister's letter."

She handed it to me and as I read the words, a dullness grew and settled in the pit of my stomach.

Dear Becky,

Just got your letter this morning and now, at 8:40 A.M., I am sitting right down to answer it.

Of course you must know this is very upsetting to me and I only wish at a time like this I lived closer to you so that I might be of help.

Rebecca, it was hard for me to understand a relationship like you and Marie had when I first learned of it, but, once it was explained to me and I saw how happy—and I do mean sincerely happy—you two were, it was much easier for me to accept. My only concern was that Marie was happy and I truly believe she was as happy as society would allow her to be.

Now she has this other goal in life that she is certain will make her even happier. I only wish I could be as convinced as she is. It would be a lot easier for all concerned, I guess, if we were as convinced of her future as she is.

Let me ask you one thing, Becky: I can't understand why you can't at least stay with Marie until this is over with. What is it that has got you to the point where you are actually going to move out and divorce yourself from the beautiful relationship that you did have? We both know you can't turn love on and off—and in this case who is to say that you couldn't have a different kind of love for Marie, one that might enable you both to be more completely happy than you've ever dreamed you could be?

Can you possibly put the shoe on the other foot and see what it would do to Marie if sometime in your life together *you* might find some male that you were attracted to? Maybe you could compare it to a husband and wife and say the wife was having an affair with someone else. Now that's a pretty big thing, but I'm sure there have been marriages that have been able to be saved even after something as terrible as that happened. I guess what I'm trying to say is, can't you at least give yourself a chance and let the change happen before you make up your mind that this really isn't what you want? What could you lose out of it?

Where, in Marie's case, she could lose a life if she is driven— and in not having anyone as close as you are now to turn to.

Please, Becky, I'm begging you: Stay with her and try to see it her way. Even if you can't, maybe you can make it a little easier by just being there so she can hold your hand when she is really going to need someone's hand to hold.

I love my sister Marie very much and I feel that she has a lot to offer to this crazy world we live in. And if you leave her so all alone maybe she'll give up before she ever has a chance to start.

Please, please, please. Oh God, how I wish I could be there! You know lots of times it is easier when someone who is on the outside looking in can help you.

I hope this letter doesn't cause any more problems than there already are in your home. I'm sure Marie will know that this letter is from me but I just had to write you, Becky, and let you know how we feel. I'm sure you realize how much Jim and I care for you too. This is why we are hoping that things will take a change for the better.

Is there anyone that you have been able to talk your problem over with, or are you alone too?

Please answer this. I've got to know what's going on as this situation has become very important to me. Write soon.

> *Love,*
> *Jan and Jim*

Rebecca stood up from her chair, looked at me, measuring me. Then she left the room.

Surgery was only a month away. Within this time I must put

my own life in order. I must talk with Mrs. Wallace, our director of nurses—but how would she take this whole thing? Well,
even if she didn't understand, she wouldn't make life difficult.
I could count on that. Had she met this problem before? What
about my job? And how would I find another as a new person,
a new identity?

Was I imagining a slight change in Becky? A lessening of
tension? Was it because she realized I was going forward with
my plans in spite of the near-insurmountables? Rebecca was
making an all-out effort to speak normally. What a welcome
change—if, truly, it was a change. And, knowing her honesty,
I was sure she would never indicate an attitude unless it was
real.

Her less biting tones were enough to lift my spirits. Still, I
did not know if she was leaving me as she had said and as she
had written Janet.

So many plans had to be made, and bills must be paid in
February for two months, since I was to be hospitalized the
third day of March. My position had to be reckoned with: As
supervisor I must give a month's notice of any absence from
duties.

I decided to take another supervisor, Clair-Marie Shannon,
into my confidence. We had a rare working relationship and
we shared the benefits of our understanding director, who
always listened to both sides of a story when called upon as ar-
bitrator. Even so, just how would Clair, who couldn't have
been more Irish—and so fresh out of Ireland—respond to this?

Well, I was counting on her sunny temperament and good
will. Knowing her as I did, I could ask her to listen to me now.

Clair had one quality that made me wonder about telling
her of my sex change: If she made a judgment she stuck to it,
and no one could change her mind. My quandary: Tell her
now—or wait? If I told her too soon and she felt anger or disgust, then the next month would be hell. This was another
chance I had to take.

A few days passed before there was a quiet time. Quite
abruptly I said to Clair-Marie, "I want to discuss a matter of a
very personal nature with you. Could we meet in the office for
a late coffee break?"

She agreed in her happy way, and at the end of that afternoon we talked over steaming mugs of black coffee. I began by telling her of my earliest feelings. When I finished an hour and a half later (with frequent phone interruptions), she sat almost motionless, not speaking for the moment.

"There's just one thing, Marty: Make sure this is what you want because you have to live with yourself." She reached over and lightly touched my hand. "As for the problem itself—well, I've seen it resolved a few times in England, so this doesn't come as a shock to me. And don't worry too much about Becky. Knowing how close you've been, I don't think she'll leave you now."

"Clair, you are amazing. Unbelievable. You make me feel that maybe Becky won't leave me."

"I'm sure of it!" Her lilting laugh seemed to lift the weight from my being. "Now, Marty, let me help you. But what can I do? Do you need money? And when are you telling Mrs. Wallace?"

"You're helping by just being you. By listening. By bolstering my faith. No, I don't need money. And I'm staying over to see Mrs. Wallace after the shift ends."

Clair blew a kiss my way and left then, and I waited for our director.

I spared the details but did explain my feelings, the hormone therapy I was going through, and the surgery scheduled for next month. When I finished she looked me straight in the eye and said, "Miss Martino, you have a great deal of courage. I don't know that I could face what you're facing, even for something I so deeply believed in."

How glad I was that I'd decided to confide in this remarkable woman. As a professional she couldn't be topped.

"I'll hire a replacement immediately and you can train her before you leave. Now don't you worry about your job or any future reference. I'll change the name and gender on the necessary papers myself, and, of course, you'll get the excellent recommendations you deserve."

I left the office feeling tops. Despite all the other transsexual cases I'd heard and read of—and feared!—everyone was actually on my side. Except Becky. As much as I needed and wanted and appreciated their support, I needed and wanted Becky's even more.

I had one last thing to do: tell Dom and his wife, Barbara, and Tim, their first son. I'd not seen them for almost a year, but now that I was going into surgery, telling them could not be postponed. It was important to me to tell them. They lived near us and time was brief. I called and asked if I could visit the following weekend. If they thought Becky's not coming was strange they made no mention of it.

Dom picked me up on Saturday morning and, as we drove back, I told him I had something to discuss with him and Barbara. I planned to talk privately with Tim, who was special to me. The other three children were too young for adult talk and Dom and Barbara could tell them when they were ready for it. This was fine with Dom. "The three of us will go out to dinner and we can talk about whatever's bothering you."

Theirs was a beautiful suburban home, their privacy ensured by an abundance of trees and shrubs. All were encircled by an emerald stretch of lawn. I never envied Dom more than at that moment: married to a marvelous woman, children, a home in the suburbs, a place in the community, a brilliant professional life. Perhaps mine would be on a less grand scale—still, mine would be a similar one. Some day. A part of the fatigue I'd known from the burdensome past months began to slip from my body, from my very soul.

Over drinks at the restaurant that evening I told them about my change. Their lack of surprise was gratifying, and Dom immediately asked if I'd thought the whole thing through: all the problems, moving, the new identity, legal papers, ad infinitum. And what about Becky? Dom and Barbara were fond of Becky and she of them.

"All of these things must be considered in making such a gigantic decision," Dom cautioned.

"Of course, Dom." I was almost annoyed. Did he still think of me as that kid sister, that tomboy who appropriated his old Army shirts and hat? Concealing my momentary annoyance, I turned the conversation to Becky.

Dom's reaction startled me. "You didn't give her a choice at all. It was either stay or go—there was no alternative."

"You're absolutely right, Dom." I really hadn't thought of it that way. "But what alternatives could I have given her? There were none."

"Marie has started this, and it's what she's wanted all her life, so she has to follow through." Barbara came to my defense on this point, yet she could see the other side too. "Becky is fearful of the outcome—and how it's going to affect their lives."

How could I have been so consumed with self-pity that I failed to accept her withdrawal as struggle within self? "You're right, both of you. Becky has had to suffer it out alone. You have given me new insight into her reactions. And you know I love her. Because I do, I resign myself to moving out of Becky's life. This ordeal is costing us too much."

"Now you're being hard on yourself," Barbara said. "We're interested in *your* happiness *and in Becky's.*"

"Barbara's right, of course. Whatever we can do to help we'll do. You can count on both of us." Good ol' Dom.

I could always count on Dom—and Barbara, since the day we'd met.

On the way back I said I'd like to tell Tim tonight. A fine idea, they agreed.

At sixteen Tim was almost as tall as his six-foot-two father. Tim was easy to talk with and, since he was a favorite of mine, there was a happy camaraderie. In straightforward talk I told him I was to undergo a sex-change operation: something I had wanted all my life. I wanted him to know before the change actually took place.

His eyes lighted up, and his face became as alive as if he'd just made a new discovery about our universe. "Gee, Aunt Marie, I think that's neat!"

Surprising: the resilience of today's youth. Their sophisticated acceptance of the extraordinary. A transition from one sex to another was a phenomenon as comprehensible to him as stepping off onto a virgin planet.

"This won't change our relationship, Tim."

"The opposite. Because you've told me yourself I guess we'll be that much closer."

Confiding in Tim was to give us an even stronger bond, one that was to help me understand his problems later on.

The hospital staff had been told that I was moving and leaving my work there. On my last day, at a great farewell party, cameras clicked and I remember thinking that any pictures of me would soon need to be destroyed as I went about the business of seeking my new identity. But, without photographic benefits, the memories of this leave-taking were to stay with me.

The dateline was drawing near.

One night, lights out, before we fell asleep Becky said suddenly, "I'm staying." As suddenly as she'd said months ago that she was leaving.

My body stiffened as I lay there beside her in the darkness. Dare I believe what I heard? Or did I only imagine I heard it?

Becky began to cry. Softly. My own tears ran down my cheeks, yet I could not bring myself to reach out to her. The distance of hurts was far too great.

Why, after all this time, had she changed her mind?

She sensed my unvoiced questions. "I just realized I love you. That's all. And I want to stay with you."

Oh, I slept that night! The first good night's sleep since her initial pronouncement an eternity ago.

"Dump the broad!" that dumb cluck of a doctor had said, and now I wished fervently that I had socked him in the teeth.

This morning was like the mornings of our good years. And the day was a good beginning of a new life, a renewal. With determination and new perspectives and the hurtful experience of near parting, we renewed our pledges to work at making our life better than it had ever been.

With light hearts we talked. I was happy just knowing I would have Becky next to me through this most important time.

But it didn't quite work out that way: She came down with the flu on the very day I traveled the fifty miles to the hospital.

Never having had surgery before, I was like everyone else facing it for the first time: scared. Having worked in many hospitals, I am aware, perhaps more than those who have not, that patients try to cover their true emotions. I was frightened and I didn't know why. One cannot realize pain—or one's ability to endure it—until he has experienced it.

I was on the female floor and this gave me an uneasy feeling. The patient in the other bed looked like a female. Later I was to learn she was a sex-change patient and had until now been a male.

How did the nurses feel about this type of surgery? And why was I wondering how everyone in the world would respond not only to the surgery but to me in particular? My short haircut and deep voice set me apart from others on the floor and I felt and looked funny. Well, I'd stay in my room—my first venture out would be the next morning at five o'clock for a shower when, perhaps, no one would see me.

But little time for such fretting. Lab work and X-rays, supper at five. I read the paper. And then Dr. Lake came in. The doctor marked my breasts with ink to serve as guidelines in removing these unwanted appendages, offered words of cheer and said he'd see me early next morning. Then I called Becky and she wished me luck. I read and kept my mind occupied until I grew drowsy, refused the sedative, and slept through the night without wakening.

The nurse came in at seven, raised the blind on a bright sunny morning, and gave me the preoperative medication. She fastened me into the familiar hospital gown and teased about my eagerness to go to surgery. "Most patients are terrified. You treat it as a great adventure."

"It's the adventure of my lifetime!"

The haze was closing in now as she covered my short thick hair with a green cap, and I moved, without need of assistance, onto the stretcher which was to take me downstairs and, happily, into a new life-style.

"Today I am being born again," I remember telling someone.

The blinding lights centered on the operating table where I lay, and I saw Dr. Lake just before the anesthesiologist inserted the needle.

"All is well," Dr. Lake was reassuring me. "When you wake you'll be a new person."

The clock on the wall read 8:05. Then everything went blank.

The nurse was taking my blood pressure.

"Are they off?" I tried to look down at the massive pressure bandages covering my chest. Yes! Now I had a chest as opposed to breasts. I felt wonderful—and immediately dozed off. When I next opened my eyes the same question: "Are they off?"

"Yes, your breasts are off. Surgery is completed. But there was a little problem on the table: You became shocky. Because of shock you must stay in the recovery room for a while."

Somewhere in my fuzzy mind I knew what she meant. My blood pressure had gone down, my body had not responded normally. Apparently, though, everything was all right now, for only one nurse was caring for me—and I was conscious of other patients in various stages of wakening from anesthesia. Yes, I was OK. Soon I'd be back in my hospital room and could call Becky and ask how her flu was. In my half-conscious state I wondered if this nurse could even slightly imagine how I felt and what had led to this moment. Did she too think this change had taken courage, as others had said?

When I could answer her questions without falling asleep in the middle of a word, and when I started complaining of thirst, the nurse decided it was time for me to go back to my room. The day, still bright, looked cold and strange. During the move from stretcher to bed I saw Dr. Lake and asked if I could call Becky. Once I was settled in bed, he examined my dressings and the nurse handed me the phone. I remembered only saying I wanted to call but had no recollection of doing so, for suddenly I felt very warm and was sweating profusely. Would someone please open the window?

And suddenly the room filled with nurses rushing about. I was pushed onto a stretcher and a doctor kept yelling for the *aramine*. Aramine—the medication to bring up the blood pressure . . . was I in shock a second time? I didn't feel I was in shock.

Dr. Lake was there again. "Take him to ICU. I want a cutdown."

"ICU"—why the intensive care unit? And oh, no—not a cutdown! That hurt: I'd assisted at many such procedures and knew it had to hurt—cutting along the inside of the elbow, inserting the thin tubing for IV (intravenous solution) to run into the veins.

It was Dr. Lake again: "Get him over. Quick!"

If this was dying it was not unpleasant. No pain. I couldn't talk, though I kept trying to tell someone to open a window and then I'd be all right.

Dr. Lake was still calling for the aramine and I kept trying to whisper: "Forget the aramine—someone call a priest." But the words would not come out.

I could hear everything, see everything. And yet it was as if I weren't really there. Frightening. . . .

In ICU they shifted me over to the bed without incident. Miss O'Callahan, the charge nurse, appeared as if from nowhere and was taking my blood pressure. Dr. Lake called for a medical consultation and one of the medical men suggested they insert a central venous pressure catheter into the cut-down. Again I wanted to protest—but things were out of my control. Too late. The tubing was being passed up my upper arm into the right side of my heart, and by a special measurement they could determine the pressure of the blood behind the walls of my right upper heart chamber.

No pain. Nothing. Unbelievable. But wait: Was I so near death that nothing caused pain? That must be it. . . . Everything they did, like pricking the end of my fingertips for blood samples, was without feeling.

I had to call Becky. But who was to know, for I could not speak? I drifted off, intermittently, and on waking would feel no pain. Had there actually been surgery—or was I still wearing those unsightly breasts?

I must call Becky—

Was it evening when Nick came? It must have been because it was dark outside. What was he doing here? Why wasn't he at night school after his daytime trucking job—and why had he come the fifty miles only to drive right back again? How did he get there? He could stay only a half-hour, he said. What a buddy. Without words we could communicate: that special indescribable something which comrades share.

After Nick's visit I began to feel better. Even so, the tightness binding my chest seemed to tighten even more and to breathe was excruciating. Except for this, no pain. My right arm was growing stiff from being stretched on the armboard and then I noticed blood running. *Oh, God, I'll have to pay for blood*—and who knows how many units they may already have given me. A sudden nausea. Was this a reaction from the anesthesia? Or from trauma? Perhaps both. A nurse gave me something to ward off the nausea.

And now I was talking. Was it possible? Had the shifts changed? Of course. It was morning, the next day. Well now, I wasn't going to die after all. I slept, this time more naturally. I was unusually warm, but happy.

Dr. Lake had been in and out countless times. They had first thought the shock was due to loss of tissue fluid because of the largeness of my breasts. Well. Consider, though, I had worn size 44 bra—and man! that's a lot of tissue. Later it was found I was allergic to the anesthetic. And I learned that the only other known case of sex-change surgery shock was dealt with as successfully as my own.

During the night I must have moved around, for now the central venous pressure and IV tubing were dislodged, accounting for my high temperature. Now that I'd managed awhile without either, couldn't all that be left out if I could tolerate water? Miss O'Callahan said we'd ask the doctor.

I credit Miss O'Callahan with saving my life. Of course many hands go into such a thing, but she was soothing and all kindness and talked to me about the joys and sorrows in our profession. Now I could more fully understand how my own patients felt when they said they appreciated my manner and concern for their well-being.

Dr. Lake was in before eight that morning. Could we leave out the IV? Yes, if I could tolerate water. And could I go to the bathroom instead of using that despicable bedpan? (Psychologically, I hate the damn things! Women use bedpans, men use urinals.) Yes, he said, when I could sit up. I could. And I was beginning to feel quite normal.

The pressure bandages were too tight, but I sat up that morning and again in the afternoon and was rewarded by being transferred back to my room. I felt great. I wanted to shout from the housetops. I was *happy*.

"Everything clinically is now under control. The surgery has been a success." Dr. Lake was congratulating all of us.

What more could I want to hear?

I called Becky and said everything was fine and I couldn't wait to get home. She wasn't well. But her voice was soft and warm and she seemed to feel guilt at not being with me. Who knows, perhaps she even sensed that God had almost taken me from her? (What was it she'd said—eons ago—about man's stepping in and reversing the processes of God—without penalty?) I didn't know. Not then, not ever. But she did try to cheer me—and I tried to sound as if nothing extraordinary had happened here.

Opening my eyes after a short nap, I saw a nurse standing over my bed. Oh, God! A former classmate from the University. What the hell was she doing in this hospital far from where we'd trained? Was she doing private duty? No, she said, she was assistant director of nursing in this hospital. "I saw your name on the operating room schedule and just knew it was you."

We'd not been close in school and, as I remembered, she had a sullen poor-me attitude about life, and when she laughed it was not a real laugh. No, we'd never been friends, and I did not want to see her now. How small the world. Sensing my disquiet—and her curiosity satisfied—she cut her visit short.

Dinner came soon after her departure: Steak, baked potatoes, the works—and, for the first time, I was hungry. I couldn't finish it but made a good try. And that evening Dr. Lake said I could go home the next day. Home? Almost dead one day and discharged from the hospital two days later? I was stunned, delighted.

Doctor set a time for me to see him the following week for taking out half the stitches. This would mean that first look at my chest. I'd never seen plastic surgery done before, and the only breast removals I'd seen were on cancer patients. Often that type of procedure had meant going down to the bone and removing other muscles—and was not to be compared with plastic surgery.

Soon after lunch the third day, in walked Becky. I wanted to hug her tight, tell her how happy I was—but I was still very weak and she had that bad cough, so we settled for the small peck on cheek. We talked and began the tedious process of getting me dressed to leave. Slow going. I could scarcely raise my arms, but there was no pain. Many patients who have this surgery require no medication postoperatively, perhaps because the psychological uplift (no pun!) is so great as to block out pain.

I was going home. That was the important thing. Lots of time to figure out the reasons for no pain. For now I was thinking of the new life for myself and the woman I loved.

It had snowed while I was away and the roads were icy and very bumpy, but we were happy. We complimented ourselves that the cab driver had given us a flat rate on that fifty-mile trip home, permitting us the luxury of not worrying about the cost.

Dr. Lake had requested I go to bed immediately on reaching home. He knew Becky's reputation as a nurse and was assured of her ability to handle any unexpected problem. Now, for the first time since the operation, I looked at myself in a mirror. What a shock! How pale I was. Like Death. Eyes sunken, skin blanched—white, like alabaster.

Oh, well. Some of Becky's unbeatable home cooking, and I'd be as good as new.

Did I sense a threatened strain? God, no, not that! Could she be thinking that God was imposing penalty on me for trying to alter His work? Or was I overdramatizing?

We said very little those first few days, but by the weekend the old warmth between us was returning. And, miracle of miracles, Becky held onto my hand as we fell asleep!

Our transsexual friends were invited to dinner that next Sunday evening. Our group was growing more and more disenchanted with Dr. Patterson and his monthly sessions. He was still saying about the same things and, though he promised legal help and counseling, he was incapable of giving either. He had little to offer us in terms of understanding the very real problems which beset those changing from one sex to another, in that his knowledge of law seemed minimal and he also lacked the human touch. And there was altogether too much talk about sex and the sex act.

Most of us had already reached a satisfactory level with our mates and were more eager to learn how to handle the emotional conflicts in this transitional period. How were we to cope with the hurts inflicted on us by an unthinking—or sometimes intentionally hostile—world?

So we had turned to one another and worked on our own to find ways of getting diplomas and transcripts and birth certificates properly altered. The lawyers we had heretofore contacted had made fools of us, charging staggering fees for almost nothing in return. A select few transsexuals started meeting privately at our house. Almost without exception, we had college degrees or were in various levels of undergraduate work.

It was good to be with our people. I enjoyed the professional exchange, and laughter punctuated the meetings. Not too keen on the idea of forming the group in the beginning, now Becky was joining in, and my contentment reached a new high. It was obvious that my friends liked her and that she could at last communicate with them. She no longer rejected their encouragement to me. Privately, I decided she was pleased to see that these couples with their common problems were as normal as any next-door neighbor. Most of the men were already masculinized and, in fact, married—and it was evident that they were adjusting to the various stages in this long procedure and meeting the goals they'd set for themselves. Yes, our group was a great idea.

The following week I made the long tiresome trip to Dr. Lake's office. I was nervous at the prospect of having him remove half the wire stitches—and waiting in the outer office for some two hours didn't help matters.

I watched carefully as he removed the bandages and I saw the thin red suture lines. Each nipple was covered with a gauze pledget, a small pressure dressing, held in place by black sutures. I tensed as the doctor asked the assistant for the wire cutters but felt nothing as he pulled out the long retention wires. I felt nothing when he applied a thin gauze dressing.

"OK. You can get dressed now," he said.

The room went black. When I came to I was lying on the black leather couch. Undoubtedly it was anticipation of hurt which caused the tenseness, plus the long wait beforehand. A light tranquilizer might have prevented the fainting.

Dr. Lake explained about the pledgets. "I had to do a free nipple graft—transplant the nipples. The dressings are used as pressure against the nipples until the graft takes. Next week I'll remove the pledgets and make sure the graft is satisfactory."

"Oh?"

"I've never had an unsatisfactory one, so let's not worry."

What would we do if mine proved the exception? My shock after the mastectomy had been exceptional. The ominous words of one authority came suddenly to taunt me: "Not all transsexuals survive—but the survivors are indestructible!"

"Not all transsexuals survive," he had said. What did he mean by that? Was he saying that some would die before the final surgical procedures in sex change? Or did he mean some would choose to reverse the hormones and accept the body as it was? (Choice of reversion was supposed to happen sometime during that first year *before any surgery took place*.) Neuterization? Those pathetic cases were primarily the responsibility of the doctors who indiscriminately approved them for sex change.

If he had meant death, then I'd die trying. . . .

But wait! He went on to say that survivors are indestructible.

Well, *I would be an indestructible survivor*. That settled, I wanted to get home to Becky and sport my new chest. The prospects of a hairy masculine chest filled me with new manly pride.

I'd planned to visit Janet and Jim and the kids after my stitches were out. I called them to report my progress and said I was making plane reservations to leave within a few days. How great to hear the airport operator call me *Mr. Martino*. This would be my first public appearance as Mister and the thought was both exciting and frightening.

Becky went with me to Dr. Lake's office and again the long wait. I'd fortified myself with a tranquilizer. Three hours passed before we were called in. No pain, no fainting—and the remaining sutures were out. The gauze pledgets were lifted: The nipples were black!

"Oh, my God! The transplant didn't take!" I felt sick.

"Oh, but it has. This is only the dried blood and it will wash off as you shower. Now don't pick it off, *wash* it off." The doctor sensed my temporary disappointment.

Black nipples would not deflate my image, new or otherwise, in Becky's eyes. The normal brown and pink would return within days, and then, except for the thin scars, mine would look exactly like a normal male chest.

All we'd heard about Lake was true: He was master of his profession. Now, if he could only create a penis, I'd be in the promised land.

(Although vague rumors about surgeons who were creating the artificial phallus, or penis, reached us from overseas, nothing could be verified. As with the elusive fantasy of the dreamer, reality was never quite within our reach. Not yet. But we'd already learned the game of patience. We could wait. . . .)

Becky came through like a trouper: She changed my dressings, helped me in and out of the tub, gave the moral support I so needed and wanted.

I was indeed a self-satisifed man when I kissed Becky goodbye for two weeks and set out for the airport en route to Janet's. As I was waiting to board, my ego was unexpectedly inflated when a nice thing happened: A group of young girls were looking my way and one of them said: "Isn't he cute?" Another said: "Yes. But he's too short."

Short or not, this proved I was like any other Joe—which was exactly what I wanted to be!

Janet and the kids were waiting at the airport when I disembarked. She ran to me, arms wide open, hugged me, and began crying. Crying for both of us, perhaps all of us.

The children were too small to notice Auntie Marie was wearing a small beard. Taking the elevator to street level, the five-year-old expressed his pleasure at seeing me again: "Gee, Aunt Marie. I'm sure glad you've come to visit us."

His mom whispered something in his ear.

Since he was accustomed to my short hair and rather masculine clothes, the beard seemed not to denote any change in gender to him.

Once the car was headed for home Janet said simply: "Kiddies, this is now Uncle Mario."

One wonders what it's like to be a kid and have to start calling an aunt an uncle. But kids adjust. It was Jim who was in trouble, and he spent most of our two weeks apologizing for stumbling over my name.

Janet was anxious to see the results of my transformation and I was eager to accommodate. She had to change the dressings. Funny: As a female I'd always tried in every way to hide my breasts. Now, with my new chest I felt no embarrassment and looked forward to the day when I could take off my shirt, just like any other guy—and just as my father had done!—when working in the garden or lolling on the beach.

I put in a call to Pa to say the surgery was over and done with and I wanted to visit him and Lenore. Waiting for the connection, I agonized. Were he to look back, he'd remember that I never acted or dressed like a girl: a thorny cross for him to bear. He'd been so pained, later asking why I wasn't like other girls who wore dresses and dated boys—and I'd told him I didn't feel like other girls. Couldn't he remember that from the very beginning I'd been aggressive, a tomboy? That I'd never been a real girl? Why, then, should he expect me in adult life suddenly to change into a normal woman? Last summer I'd told Pa about the eventual sex reassignment and he'd brushed it off. "You're cra-zee! Just cra-zee." He couldn't accept that these things were being done. He refused to believe I was like Jorgensen, in reverse—the sensitive young boy my father had derided when he read of the transformation into Christine.

Lenore answered the phone. She had known I was undergoing sex change, yet seemed surprised at my more masculine voice. "Who is this?"

"It's me. Mario."

For a moment the name did not register. "Marie! It's you."

My ears burned, my temper ignited. No, I must keep calm. I wanted to see my father and it would be hard enough without a big scene.

"May I speak with Pa, please?"

She called to him: "It's Marie."

I could hear the receiver as it changed hands.

"Hi, Pa! This is Mario."

"Mario who?"

"Come on, Pa. This is Mario, once Marie. I told you last summer what I was going to do."

Dead silence . . . had he dropped the receiver?

"Pa, are you there?"

"We won't talk about it."

"But, Pa, we have to talk about it. I want to come out to see you. And Lenore."

"If you want to come, come. I don't care. . . ." All went silent. He'd handed the receiver back to my stepmother. "He won't talk about it," she said.

"Look, I want to see him. What do you think?"

"Come on. After all, he is your father."

Yes, he was my father, no matter what our differences. Why couldn't Pa see my side of the picture? Or even meet me half-way? Even listen? . . .

Oh, Dad! How can father and son, or father and daughter, reach such an impasse? How can the love you once held for me, and I for you, now do so complete a turnabout?

I was worried—angry and depressed. Torn by this destructive love-hate thing. But I must try once more. After all, my father was ill—it was time we made our peace.

Next day Janet and I drove out to our old town to see Pa and Lenore. Pa was sitting in his easy chair watching TV when I walked in. As he looked up at me, the tears welled in his eyes and I felt a great tenderness for him, wanting to rush over and embrace him and tell him to be happy with me. But now his eyes avoided me and dropped, then lifted in the direction of the screen. His attention seemed riveted there and attempts at conversation were futile. Because of his Parkinson's disease, he'd lost facial muscle tone and seemed incapable of expression. Perhaps he could not have smiled had he wished. Was his bland countenance from the disease—or utter disgust?

I took off my suit jacket and loosened my tie and did my best to relax. When Lenore called us to her bountiful table, I found it difficult to swallow the food so lovingly prepared. How does one eat under parental rejection?

I was a lost child, again, a lost soul.

Pain, hurt, this sense of being cut adrift. I wanted so very much to explain, but tension reached such a pitch as to become unbearable, and there seemed nothing to do other than say thank you, all-good-health-and-happiness, and good-bye. At the door my father limply took my hand and shook it. I hugged him without emotion and we left them standing there at their apartment door.

But Becky was almost herself again. Little by little we'd talked over our past conflicts.

"What explains the silent treatment, Becky?"

"Up until then, sex reassignment seemed almost an intangible. When I was faced with it as an actuality I panicked."

"But hadn't we been waiting for this actuality?"

"Of course. But now that help was available—that you were actually to reverse a process of God's. . ."

"Couldn't we have talked about it?"

"I froze inside, I guess."

"And I was too involved with self. . . ."

"This was something I had to face and resolve myself. So many moral, ethical, and philosophical feelings are involved when one begins to think of tampering with nature."

"Well, aren't we tampering with nature, or God, when we consent to abortion or euthanasia?"

"These things overwhelm our capacity for rational debate. I wasn't thinking of your sex-change surgery as a matter of life and death—although it did turn out to be close to that, Mario."

"At the time, you *were* thinking it might be a penalty from a Higher Power?"

"Yes, that thought stayed with me. I had all these doubts as to the morality of sex-change surgery. And, if *I* questioned it, what about our families and friends?"

"Why couldn't we have talked calmly about all this before?"

"My conflicts were very deep within me. I had to think them out alone."

"But you did write Janet, confide in her?"

"Yes. And her letter restated things I was sure of: your love for me, my love for you. Janet was the outside force that helped me put things in focus."

"God love Janet!"

"I was finishing my thesis on passive euthanasia. . . ."

"I remember."

"And I realized that if the patient has the right to choose between life-sustaining procedures and dying with dignity—well,
then, didn't you have an equal right to correct your mind-body
problems? . . . ."

"Brilliant summation! And, having resolved your own
doubts, you decided to stay with me?"

"Yes, Mario. I decided yours was the right to choose what
you, yourself, considered right. That yours was the right to
pursue your own life, liberty, security, happiness. . . . And
you were offering me the same love we'd known for eight
years. You were offering me, at last, that which we both wanted: a normal life in home and community."

"And . . . ?"

"And—we love. After all, isn't this *everything* I've truly
wanted most?"

Three weeks had passed since my mastectomy and there was
now much to be done. We were going to need money and
need it in a hurry. I must get a job. How would I manage this
with the name "Martino, Marie Josephine" on my nurses license? I slipped my picture over the name Josephine—to
change the *e* to *o* would deface the license, make it illegal. No,
I couldn't resort to that.

I thought of Nurses Registry, an employment service. And I
remembered Mrs. Paul, that unusually nice woman, who was
in charge of the service. Perhaps she could help me now in finding work.

But first, I must get a haircut: a man's cut. Going to one's
barber sounds simple enough. . . .

The shop was empty except for the man behind my accustomed chair. Having always affected male shirts and short-
cropped hair, I hadn't realized how different I really looked
until settled in that chair. When the barber turned and unfold-
ed the cloth to fasten under my chin he stopped short, the
cloth sagging in midair.

"They're gone!" he almost shouted, then his mouth hung
open.

I went weak inside. I struggled for composure and managed

to say: "Yes. If it bothers you, I'll go elsewhere." This problem had never occurred to me until this very moment.

"Of course not." He was anxious to get on with the job, pretending this was business as usual, and when he finished I looked like the average guy.

Even so, that day my barber lost a customer of six years' standing.

The following morning I was up and out and at the door of the Registry as Mrs. Paul was opening her offices. Inside I lost no time in explaining my reason for being there: "Can you help me in getting private duty assignments?"

"Of course I can, Mr. Martino."

"Will my license pass with the picture over it?"

"I don't see why not. You are a nurse, you're not being fraudulent about the license. And any prospective employer can call me and I'll tell that person what I've just told you."

"Thank you, Mrs. Paul. You are a warm and compassionate woman."

"You'll hear from me," she promised and I took my leave.

So many people had accepted the situation, I was becoming more confident that there would be few problems with my transition. This assurance added to the excitement of discovering the subtle changes of facial and body structure as hormone therapy continued.

Mrs. Paul called later in the day and assigned me to special duty at a downtown hospital that very night: midnight to eight A.M. The patient had had a prostatectomy, or excision of part or all of the prostate, and needed a nurse for three postoperative days.

When I signed in the supervisor asked for my license. She seemed to study it very intently—and my heart stood still. Slowly then—almost reluctantly, it seemed—she recorded the name Mario and the serial and handed it back to me. I hoped my heavy overcoat concealed my shaking body.

Many things were running through my mind. One of the nurses who'd worked under my supervision with Mrs. Wallace was now at this same hospital. She wouldn't recognize my face but what about my name? All nurses wear name pins. And there was the patient: Was I physically up to lifting a heavy man and the three-gallon jugs of water that hung on the IV pole? Assuming a calm I did not feel, I went to my patient's room and took the report from the four-to-twelve nurse. The phone rang and, instinctively, I knew it had something to do with me.

One of the male nurses answered: "Yes, he's here."

My heart sank. He turned to me and said, "She wants you to spell your last name for her—she can't read your handwriting."

I reached for the phone and spelled my name for the voice at the other end of the wire.

"Thank you," the voice chirped.

My legs were like rubber. Could I take the trauma every time the phone rang?

Was there some other way? . . . .

Fate was kind and I finished the three-day assignment, which became more and more a chore: I had to get into the dressing room before the others came and was always on the alert for the nurse who would recognize me. I was almost done in. Physically it was not such a strain, for my strength had returned. No physical problems, just the frightening emotional ones.

A few days off to get myself together and I was ready for the next case, this time a patient in full body cast at a large medical center. This work could last as long as I wished but, on the third day, the head nurse returned from vacation and recognized me on sight. It was Mrs. Myerson, the nurse I'd trained for my former job as supervisor, now head nurse of the unit at this hospital. Mrs. Myerson was not unkind, but later that same day one of the supervisors came up and asked how long I'd had my beard and where I'd worked before. Her lack of subtlety indicated she'd been told about me, and this made for so much discomfort that I signed off the case next day.

Well, certainly, I couldn't run every time someone recognized me. I must overcome fear of discovery. And the only thing to fear was the fact that my license did not correspond with my name—and until this was changed legally I couldn't afford the risk of having someone write the Nurse Licensing Bureau.

Dr. Lake was pleased with my chest. Hair growth was plainly visible and gave indications of a dark nappy covering. It was expedient to tell him I must have a full-time job and that it was difficult because of my license.

"Why not come work at my hospital?"

"Your hospital?"

"Yes. Why not? I'm a major shareholder and in a position to ask that you be hired under your male name and paid under your once-female name. Until your papers are in order. After your papers are changed there should be no problem."

"Dr. Lake, you're just too much!" Suddenly words didn't come easy: They seemed stuck with emotions—the humanity of this great, great man.

"This would mean moving from the city, where Becky is registered for fall classes at the University. We'll have to talk it over. Together."

"I'd like you to. Be in touch."

Becky and I talked about it into the night and again for the next two days. Somehow it would all work out: She wanted to stay at her present job until August and get the vacation that would then be coming to her. On that time off we could move our belongings to our new location in the suburbs and, till then, I could come to the city on my days off. This would mean, however, that we'd be living apart more than half the time. Having tempered and forged our bonds during that awesome trauma of a half year, we knew we could now survive this minor, and temporary, separation.

Dr. Lake arranged for me to meet Mrs. Savage, Director of Nurses. As I traveled the fifty miles I wondered what it would be like to be back on the floors again.

The director here was the opposite of Mrs. Wallace. Perhaps Mrs. Savage resented a superior pulling strings, for Dr. Lake had asked her to find a place for me. Perhaps her fifty-plus years had conditioned her way of thinking. She was not pleased with me and I was ill at ease. I found her cold and unyielding, her speech clipped, her voice a monotone.

Mrs. Savage assigned me as a charge nurse for the male floor, with two days off per week and three days' sick leave per year, three days off for death in immediate family. One meal free for every working day. No, this hospital did not give college reimbursement, although they did give a four-week vacation after the first year's anniversary. This information relayed, she looked at my license. And fell silent. Our interview was over. She did not look up as I left her office.

What a prude! Or maybe I was being unfair, comparing her with Mrs. Wallace. But I'd never been treated like this before and it wasn't easy to take. However, one does learn to catch the breath and breathe again.

Where to live? Mrs. Savage had no recommendations. After looking for three days, a friend and I stopped at a house on the corner across from the hospital. The place was run-down, dilapidated. Weeds had smothered any sign of grass, and broken glass and bottles protruded crazily from the ground, reminding me of a miniature cemetery in decay.

An elderly black woman answered the bell and called the manager, a grubby little man. The hallway was dingy and dirty and the door to the one vacant room was padlocked. When he opened the door I damn near fainted from the stench. The mattress—coverless, stained with yellows, browns, and blues—lay in the middle of the floor. Mounds of empty cans and bottles and filthy clothing lined the walls. Hell, what was I getting myself into?

The woman invited us into her tiny overheated apartment and served lemonade in spotty glasses. The grubby little man quoted a $20 per week rental.

"Never! That room makes skid row look like Alice's Wonderland."

"A little soap and water—and elbow grease . . ."

We haggled. I said I'd clean up the place at $15. The woman snatched at the offer.

How could I tell all this to Becky?

Amazing, my Becky! A thoroughbred. Laughing at the thought of my strange new accommodations, we packed bags of rags, cleaning powders, and disinfectants, a gallon of paint.

Another three days and my room was scrubbed and painted, new curtains were at my one window, and deodorant bars swung like so many banners.

Meanwhile, my neighbors had made themselves known. They might have been lifted from a film script: a self-pronounced homosexual, alcoholic, on the make—the once-brilliant man just out of an asylum after a divorce—three old-ish sisters, who took shifts at street-spying from their front windows—two boys who urged me to join their daisy chain. My landlady, as it was to turn out, was the most respectable lodger in the house, with a kind Christian patience and a demented nephew. Every Sunday morning I would hear the weathered floorboards down on the first floor, groaning under the joy of abandonment in religious spirituals.

New life-style, indeed!

9

Male (first) Nurse (second)

I had a new identity, a new home, a new job.

After the preliminaries on the first day, I was taken to the unit of which I was to take charge: a small twenty-five-bed medical surgical unit for men. Before we even reached the time of a report (all tours end with report to the oncoming nurse on the condition of patients), a man suffered a cardiac arrest.

Lord, I didn't know the code to call, having arrived less than five minutes ago. I didn't even know where the phone was.

In all hospitals a special code is set up for such emergencies. The arrest is called down to the switchboard, the operator announces it, and the personnel assigned to cover this code respond within seconds.

I immediately began pumping on the man's chest, someone called the code, and the team arrived promptly. The patient did not survive.

Cardiac arrests are difficult. To lose a patient is to throw the whole floor into despair, for each feels a share of responsibility. To have had this experience during those first few minutes at a new job had an especially depressive effect on me.

In any small hospital (two hundred beds or less) a nurse is called upon to employ many skills. I liked the challenge of diversification: The sicker the patient, the harder I worked, using every skill and technique I'd learned for his care and comfort. I was always to feel a sensitivity toward my patient and to take time for understanding his problems.

The aide assigned to me had been at this hospital for several years. She was to show me the ropes, and I could only hope that Mrs. Murray's approach was not rigidly molded. Dimmed hope: Mrs. Murray was no different from others I'd known who'd been around too long with outmoded ideas.

I tried to be optimistic: Maybe I'd been adversely affected by the dyed red hair crowning a stout body, her rasping speech, her less than genteel manner. Forget that she could be typecast as a gun moll in a B-movie. . . . The showdown came on the third night.

"I expect all incontinent patients to be changed immediately, washed, and powdered," I told her. "This means checking them every hour."

She looked at me in disbelief. "But—but we don't do that here."

"Perhaps not in the past. But we will from now on—for as long as I am on this floor."

Such news will spread in a small institution, and the following night, personnel seemed to be making pilgrimages to our floor, talking in rather loud voices and saying uncomplimentary things they must have wanted me to hear. What did these gals have up their sleeves?

Whatever, I was sure I wouldn't like it.

From the nurses station I could see down to the other end of the floor, and it was a shock to see a nurse, an hour after coming on duty, bow her head and doze off and on throughout the night. Mrs. Murray also had trouble staying awake, but I almost welcomed the quiet. The seriously ill I took as my own patients and asked for help only when necessary.

It wasn't long until I noticed that all conversation ceased when I entered a room. Was I becoming paranoid?

Unthinkable. Still, how could I be sure? I'd come to this dreary little hospital because I knew no other place to turn at this point in my life. I'd hoped no one would remember my last name—that they would not remember I'd had sex change here. How could I have been such a dope?

It seemed everyone had had advance notice, even though I'd specifically asked Mrs. Savage to keep my reassignment confidential. The fact that Dr. Lake and I were friends only worsened matters, and some staff members were blunt enough to say they felt I was carrying tales to Dr. Lake.

The ultimate humiliation came one morning in the cafeteria. I carried my tray to a table where other members were assembled, and when I sat down, everyone got up, picked up his or her tray, and, en masse, moved to another table and casually finished breakfast.

This couldn't be happening to me. That people dedicated to easing the pains of humanity could purposely inflict such mental anguish on one of their peers was beyond belief.

Bad enough I was a male nurse. Add to this that I was a transsexual and a friend of Dr. Lake's. The sum total in their books was that I was a spy of the lowest order.

A week or so later a supervisor and Mrs. Murray were discussing a new case, speaking in voices loud enough to be overheard. "You should have seen this one," the supervisor said. "He must have been at least six feet tall and the only thing he could do was curse and fling himself around the bed. Oh, we had quite a time with him!"

I asked: "Is that a patient on the other male unit?"

"No, it's *one of those!*" She did nothing to disguise the scorn she felt.

"By *one of those* I gather you are referring to a transsexual?"

"She sure is," piped in Mrs. Murray, almost gleefully. "This transsexual . . ."

But this was the supervisor's story and she wasn't letting Mrs. Murray take it away from her. "They put this guy into a room with a *normal woman*, a young woman. And when her mother heard that male voice, she had her daughter discharged from the hospital."

"Sad for everybody concerned, I'd say."

"Especially for that normal young woman and her mother, Mr. Martino." As if on second thought, she added, "Since you're such a close friend of Dr. Lake's, it would behoove you to tell him to keep *those patients* away from the normal ones."

"You're talking now about a male who is changing?"

"Yes!"

The picture was clarifying. What was happening here was just this: Males who came in for sex-change surgery were being put on the female unit, females on the male unit. Why, I wondered, didn't Dr. Lake have a few rooms set aside for this type of patient with specialized staff to look after them?

Certainly this picture gave the hospital a blackened eye. Just how black I was yet to learn.

Care, or lack of it, appeared to be by rote. Any attempt to implement a more progressive care was rebuffed with the same old cliché: "We don't do that here."

The family of a dying patient was still at its long vigil. How long had they been here? No one seemed to know. And no one stopped by to speak with them, so I went to ask if anyone would like cold juice or a hot beverage. The wife was so grateful she almost kissed me.

I went for the refreshments.

Mrs. Murray, in hazy sleep, lifted her head at the sound of ice tinkling in glasses and chimed out her complaint: "We don't—Mrs. Savage doesn't approve."

I doubted this. Mrs. Savage had some sensitivities, and I was assuming she'd consider this proper procedure. "Nonsense. I'm sure if this were Mrs. Savage's own family she'd approve. Frankly, I doubt very much that Mrs. Savage ever made such a rule."

When I returned with the juices and hot coffee, the wife said to me: "How kind you are. We've been here for three days now and no one else has offered us so much as a glass of water."

Staff members were permitted to visit different floors, yet my supervisor said I was not to leave my unit. Actually, there was small reason for my leaving, since very few on the staff spoke with me. Everyone knew my identity now and my supervisor began the habit of addressing me as *Miss* and then elaborately correcting herself. I got the message.

I no longer had any desire to get to know any of these people personally. I just wanted to give my best to my patients and then go back to the room I must think of as home. Temporary home.

My loneliness was almost unbearable. Becky was living alone in our city apartment and would stay on there until time for her terminal vacation and eventual training for an R.N. I continued the search for a small apartment here.

By the end of the second week at the hospital I'd had it. The staff was now openly hostile; the weather was miserably humid. I felt beaten down.

Dr. Lake had said I could work at this hospital until my papers were finished—but when would that be? And my hysterectomy must wait indefinitely while Becky and I prospected for a surgeon who'd do it. I had to hang in there. . . .

That weekend I told Becky I wanted to quit.

She couldn't believe it. "Quit? Why, Mario, I've never seen you walk away and quit anything. You can't know what you're saying. . . . Think of your accomplishments—in spite of incredible odds."

That knocked some sense into my head. "You're right, Becky. I'm not a quitter. The moment the words were out I guess I knew I didn't really want to quit. I need you to understand and side with me. I need encouragement in my new gender."

"But this new role is what you've wanted even more than life. And now you have it!"

"And now I have it. God, how I've worked for it—and you've stood by. Help me now, Becky."

She held me tenderly then.

Becky. So little, yet with strength as comes to those who are strong in faith. As if by miracle, her strength seemed to transfuse my every fiber.

I'd stick it out at Dr. Lake's hospital for a year and see what developed. But first, I'd talk with Mrs. Savage and let her know how I felt about some of the procedures here and discuss ways in which we might improve them. And, not without some malice, I decided to give Mrs. Murray enough rope to hang herself. In the meantime I'd keep looking for that apartment.

Still struggling with my new life-style, I was not prepared for the urgent call from Janet. "Dad has had a stroke," she said, "and we don't know how long he will last. I don't know if you should. . ."

Before she could say more, I asked the name of Dad's doctor. Noting it, I said, "I'll call Dr. Scheff and see if he thinks I should come home."

I put in a call to Dr. Scheff. He could not be sure of the seriousness of the stroke at this early stage, nor would he express himself as to Dad's possible recovery.

"I'll come," I said. And then I examined my motives for going to Dad's bedside. Was it to seek final approval?

Yes. Along with familial loyalty. One incentive was as strong as the other.

My third call was to Becky. We decided I could afford to make the trip and stay for a week. Mrs. Savage agreed to this arrangement.

"Take whatever time you need, Mr. Martino. Suppose you take the week off without pay and return the following Monday. If you cannot, please phone. I do hope you find your father better."

Janet and Jim were waiting at the airport and now they filled in the details. "You know how Dad is," Janet said. "Independent. He came to our house and I told him not to go to the bathroom by himself in the middle of the night. Just call and Jim would help him. Well, he got up—without calling Jim—"She broke into tears.

Jim went on with the explanations: "He had a stroke and fell. By the time we reached the hospital he didn't know us. And since he's been there he's had a heart attack. You mustn't be upset when you see him: He's lost a great deal of weight, and he can't speak."

This was worse than I'd feared and we rushed to the hospital. The supervisor, appreciating the fact that I'd traveled for hours to reach my father's side, permitted us to see him immediately in spite of the very late hour.

Standing by my father's bed and looking down at this small, shrunken figure, clean-shaven, eyes closed as if in sleep, I felt a sudden urge to tell him everything would be all right. He'd see: They'd let him go home soon. . . . Yet, this was false. I couldn't lie to him.

No matter what our differences had been, it was painful for me to see him lying there. I bent over his silent figure and took his withered hand. "Dad, it's Mario. I've come to care for you."

He opened his eyes but remained mute.

"If you hear me, squeeze my hand. I know you are too tired to talk now, but that can come later."

I felt a slight pull on my hand, and, for an instant, the glassiness lifted from his eyes. Recognition!

There was so much I wanted to say: that I'd made the right decision about sex change—even though the going was rough. Perhaps it would take time for people to accept me, but I was going to make it!

The words were never said.

Dad sank deeper into coma and it was sad to see him as he lay dying. All my life I had sought approval from this man before me. Approval withheld or forfeited by death was a waste, a tragedy that surely the two of us could have avoided. Why had Fate played this trick on us, never allowing that meeting of minds between father and child: that chance to prove ourselves to each other?

I remembered Dad's taking my picture down from the wall in their hallway after my surgery. Disclaiming me. That act had cut deep. But now I could see he was right. *Marie* was no more. Now it was *Mario*.

By week's end, I knew this would be the last time I would look on my father's face. I would not return for the services: My coming would cause his cronies and former neighbors to jeer and tarnish their memory of him.

One month later, after receiving the sacraments of the Church, Dad died in his sleep. I did not cry tears, but, remembering the many ways in which I'd disappointed him, I felt torn inside.

I had wanted to share a man-to-man relationship with my

father—and in that brief moment at his bedside, that slight pull on my hand, our relationship seemed to span that lack of a lifetime. I hoped I had made peace with my father.

During these dark times we found a silver lining: the ideal apartment in a private dwelling not far from the hospital. Far less expensive than the one we had in the city, far more room. The landlord and his wife were Jewish: Hyman and Millie Cohen. No pets, they said. "But," whispered Mrs. Cohen in an aside, "why don't you bring your little Jo-Jo over? And we'll see."

Our pooch had a sense of showmanship—he carried himself in grand style and greeted Hyman and Millie as if they were bosom buddies.

The Cohens were captivated, and, before we left, we signed the lease on our new apartment. As Mr. and Mrs. Mario Martino. This did not seem wrong to me, since we'd been together for eight years and would legalize our union as soon as my papers were in order.

We wrote Becky's mother the whole story about my sex change. It was fair to her and the only right thing for us to do. Her response was as we had feared: She could not accept the change, a contradiction to God's Plan. "If God had wanted Marie to be a man He would have made her one," she insisted. Even my letter was not to change her mind.

> *Dear Mother Harrison,*
>
> I know this situation is difficult for you to understand, but God's ways are strange at times. I know too that you feel if He had wanted me to be a male He would have made me male— but God allows many sorts of suffering as in cases of the blind and mute. My problem, although not as simple to explain, is not something I would have chosen. But, Mom, who does choose to suffer?
>
> There is only one thing I want to defend and that is my attitude toward Becky. I've loved her more than life itself. She walks beside me and is a true mate in every sense. I have great respect for her judgment. The years we've been together have been very good to both of us.

Years ago you told me that of all your children you felt Becky had made the best choice. I hope nothing in our present or in our future will ever cause you to feel otherwise.

Thank you for having your daughter, Becky.

I love you for it.

My love always,
Mario

The week before Becky went off to take her turn at school, we moved all her things from our former apartment to our new one at the Cohens'. This remarkable man and wife were to live up to their guarantee not to interfere, and we lived very much as if this actually were our own home. They came only when invited to drop in for a drink and for holiday or special partying. In turn, I shoveled snow, trimmed shrubs, and weeded and mowed the lawn. A welcome change from my professional work. This was a good time for learning to care for a house and grounds and it was a help to Mr. Cohen, who was not well.

Mrs. Silver was head nurse on the day shift. She took no sass or fooling from anyone, and it was a great relief having such a free-thinking soul on my side. It was a personal loss when she fell and broke her hip that winter.

Carolyn, a university classmate of mine, temporarily replaced Mrs. Silver. Now I had someone with whom to share my professional life, even though the staff lost no time in telling her: "He is one of those!" or "He's a sex change." Ad infinitum.

In an attempt to squelch the backbiting, Carolyn called the staff together and suggested that they cool it. Unaccustomed to discipline, the disgruntled members drew up a petition, stating their refusal to work with either Carolyn or me. This further undermined our staff morale, and the dissensions continued until I suddenly became a supervisor—and was as suddenly beset with problems that became multifold.

On one of my visits to her room, I found courage to ask: "Why, Mrs. Silver, is everyone so hateful to me?"

"They dislike you for several reasons, Mario. First of all,

you're a damn good nurse and that they can't deny. You are young and enthusiastic. Furthermore, you are a friend of Dr. Lake's. The fact that you are a transsexual gives them something to hang you on, so to speak.

"People in this hospital have been working with transsexuals for a long time. The only patients they have really learned to know are males who change to female and, believe me, a few of these patients overreact. The behavior of these few has soured the whole staff on the problem."

"But this is reputed to be a progressive hospital."

"Yes. But some of the old-timers rebel at change. So, you see, Mario, if you took away your transsexualism, they'd attack your other attributes because you're a threat to their own security on staff." She brightened the early hour with what she said next: "It may be of some small comfort to you that I have already told Mrs. Savage that the nursing care on our floor has improved a hundred percent since you came. The patients are pleased with you—what more can you ask?"

"I'll tell you what more: I'd like to have someone talk to me during the night. I don't like being the butt of snide remarks which are loud enough for me to overhear. I want to work in a professional atmosphere, with discussions about patients, not the latest local gossip. All this nonprofessionalism is new to me —very unlike the atmosphere in large hospitals and teaching centers I've worked in before coming here."

"Trust my word, Mario, things will change. Give them time. But do yourself a favor: If you ever think of quitting, well, don't! That would be the worst thing you could do, adding fuel to the embers. Just fight the battle like any other man who is under attack. Now that you have gained your new gender, don't let anyone threaten you."

"You have my promise, Mrs. Silver: I'll never let my old character disintegrate in my new body."

10

Legally, I am a male!

Soon after my bilateral mastectomy, Becky and I joined group sessions with other transsexuals. But too much information disseminated there on gender identity could not be verified or was found to be inaccurate. There were too many half-truths. Doctors gave too much hope, which could not be substantiated: Rosy promises of cleared pathways seldom materialized—instead, the directions were thorny and often led to frustration and despair. Not from intent, but because the whole thing was so new to all of us. It seemed to me that we needed facts and figures from driver's license bureaus, departments of vital statistics, universities, research teams, medical centers. We needed it firsthand, not as hearsay.

Dissatisfied with the little that was accomplished in these meetings, I mentioned to Becky that we should start something of our own.

Becky and I discussed the idea of our own counseling service with Dr. Lake and he was all for it, going so far as to allow us to use his own office address for mailings. We asked a small fee from each patient—if he could afford it. If not, he was to be placed on the free list. We thought of this service as a child of sorts: a brainchild, one that would help compensate for the children we knew now we'd never have.

Contacting the newspapers, we met with refusal. They would not accept our ads. It was still too early in the sexual revolution. We appealed for financial assistance to a foundation already active in this area, but their reply was that they did not dispense money to private individuals. Yet, sometime later, we were to learn of such a service actually sponsored by this same institution. Their service, however, was for the male-to-female transsexual. Ours was designed for the female-to-male. It seemed evident to us that interest in transsexualism was predominantly in male-to-female.

Before my legal papers could be changed, I was required by law to have a *pan hysterectomy*, or removal of the uterus, and a *salpingo-oophorectomy*, the excision of tubes and ovaries. There was no area in our state where I could find a surgeon to perform this operation. Desperate, I wrote to Janet, asking her to contact her own physician, Dr. Jonas, for recommendations.

My insurance was under the name "Marie" and I kept it that way until after this second surgical procedure in sex change. (And who ever heard of having male insurance to cover a hysterectomy?)

Any skilled surgeon could do the operation. And aside from the legal requirements, every female-to-male transsexual requested these surgeries for reasons identical to my own: 1) to remove the unwanted organs, 2) to eliminate the hormone-interacting process of menstruation, 3) to remove an organ high in cancer susceptibility, 4) to enhance testosterone utilization in producing secondary sex characteristics, such as the deepened voice, hair growth—in short, increased masculinity.

Surgeons usually made the incision in the abdomen, but the transsexual usually wanted it done vaginally, thus leaving the abdomen unscarred for an eventual phalloplasty.

We waited impatiently for Janet's Dr. Jonas to make a recommendation. He had taken time to contact the surgeon, Dr.

Adam Brown, before giving us the name and was pleased to say Dr. Brown would do my hysterectomy. I was to send a detailed background, listing goals already realized and goals yet to meet, directly to the surgeon. After reviewing this data, Dr. Brown asked that I come to his state, his hospital, for a personal interview and examination, with a tentative date set for surgery during the Thanksgiving holidays. Becky would have some time off then and could stay with Jan and Jim.

In the interim we bought a car, a luxury on our tight budget. The change of name on my driver's license was handled without incident. And now we left for Janet's home with the realization that we were taking still another step toward my sexual reassignment. I was to be in the same hospital where my father had died. I would be the first transsexual (but not the last) to have this procedure in this hospital.

The woman in Admissions checked my name against the operating schedule and became flustered. Looking at me, at my full-face beard, she couldn't understand my feminine name. Regaining her composure, she registered me and sent me off for a chest X ray.

Dr. Brown had informed the professionals on the unit but felt no need to brief the auxiliary staff as to the nature of my surgery. Becky was to be my nurse, and I would be a patient in a private room. Nor did Dr. Brown inform other departments with which I'd be involved, and some of the incidents there were not without their chuckles.

The X-ray technician became unsettled to the point of tearing the request in half, after which I helped her tape it together. Though I tried to maintain my calm, it came close to shattering when I noticed everyone outside the department lined up to take a look at this new specimen: *me*. In the laboratory for blood tests, the young woman dropped all her test tubes.

"Don't be nervous," I said to her. "I know exactly what you're going through because I used to draw blood."

Reassured, she had no further problems. In spite of the curiosity, everyone in this hospital treated me with professionalism.

Mrs. Thompson, the head nurse, came in almost as soon as we'd reached my room. She said my genital area must be shaved and I must have a vaginal suppository (as a safeguard against infection) and an enema. She agreed to Becky's helping me with these preparations.

Mrs. Thompson advised us as to hospital procedure, when we could expect Dr. Brown to visit that evening, and the time set for surgery tomorrow. Both my history and final examinations would be by Dr. Brown himself, not by one of the residents, to avoid any embarrassment on my part. His sensitivity endeared this man to both Becky and me.

I wakened in the early hours and was happy to see Becky, Jan, and Jim before going too far under from the preoperative sedation. More than anything else I was vaguely aware of the orderly standing at the door, squawking in a voice approaching terror: "I ain't never taken no man for a hysterectomy!"

"Get him out of here," I croaked. "God! This man is going to mess me up."

Janet ran to the orderly and asked him to see the head nurse —she'd explain. Within minutes, the man, sobered and wordless, returned and helped me onto the waiting stretcher.

Dr. Brown had been told that I'd gone into shock the first time I had surgery, so he was prepared for such an eventuality the second time. I remembered nothing about the operating table. On waking, I was happy this second procedure was over and that I was apparently doing well.

By the second day I was asking to get out of bed and on a regular diet. I was feeling great, anxious to get back to normal. And I was hungry. A liquid diet was simply not for me.

It was something of a surprise that Dr. Brown had not put a large dressing over the classical cut he had made in my abdomen. (He preferred the abdominal procedure, not the vaginal.) The incision ran from the navel to the hairline of the pubis and Dr. Brown had covered it with a Band-Aid and dispensed with the old-fashioned binder we'd always used after this type of surgery.

No incisional pain, but great discomfort from gas. Abdominal cramps were so severe I couldn't laugh. The cramps were to stay with me for about a week.

Up for the first time on the third day, I examined my face in the mirror. It looked as if it had been burned.

"What in hell happened to me up there, Becky?"

"You went into shock, Mario. Dr. Brown and his team simply revived you, then continued the procedure."

"Why in the world didn't you tell me I had a *subcutaneous emphysema*?" (This is the term used to describe presence of air or gas under the tissue, with consequent distention or swelling.)

"The problem came up when they tried to insert a tube in the trachea—when you were in shock."

"In shock? But why haven't I been told?"

"Dr. Brown thought we should wait. . . ."

"Well, I still think you should have told me."

Examining myself more closely, I realized how puffy my face was, and the dark circles around my eyes resembled those ghostly sockets on a Halloween mask.

"I frighten myself." I grinned at Becky.

Becky grinned right back at me.

"What's a couple of little old smudges when you've almost reached the top of the world?"

I was discharged five days after surgery. My experience here at this hospital had been exemplary and we had only praise for every staff member we met. Dr. Brown's splendid stitch work was removed on the seventh day. He asked permission to present my case to the surgical board meeting that month and I granted it, of course. I would even have appeared before the board if it would have been helpful to other transsexuals.

Becky went back to school, and I had a few days with Jan and Jim, then home again for six weeks' rest. Already I was restless, wanting to get busy again.

I'd taken the second step in affirming my male gender. It was something I'd anticipated and worked toward and now I felt positively wonderful. Wonderful!

Lots of time to think during my convalescence, and I wanted nothing more now than that Becky and I marry.

Never having had a problem with the law, I had supposed that lawyers were akin to my old-fashioned ideas about doctors: professional, humanitarian. An appointment with one lawyer was to shatter these illusions. Insensitive, cruel. Crude. Upon hearing my reasons for needing name and gender change on my legal papers, he exploded: "Why did you have your tits whacked off?" He did not wait for an answer. "You must be sick—or somethin'. Why don't you just go on livin' with the broad?" (Echoes of Dr. Patterson!) But he hadn't finished. "Resign yourself to being a lesbian!"

Why bother to explain that the woman who believes herself to be a man, who wants in every way to be a man, is not a lesbian—she is a transsexual? I couldn't get out of there fast enough.

A most disconcerting experience. It was to leave me wary. I hoped I'd rid myself of that apprehension with a more reputable attorney.

Never would I have more time than the present. I gathered up my courage, sought out another legal man, and took Bill along. His problems were identical to my own.

The office of counselor Wentzel was in the shopping center, and the waiting room, dreary and windowless, should have forewarned us. No evidence of a secretary. Still, I told myself, we can't judge books by covers—give the man a chance. Maybe he's so honest he makes no pretense at show.

Wentzel personified *the mouthpiece*. His mouth was loud, his words came too fast, his vocabulary peppered with obscenities.

How could I possibly have found my first and second lawyers so lacking in professionalism? Well, we're here in Wentzel's office, I thought, let's get on with it.

"You are reputed to be knowledgeable in name and sex change on legal documents for transsexuals, Mr. Wentzel. What is your price?"

"Four hundred dollars. But first, I'll have to see what judge will even listen to me about your cases. Damn controversial, y'know." He smirked. "When we find that judge, then we can work out a plan of payment."

"When do you think you'll find that judge?"

"Damned impatient, ain't ya? How do I know—I can't promise swift action."

We had to be satisfied with that. Bill felt as defeated as I did. Something was very wrong here. The waiting was ridiculous.

Six months went by and we called and visited Wentzel's dingy little office as often as we dared, admitted because we always brought in our payments. And then, one day, his announcement came almost as a surprise: "You're papers are finished—but, well, the judge struck out that part of the order which says that the birth certificate must be amended to now read *male gender.*"

"I can't believe it!"

Wentzel began his usual whining: "You sound just like damn crybabies. You can't have your cake and eat it. Be happy with what you got."

"You've made fools out of us!" Bill exploded.

"How dare you play us along like this? What we got is a mess. We've paid our money because you led us to believe that our papers would be done as submitted. Now: nothing more than a name change—and out $400! We're very little better off than before."

He looked at us with those sly eyes. "Heh-heh! I guess the reason you had to wait so long was the judge's way of getting back at *me*. I'd promised him a male-to-female so he could write a test case on it—and when I came up with two females-to-males he got mad as hops. He could've signed those damn papers in one minute but he wanted me to sweat."

How could this man have passed the bar? It had just been our bad luck to meet up with two shady lawyers.

Another goal for myself: I'd learn about law.

Now Wentzel quoted an additional fee to continue with our cases but we said we weren't interested. Since it was up to us personally to get all our papers (letters from physicians and psychiatrists, old birth certificates and similar documents), we decided to write our home states and ask requirements for sex change on our respective birth certificates. Replies from both states came promptly and read something like this:

> Send a court order for change of name and the letter from a physician and we will amend your certificate for $2.

Just as promptly we wrote our own affidavits, and the doctors and surgeons involved affixed their signatures. With this signed affidavit, check for $2 and an eight-cent stamp our sex was changed on our birth records and new copies forwarded posthaste to both Bill and me.

Literally, I jumped for joy when my little piece of paper arrived. It helped restore the dignity I'd been in danger of losing along the way, through the hostilities at the hospital and the shenanigans of the shysters.

I traveled to the state capital to have my nurses license changed and stayed overnight with friends. Connie, the wife, offered to go with me. Changing one's sex legally was not without its complications, and I felt apprehensive on approaching the building where, earlier, I'd taken state boards for my R.N. An armed guard stood at every door, and I broke into a sweat as Connie and I neared the desk just outside the door of a room filled with the shrill of phones and chattering people. We were asked to register before entering the room, and just signing my name added to my agitation. What would I say if this unknown woman, this Miss X, should break into raucous laughter or utter some unkindness after reading this court order?

How would she handle this delicate problem?

I handed the order to Miss X and sat down in the chair beside her desk, Connie close enough to press my knee for reassurance.

"What is your name now? Is the last name the same?"

"My name is Mario Martino—the last name is the same."

She was courteous and kind. My good luck. She excused herself, went over to a long file and pulled my pink card with all the vital statistics of my professional career, starting when I first filled it out four years ago. How vividly I recalled having written *female* on that card! However, this admirable creature did not flinch as she compared my license (which read "Martino, Marie Josephine") with the court order.

"Well, Mr. Martino," this blithe spirit commented, "it must have been difficult for you to go through life with this name."

"Yes. Something like that. . . ."

The tensions released, the three of us laughed happily together, and people turned to look and wonder at our light-heartedness in this strictly business office in the state's capitol.

Miss X excused herself, took a new license form to the typist, and waited for her to finish before returning to her own desk.

"If you should ever want your large parchment license for framing you will return the original and pay a fee of $7."

"Should I! Sooner than you think."

Miss X wished us luck and turned to the next applicant. Signing ourselves out, Connie and I embraced openly in the hall and were sure any onlookers would naturally assume we'd just come from the marriage license bureau.

Mine was the first request on record for name change on a nursing license. Next on my agenda was that social security card. In each case it was necessary only to present the legal court order.

All my papers were now in order. *Legally, I was completely male!*

On a lark I called Becky at school.

"Becky, will you marry me?"

"Well," she teased, "do you think we've known each other long enough?"

We'd marry in January, we decided. We'd waited a lifetime, it seemed to us, and we hoped we'd be happy ever after.

Could we measure up to the fairy tales?

Well, since ours was a world of reality we'd have to work at happiness.

Becky could no longer postpone the letter to her mother.

Dear Mom,

I have been wanting to write for a long time, but haven't had a chance to sit down and really say the things I've wanted to say. We don't want to upset or hurt you in any way—guess that's the reason I've put off writing.

All the papers have been changed legally to the masculine name "Mario," male sex. We know how you feel about this and we both understand that we can't ask you to accept it just now. But we both pray that in time you will understand and accept us as a part of our family.

Please don't hate me for what I'm about to say. I love all of you very much and, as you already know, Mario thinks you are the greatest people in the world! *I say this because it is true.*

Mom, Mario and I love each other very much and are completely happy together. To have someone who really cares for me is one of the best things in my life. There is nothing Mario wouldn't do for me. I don't know where I could find a better man, one who would treat me as wonderfully as he does—and always be true.

I really don't know what it is that you don't like about him, but you say he might take advantage of me. Mom, that just couldn't be. Mario would give me the world if I asked for it. He is concerned enough about my welfare that, before surgery, he drew up his will. He did this to protect me should anything happen to him.

I would never be as far in school if he had not kept his word about my getting an education. Yes, you said if I married someone other than Mario I wouldn't need all this schooling because we'd have a houseful of kids. Well, you don't have to worry about that because we've decided against having children of our own. Not that we wouldn't love having them—it's just that we feel that there might be too many problems later on for them to understand all that Mario and I have faced together.

All these changes are difficult for parents to understand, let alone children. It was difficult for me to understand at first and, you may remember, only last summer I told you I was planning to come home. And then, finally, I saw it all clearly: My love for Mario was too great for me to leave him. I've been with him for so long and, loving him as much as I do, I made the only possible choice. Every day since then I realize more and more that my decision was the wise one.

I see no reason why anyone there needs to know about this. We understand, of course, that you don't want Mario to come home and he won't. However, no one would recognize him, for he looks quite different now—and even better than he did as Marie.

Please try to understand, Mom, all of you. Just remember that we are very happy. I feel that nobody will ever love me as much as Mario does. This is the life I've chosen and we are to be married in January when I am on vacation from school.

We both love you.

Love,
Becky

We said a prayer together, asking God to help Mom understand. We posted the letter and went off to work.

Needling by the staff was often hellish, but I tried to underplay it for Becky's sake. To Becky, my hurts were her hurts too.

One thing was in my favor: rapport with the men on my unit. I learned firsthand how male patients react under stress, what they expected of themselves, of their peers, and of me. They needed to verbalize their fears: banteringly, if they were seriously ill—thinking of last rites, if mildly ill. They respected honesty. I was their brother, father, confidant—and, yes, sometimes their confessor.

The day people were softening toward me, but those on my own night shift still spat out their words when speaking to me. Well, things would eventually work out.

Nothing could down me for long. I was legally a male, free to marry my Rebecca. In January we'd marry and have a honeymoon. In February I'd get back to work on my bachelor's degree.

Life was opening to full blossom.

11

"... Always."

"One of those heavenly days that cannot die."

I'd no way of knowing on that fateful first day of our meeting at Renner that a sanctioned marriage between Becky and me would have to wait nine years.

Now, legally a male, I visited Father Conklin, a priest who was known to marry transsexuals of the Catholic faith. As I sat in his office, nervously chain-smoking, I wondered what his response would be to my problem. The friend who sent me to Father Conklin had cautioned me not to let his secretary know the nature of my visit, so, with my prefabricated story of "conscience matter," I was ill at ease.

The door opened. In he strode—six foot five of him!—who, in secular clothes, might easily have been mistaken for a linebacker at Notre Dame. When he gave me his powerful handclasp, I relaxed. What a nice guy. He took me into his office-library and, seating himself behind his massive desk, motioned me to the facing chair.

He opened the conversation. "Now, tell me your problem."

"I am a Catholic. And a transsexual. I've been told that in the past you've married others who have undergone sex change."

"Yes. But, first, I'd like to ask a few questions."

"Anything, Father."

Whatever jitters or fears I'd had in facing this man of the Cross were abruptly dissipated. Here was a man of understanding, and I wasn't about to ask him why he wanted to go out on a limb to help me, a transsexual. And others like me. I was sure as hell glad he did.

He asked where I was born, my ethnic background, the extent of my religious training. He was surprised to learn I was once a nun but made no great point of it and proceeded with his questioning.

"Do you recognize marriage as a forever-thing?"

"It's the only way I've ever thought of it, Father." It wasn't always practiced down to the letter in my own home, I thought, but we were aware that man's first duty was to wife and family. My inherent sense of duty I credit to my father.

Father Conklin interrupted my thoughts of Dad. "We must make sure of your convictions, for, as you know, there can be no divorce as far as the Church is concerned."

"I fully understand this."

"Do you plan to have children? If so, by artificial insemination or adoption?"

"We're undecided. Becky is now enrolled at the University. Since we are not yet married, we haven't discussed the method at any length."

"What is Becky's faith?"

"Protestant."

"Was she baptized? And does each of you have a certificate as proof of baptism?"

"Yes. And we have our baptismal certificates—but wait! Mine is under my christened name. That's something I hadn't thought about, Father. You can be sure I'll write for it today."

"Good. I need a copy from you to keep as part of the Church record."

"I'll take care of it immediately."

Father Conklin was satisfied with my answers. "Of course,

I'll marry you—or any transsexual—but only *after* I am sure of your understanding of a Church marriage, of your responsibilities to yourself and your mate and to God. I must be sure you are emotionally stable and that you live by the precepts of the Church."

Father would marry us! I found it difficult to contain myself while we talked in some detail about Becky's work and mine, our goals and aspirations. Another bone-crushing handclasp and I left his office.

We had arranged that I was to call him after speaking with Becky as to the date and as to when we could start our pre-Cana conference, a custom in the Catholic Church. Briefing her, I then telephoned my hometown priest. He said to send a copy of my new certificate to my sister at her address and she could deliver it directly to him. Attaching a copy of the court order to the certificate, I posted a letter to my sister that very night.

I heard from the priest. His reply was prompt, kind. *Negative.* The canon lawyers, he wrote, would not permit it.

I had called Father Conklin and told him we'd have to wait on the baptismal certificate and that, to accommodate the delay, we'd set our wedding date ahead to January 3. He was genuinely sorry, he said, but he was heading a pilgrimage to Europe over the holidays and would not be home in time to officiate. This was distressing news—and came at about the same time as refusal from my home parish to change the name on the baptismal certificate.

Two counts against us. I wanted to bang my head against the wall. Someone at the rectory referred me to Father Reilly, who was now away on a peace mission.

Couldn't anything go right?

I wrote a second letter—straight from the gut!—begging the priest to understand our reasons and our great need for that baptismal certificate. Perhaps (after much prayer, I suggested), he could put canon aside in making his decision? I enclosed our pictures and sent the letter.

And waited. . . .

Our life seemed so designed: always waiting for things to happen.

His answer arrived two weeks later. I was outside when the postman brought it, and I stumbled unsteadily in the December snow. I cut short my usual chatter with the postman—I was anxious for him to be off. I wanted to tear into that envelope, half scared to death!

My hands were nearly frozen, more from fright than cold, and I tore at the envelope. Inside was the certificate: "Mario Joseph Martino." His personal message was contained within two lines: "I hope my messy handwriting will lead to your happiness."

I wanted to jump up and down and shout to the world: "I'm going to marry Becky!"

It's at times like this that I look up at the sky and in the single ray of a winter's sun I swear I see God. And He is smiling with a twinkle in His eye.

Armed with this piece of parchment—heretofore the missing piece of our new pattern—Becky and I set off for the next town to see still another priest, Father Joseph. Our meeting followed the general pattern set by Father Conklin, except it was devoid of any personal warmth. It was arranged that we could meet on several occasions before our banns were announced the customary three times at St. Paul's Church.

We were walking to our final meeting with Father Joseph before the wedding. A soft snow was falling and Christmas lights were strung along the street and in shop windows. Our footsteps crunched as we approached the last hurdle: pre-Cana. This was the night Father was to take us aside, separately, and question us to find out if we fully realized the step we were about to take and the responsibilities of the sacrament of marriage.

We rang the buzzer at the door of the rectory for the housekeeper. I felt the excitement that must come to every man who had stood on those same steps under the same circumstances. Although I'd known Becky for nine years, Father's portrayal of our roles in marriage over the last few weeks had given me a new feeling toward this woman beside me.

I suddenly looked at Rebecca in a different way, almost as if I had just met her: the virginal spouse who was to be the heart of our home. I felt a new tenderness toward her. She had stayed by me during these torturous years. What was happening to us was a beautiful thing.

The housekeeper opened the door of the dimly lit vestibule and we were warmed by her welcome. "Father Joseph is waiting for you in the living room," she said and took our coats and waited while we removed our boots.

The priest came forward to meet us and shake our hands and indicated a chair for me while he took Becky to his study. A Protestant, she may have had an uneasy moment, yet it was not evident. Her time with him was very much like my own with him, answering questions which Father recorded in the ledger: personal data, promise to honor the spouse and to bring up any children in the Catholic Church.

As a Catholic I was given an added instruction: not ever to use mechanical means of birth control. (Without mirth, I thought to myself: Oh, this request is quite unnecessary!) Since one priest had consented earlier to marry us and another had given me a new certificate as proof of baptism (thus, legitimizing my existence in the eyes of the Church), it was of little importance, I rationalized, to tell Father Joseph I was a transsexual.

Father Joseph gave us date and time to meet for the wedding rehearsal, advised how much we should give the organist, suggested choice of flowers and music for the ceremony. We left the rectory with warm good-byes.

Dreams were nearing fruition.

Banns were posted as our wedding approached and we were happier than we'd ever been. Overall was a feeling of peace. Peace within ourselves. With the private world we lived in. My own good relationship with men, a new rapport with women. Acceptance!

Papers in order. Personal anxieties were closed chapters.

Since Becky was in school, it was up to me to make most of the wedding arrangements. I hadn't the slightest clue as to where to begin, but I made jottings on sundry slips of paper with appropriate checks and balances and somehow everything was falling into place. And since the priests had helped me, I believed the Church was on our side—if only from a humanistic point of view.

And now it was Monday before our wedding on Saturday.

Becky and I had just returned from paying for the buffet dinner for our guests in a motel parlor—and from gift-buying for members of our wedding party. Small but appropriate gifts. We were experiencing the luxury of sharing with those we loved: initialed tie tacks for the ushers and earrings for Janet, Becky's matron of honor, and money clips for Dom, my best man, and for Dr. Lake, who was giving away the bride. We sat at our kitchen table, wrapping the gifts and discussing such minutiae as the probability that our landlady would be watching from her window when we left our apartment Saturday morning.

Becky was to wear the gown and veil that Janet had worn at her own wedding. "Why not have Janet leave the gown at Dom's and you stay there Friday night? I'll meet you at the Church—like any other respectable bridegroom."

"Yes. Let's not bring bad luck down on ourselves by having the groom glimpse the bride before the wedding."

More seriously now, I took Becky's hand. "God has been good to us. . . ."

The phone rang.

It was Father Joseph. Spitting out words at me: "You've done a despicable thing! You are one of the most despicable persons I've ever met."

"But, Father, I don't understand. . . ."

"Don't lie to me. A woman who says she knows you—in fact, works with you—has called and told me everything: You are a transvestite, you've had your breasts removed, you've had a hysterectomy. All for immoral purposes. *There will be no wedding at St. Paul's on Saturday!*"

"Father. Father Joseph! I am not a transvestite. I am a transsexual. Please let me come and talk to you, let me explain."

But he had already hung up.

I was hot. Boiling over. My pent-up emotions exuded from every pore. My body was heavy with sweat and weak with nausea, my heartbeat was too fast, and my head whirled with the *whys*. All the old angers threatened to surface . . . but angers are destructive forces. *No! We refused to be destroyed.*

With a semblance of composure I called my attorney. No, he said, we could not sue for slander. "Truth is a good defense. And the truth about your sex change is their defense, not yours. You're at the mercy of your accusers."

If I wished to pursue the matter, this reputable attorney cautioned, I could sue the hospital for breach of ethics because the staff had revealed the nature of surgery I had undergone there.

I wanted nothing more to do with the hospital or with the pettiness among the people who worked there. There would be no lawsuits. I must protect Becky from my depression, my feeling of rejection by my own Church: this advocate of love and understanding.

My next call was to our Dr. Lake, who said he'd speak with Sylvia, his secretary, and get back to us. And he'd call other friends about a clergyman.

What could we do? And what about the sixty invited guests who were coming from different states for our wedding? In just six days. And at St. Paul's. *The bride and groom would not be at St. Paul's!*

The enormity of it hit me.

Becky's voice—cool, collected—called me back to reality: "We've faced worse things before."

At the moment it didn't seem so, but of course she was right. She did not cry—but I wished that she would have. I didn't cry—but wished I could have.

And now the phone began ringing. Words of solace and understanding, offers to help. Sylvia called to tell us about Rev. Marshall, a retired Methodist minister who often visited the hospitals in the area. Perhaps we could talk with him about our problem.

I dialed his phone number. The Reverend's voice came on strong and reassuring, and I knew he would listen to me. We arranged to meet at his home the following evening.

Once more we would have to tell our story, believing in the innate goodness of this man of God. We must hold faith that his humanity would overrule any lack of understanding and possible rejection.

As we began with the amenities, the mention of Becky's

hometown brought a smile to the rather stern countenance of Reverend Marshall. He had served in China for eighteen years with a former minister of Becky's own church. Mrs. Marshall joined in friendly chatter about mutual friends. She listened sympathetically, often nodding agreement as she knitted.

The reverend was as disciplined in speech as in figure. "Please tell us your story."

I recognized the two of them as good listeners and, without interruption, I revealed myself: my life, my surgery—the frustrations, my fears and hurts. It all rushed out. I told them of meeting Rebecca, of our life together, and of our great desire to have our union blessed. To marry in a church. (I omitted only my experience with Father Joseph. Later, I promised myself—a promise soon to be kept!—but not just yet. I was too emptied.)

Reverend Marshall was somber-faced as he weighed his words: "Well, you know, it seems from what you've told me, I'll *have* to marry you—since you've been living—ah . . ."

"In sin?" I supplied the words.

This seemed to break whatever strain there may have been in our meeting. Mrs. Marshall, as if on cue, served coffee and cookies she had made. As we sat there with these new friends I could imagine myself at the movies, watching this couple act the friendly parson and wife.

Talk turned to his work with patients at the area hospitals and his several publications. Then he suggested a run-through with Becky and me standing side by side, giving suggestions as to what would be expected of us on Saturday.

This was the first time that our problem had been frankly discussed with someone who was not an intimate or a medical or legal professional.

It was good for me, and especially good for Becky, to have acceptance by a clergyman of her own faith. The very fact he consented to marry us was to prove instrumental in her family's later acceptance of our marriage.

But this time I lacked that sense of elation. Perhaps because of remembering all too vividly the last-minute upheaval of twenty-four hours ago. The rejection of my own Church— preacher of love!—still cut too deeply. . . .

And so it was that we met the Marshalls: the beginning of a

rich and valued friendship that was to endure. They helped renew our wavering faith in a Supreme Being.

Returning home that Tuesday evening, we began our list of sixty calls, sketching in the change of plans. The happenings of the last twenty-six hours were shockers, they agreed—but, knowing us, they knew we'd cope: that we'd handle this new near-catastrophe with the same good old grit. Could they possibly know the grinding that went into all this grit!

"We'll be there!" everyone said. "It'll be a great day. You'll see."

Friday afternoon. Becky was set to leave at the appointed time for Dom's home—but not before another fond look at her bridal finery. My tux hung resplendent in our front hall closet. Arrangements were complete. Out-of-town guests were moving in for the weekend, unpacking their bags and lavishing us with gifts. The nightmares blurred and were forgotten as the night wore on and the fresh snow dropped its carpet of white.

Becky left with Dom in the early hours. The snow was heavier now and gave signs of blowing into a storm. One problem was resolving itself: our landlady, visiting her daughter upstate, was undoubtedly snowbound and wouldn't make it back to her window before morning.

Dom, the perfect best man, was back with the dawn. Forgetting nothing. Seeing to it that I was properly dressed, with the required number of studs and both cuff links, even remembering that little white collar button. I might add that I was shook up—drenched with perspiration in near-blizzard weather on the third day of January.

Might something not go off as planned? If someone had called a priest, why not the newspapers?

I dismissed the fears. This was our wedding day!

Still . . .

Our guests left for the motel. Dom and I took the last car and by the time we arrived I was almost in panic. Please, God, don't take this away!

Friends and family were assembled inside the chapel. Those who loved and never failed us. Almost everyone had cameras. And bulbs flashed and shutters clattered.

How tall and stately Reverend Marshall looked in his black robes. My sister, Janet, had never looked so grand as she walked down the chapel aisle, her gown dusty pink like the roses she carried. And right behind her was Becky.

My Rebecca. Like an angel!

I remember taking her hand and whispering, "How beautiful you are. I've never seen you in a wedding dress before."

The little chapel was silenced as Reverend Marshall spoke the words: "If any man knows why this couple should not be joined in the bonds of matrimony, let him step forward."

My pulsebeat accelerated. I could almost hear the intake of breath, and the silence roared in my ears. Seconds passed—no uninvited guest appeared, unannounced, to step forward: no man, no woman.

The blessed words of the service reached their grand conclusion. I was too numb to hear much of it, yet my voice came strong as I repeated the phrases. Becky's responses were strained and she held my hand so tightly the circulation nearly stopped. We exchanged rings and were pronounced man and wife. And then we heard the baritone voice of a very special friend singing our song: "... I'll be loving you ... *always.*"...

I was king that day! Married to the most wonderful woman in the world. Fulfillment of what had often seemed our impossible dream: the sanction of a marriage ceremony, our union blessed.

Rebecca. The only one of her kind.

The laughing and kissing and camaraderie in those parlors went on until nine o'clock that evening, and then Becky and I were hustled away to the airport.

The heavens were starbright. Another good omen as we winged off on a nine-year-delayed honeymoon.

PART TWO

BEYOND
THE
LABYRINTH

12

The Transsexual Experience

The years following our marriage saw progress in our nursing careers, Becky's graduation, my bachelor's degree in psychology, many parties where we found ourselves the honored guests. We made new professional friends and personal ones, strengthened our family ties.

And during these years we formed our counseling service, directed toward the females-to-males and called *The Labyrinth Foundation Counseling Service*. We learned from our patients, they learned from us, as we worked together trying to find answers to the complexities of transsexualism.

Just back from our honeymoon, I had returned to Dr. Lake's hospital, expecting to resign. Too many old emotional wounds. But the administrator surprised me with an offer of promotion to supervisor of my shift—with freedom to incorporate my own earlier rejected ideas. This was a challenge I could not refuse. Stifling the old rancors and ignoring the hostilities of my peers, I won over the opposition eventually and, within my three-year tenure, had the cooperation and respect of both medical and nursing staffs.

It was during this supervisory period that I began to understand why some transsexuals had damaged their own repute. The females-to-males I met seemed to fall into a constructive general pattern: Outwardly, they were more or less like anyone else. They set their life goals, completed their sex reassignments, continued their education, married, built homes and families. Most of these females who came for sex-change surgery made little fuss and, when discharged, quietly left the hospital without incident.

But the male-to-female patients were another story. Too few of them acted like any other female, either in speech or in manner. The extroverts among them referred to one another as closet queens, shrilled out their demands, showed their newly constructed vaginas to anyone who'd look, and used language I'd never heard from a woman.

Could I ever accept these exhibitionists as transsexuals? Here was my first responsible experience with this segment of transsexualism, and the exposure gave me a sharper understanding of why the staff was so hostile when they first met me. Their instant rejection of me clarified as I made my own observations of these extraordinary patients.

I remember vividly my first confrontation. I had been asked to speak to a male-to-female patient. Now that her sex-change surgery was a reality, Miss Wilson was going from room to room, showing her nude body to all the patients, whether they were there for the same type of surgery or something totally different. Some of the women who formed this captive audience were in a state of near-panic.

Deeply resentful of being classified with such exhibitionists, I felt personally degraded and keeping my control was difficult as I went to see our troublesome patient.

"I would like to speak with you, Miss Wilson," I said. "Come with me to a private room down the hall."

She came along and I closed the door behind us.

"Miss Wilson, I am the supervisor on this shift and your actions have been reported to me."

Miss Wilson looked up and fluttered her false lashes. She

crossed her legs in an exaggerated fashion, swinging one foot. "Mr. Martino, the women on this floor wanted to see my surgery so I showed 'em. Everything! What's so bad about that?"

Her attempts at coquetry infuriated me. "Miss Wilson . . ."

She interrupted. "I went overseas for my original surgery. I, ah, need repairs, though, and Dr. Lake is going to fix that."

"Miss Wilson, this is a small hospital and, for the most part, other patients—both black and white—are middle class. It offends them for a patient in the buff to come strolling into their rooms, even if it's just to show off a fine piece of surgery. The patients won't tolerate it, I won't tolerate it."

"Then I'd say you're a dumb square."

"You've the right to your own opinions. But I insist, Miss Wilson, that while you're in our hospital you must restrain yourself. If you feel a great need to show off your surgery, then confine your exhibits to other transsexuals who may be having the same type of operation. Perhaps you can help them. You are not helping the cause of transsexualism, however, by exhibitionism."

Empathy between the two of us seemed quite impossible. Her show-off attitude left me with a sense of revulsion. If I, myself a transsexual, was so filled with disgust by the behavior of this patient, then how could I ever expect my medical peers (who couldn't identify with the problem) to understand? They simply refused to accept that I was more closely related to *them* in wanting a conventional life-style than I was with this person whose problem, supposedly, had been my own in reverse.

"Do yourself a favor," I suggested. "Have your corrective surgery—and keep your self-respect. If you lack self-respect, how can others have it for you? They respond to you as you respond to them."

Off in her fantasies, she appeared to hear or care about nothing of what I was saying. Was there a way of getting through to this patient? Her problem was more extreme than any transsexual of my acquaintance and I wondered how she'd ever been OK'd by a psychiatrist for sex reassignment.

Miss Wilson is etched in my memory and can never be forgotten. Sadly, this is the type of sex-changed individual the

public is inclined to remember. Even sadder, the hospital staff
was hostile toward the lot of them. It took time even for me to
soften, reminding myself that my role was not to pass judgment but to help all those, "acting out" or not, who entered
our doors.

The temptation to act out is more understandable if we
think of it as release from mounting confusions. The male-to-
female suffers greater physical risk and requires far more medication than the female-to-male. Amputation of the male organs
may result in extensive bleeding. The less skilled surgeon may
accidentally perforate the walls of the newly constructed
vagina and the bowel, necessitating a temporary colostomy and
—after healing—further corrective surgery. For weeks after a
successful reconstruction, the patient must wear a semirigid
cylinder of silicone inside the newly constructed vagina to keep
the passage from collapsing. Sturdily constructed, this "splint"
is about the size of a phallus, heavy and unpleasant to wear.
And now she must learn to sit to urinate.

Onerous as these physical pressures are, society does expect
certain standards of behavior. Adherence to these standards
varies from individual to individual, but several theorists have
commented on differences in the personality traits of the two
changed sexes. J. Walinder made this statement in an article in
1967: "Female [to-male] transsexuals are freer of paranoid
trends and feelings of persecution. Male [to-female] transsexuals are significantly more asthenic, hysteroid and psychoin-
fantile in their personality characteristics than the females."

Miss Wilson seemed to illustrate what Dr. Walinder was saying here, yet Sandy (another male-to-female) was an exception
to this judgment.

Sandy was totally devoid of sensationalism. Gentle, gracious,
longing to fit into her rightful place as a traditional female
with husband, home, children by adoption, she had traveled
cross-country for her sex change. Patients such as Miss Wilson
threw Sandy into panic and she begged to be moved out of
their shared room. The move was denied and her hospital stay
was traumatic.

Mae was another model male-to-female patient. A strikingly
beautiful blonde, she was making plans to marry a virile foot-

ball player. Apparently, they were very much in love—yet she could not bring herself to tell him of her sex change. (Later, we were to learn that the disillusioned husband started proceedings for annulment a few days after the ceremony. Concealing the truth from a prospective marriage partner is interpreted by law as fraud. Such union is nullified. And, litigation aside, what marriage based on a lie can survive?)

Not all male-to-female applicants fit our definition as transsexuals. Some openly admit they do not care what they are just so they are women from the waist up. Some of these self-acclaimed women boast of a clientele of the "the finest gentlemen in town"—and these "gentlemen" may secretly prefer their sex with males. Living as females, impersonating and working as prostitutes, these transsexuals are the ones who run headlong into the law. These are the ones who give a disreputable tinge to transsexualism. And they are the people who make all the clearer the need for caution.

I cannot stress too often the point that no patient should be permitted sex change until evaluation is completed and approved by a reputable medical team. The usual one-year period of hormones and reverse role-playing (living as male, if female) is vital.

Sex-change surgery is final. Nonreversible. With enormously profound implications. It affects how you see yourself, how others see you—and how you measure up to all these expectations.

Sex-change surgery is not without its tragedies. Sometimes, because money speaks brashly, doctors shorten the therapy period—or waive it altogether!—and patients literally rush into surgery, sometimes on a whim. These hapless persons may end up as neuters: identifying with neither one sex nor the other—realizing, now that it is too late, that what they were before was better than what they have become.

For the newly sex-changed, the problems can appear insurmountable. But, whatever the closet skeletons, the "preconditioned" patient who has lived according to the program presents a person capable of facing problems and persevering at finding their resolutions.

Even so, with all requirements met and under the most meticulous guidance, doctors report that an occasional patient may suffer depression after a few years. "My life is better than it was," one may half-heartedly confess, "still, it's not as rosy as I'd pictured."

Life for most of us is seldom as rosy as we've pictured. But I have yet to meet the female-to-male transsexual who, having met all requirements preoperatively, would change back.

Working with transsexual patients at the hospital was an invaluable learning experience: a firm base on which to build our counseling service. Becky and I were now making final plans. Our motto: *to educate the educated.* Even within the medical profession the subject of transsexualism had never been openly discussed, so how could it be understood or accepted?

We proposed to bring transsexualism out into the open and treat it with the same dignity and respect as any other medical problem.

The establishment of such a service seemed imperative. Because there were no gender identity clinics in the area, transsexuals had to rely totally on private physicians. While these medical men and women accepted such patients, they could, for the most part, offer no tried guidelines to augment their hormonal therapy and surgical procedures. Reassignment was still quite new in the 1960s. Because they had too little knowledge beyond the immediately physical to counsel transsexuals, doctors often referred patients to us. Some were more advanced than ourselves in sex change. We were largely on our own, for eight out of ten patients who came to us did not see the interviewing physician again after the initial visit, or, if they did, it was only for injections.

We started as a postoperative halfway house within three blocks of Dr. Lake's hospital. Its concept was multipurpose: The patient saved money by spending less time in the hospital, professional registered nurses were available for postoperative care, patients and wives or girl friends could ask and receive answers to innumerable questions. They could also meet other patients who were stable, well-adjusted, productive—integrated members of their communities. Cost was minimal and information was handled only in strictest confidence.

Word of our counseling service went the rounds among incoming patients of this type in Dr. Lake's hospital. Also, a private practitioner agreed to refer his transsexuals to us. Geared to the female-to-male, still we never refused the occasional male-to-female who came to us for help.

We prepared and discreetly distributed—on request or recommendation—a brochure describing our service and outlining the goals we proposed to meet. Disappointedly, we learned that newspapers would carry no advertising of our service, however discreet.

Becky and I arranged our front bedroom to accommodate the patients who came, singly or in pairs. Sometimes the spouse or lover came along and the four of us would spend long hours talking about adjustments to this new life-style. Their backgrounds and ours often had similarities: They came from patriarchal families, and their values and goals were like our own. We had had the same convictions since early childhood: that we were meant to be boys. We were tomboys, hurt by the ridicule poked at us by peers, teachers, families almost without exception.

As they still are today, some patients were too frightened to ask questions. Many wanted to obliterate their pasts as members of the opposite sex. Not knowing what might happen, or how, some from other countries had actually destroyed their passports as soon as they cleared customs. Our patients needed help in many directions.

We wrote the health department and driver's licensing bureau in every state. On receipt of recommendations from the performing surgeon and a court mandate authorizing legal change of name, many states changed both birth certificates and driver's licenses. Other states refused to do either one.

We wrote universities and asked their requisites for changing name and sex on official transcripts. To avoid embarrassment to the individual, we requested that the original name be omitted on the revised transcripts. Today the old ones are even sealed by many schools.

Major insurance companies were almost uniformly adamant against reimbursement at this time, but now even Blue Cross is paying for sex-reassignment surgery in some states. Less often, the patient is eligible for health and accident disability benefits from other companies.

Before the draft law was changed in 1974, any male eighteen years or older was required to register or face fine and imprisonment. Two years earlier I had presented our case to the Director of Selective Service, stating that it was physically and emotionally impossible for us to serve because inherent problems and prejudices would have forced us into total isolation. I was referred to a governing committee and we corresponded until the change in draft status became an actuality.

We accepted invitations from college groups to speak and show slides, but doors were closed to us in the nursing schools. Odd, for our testings indicated that approximately twenty-three percent of sex-change patients were in the medical and paramedical fields and half of these in nursing. This negativism was among our bitterest disappointments, but, fortunately, the profession is now discussing transsexualism in its journals.

Our group sought funding from private foundations, but there was that lack of general public acceptance in the sixties and our requests were usually denied. Becky and I drew on our own savings and continued the counseling—and prided ourselves on being instrumental in some of the positive results in society's slowly changing attitudes.

Meanwhile, our counseling service continued to grow. New faces appeared at our door. Heretofore strangers to us, many of these clients were to become our close friends. And it was through this closeness that the idea evolved of drawing up a questionnaire, collecting data from individuals who had been, or were, in some phase of being sexually reassigned.

Drawing on our counseling experience with roughly one hundred persons, we arrived at what we considered a characteristic profile of the female-to-male transsexual in the 1960s.

Our mean age was twenty-seven years, our height was five feet six inches, our weight one hundred forty-four pounds. The dominant ethnic groups were Irish, Italian, and German, in that order—with the English, Puerto Rican, Blacks, Polish, French, Greek, Spanish, Swedish, and Welsh following. Only one each were Canadian, Chinese, Colombian, Cuban, Danish, Hungarian, Indian, Rumanian, Russian, or Turkish. Three percent claimed more than one nationality.

Eighty-seven percent were from patriarchal families, thirteen percent from matriarchal ones. Sixty percent came from families not too closely knit, twenty from "the usual," twenty from warm and loving families.

Religion was practiced by seventy-three percent. Fifty-seven percent of these were Roman Catholic, thirty-four percent were Protestant.

Forty had high school diplomas, eighteen were in B.A. programs, seventeen had B.A. and B.S. degrees, eleven had master's degrees, six were in master's programs, six had less than high school education, two had Ph.D. degrees.

Occupations ranged from unskilled labor to college professorships.

Postoperatively, ninety-four percent were forced to change residence because of community nonacceptance. Seventy percent of sex-reassigned persons wanted to move to the suburbs, twenty percent preferred the city.

Ninety-nine percent thought of themselves as true transsexuals. All agreed that the mate should be told before marriage. Ninety percent wanted to marry "the old-fashioned girl." Only five percent of the wives had engaged in a lesbian relationship before meeting the female-to-male transsexual. Only six percent frequented gay bars preoperatively.

What is to be gained from these statistics?

They seem to suggest that transsexuals are more or less a reflection of society at large.

Then why has society been so hostile, mystified, unsympathetic? And in what general areas are people now most confused?

Not until the 1960s was there open talk about *sex*. And then, suddenly, we were all but inundated by the amount and diversity of it. Before most were scarcely comfortable with the new word in public conversation, they were hearing about heterosexuals, homosexuals, transvestites, and transsexuals and their differences. The die-hard segments of the public rejected anything they considered "abnormal," believing only the heterosexuals to be "normal."

But, in general, society looked more tolerantly on homosexuals. Perhaps long hair and the unisex clothing trends prepared the way for a more indulgent view of transvestites as well. (Indeed, one of the most popular TV weekly comedies has a transvestite character as a running gag.) But what of transsexuals? The very thought of actually changing sex organs was to tamper with divine laws—a thought the majority would not tolerate! And so people turned away, refusing to recognize the trauma—the tragedy—of being trapped in the wrong body. . . . A medical problem? Nothing of the sort, these people insisted. Anyone who attempted such a thing must be demented. . . .

Society was not merely unkind. People were still uninformed. And unready. The whole world was moving too fast.

Now, in the 1970s, we are gaining our equilibrium. We are examining this mystifying problem of transsexuality with kind and open intent. Perhaps, one day, we'll find definitive answers. For now, we continue to try, to theorize, to experiment . . . to do our best.

Transsexuality, whose recorded cases deal mostly with males, remains a rare and mystifying occurrence, its causal range as vast as the experience of life itself. And as complex. Researchers can only speculate as to whether its causes are predominantly physical or psychological. Masculine or feminine patterns are programmed during prenatal development, and, after birth, behavior is guided by learning and social experiences within the psychological matrix of parental and societal influence.

Often the transsexual becomes alienated from his or her family, and this alienation touches parents, brothers and sisters, even aunts and uncles and close friends. Parents often suffer guilt, wondering as to their own responsibility in this "difference." But, firm in their belief that the occurrence is inborn, many authorities discount parental practices as a factor. My own strongly held opinion is that *father and mother are not to be blamed*. We have only to look around at the number of less-than-perfect babies born every day to realize that sex disorientation is as possible, say, as a cleft palate, clubfoot, or other abnormality.

Wherever the cause lies, the transsexual must be willing to walk away and give the family time to adjust. It may take a year or two or three, but if the love bonds are there, given patience, they may regenerate rather than deteriorate. Only in the more extreme cases will the familial roots be completely severed.

As they move through life, transsexuals are often mislabeled homosexual or transvestite. Some theorists believe the homosexual and transvestite have no confusion of gender role, that they accept their physical form and only choose partners and dress contradictory to convention, but the transsexual is confused to the point of desperation. A significant difference then, they contend, is this confusion and the lack of it.

A friend of ours, a psychological therapist, takes an opposing view: "While many overt homosexuals claim no gender confusion, there are many sensitive covert homosexuals who suffer the tortures of the damned because of ambivalence regarding their identity."

Because all are so grievously misunderstood, transsexuals usually empathize with homosexuals, male or female. All suffer ostracism in the form of needling or gossip and face discrimination in the labor market. The majority of these individuals live very private lives, working to fulfill their potentials, minimizing their social differences.

One area of public ignorance or confusion concerns how the female-to-male transsexual differs from the masculine-acting lesbian. I think I can clear that up quite easily. In female duos of that type, the partner who acts in a sexually aggressive manner may be doing so without any desire whatsoever of changing her sex. Proud of being a woman, she makes love to another woman who responds to her as a female. Their sex life may include mutual masturbation, oral sex, perhaps even the use of a dildo or store-bought phallus. Yet the masculine-acting lesbian is happy with her femaleness. The lesbian's satisfaction is the woman-to-woman contact.

Julie Lee, who talks with and advises thousands of women in her capacity as Lesbian Peer Counselor, gives us this definition: "A lesbian is a woman who loves women. She is a totally woman-oriented woman, who loves her own gender, who loves her own body as she loves the bodies of other women. The woman who wishes to be a man is a female-to-male transsexual. There really are no similarities and there is very little overlapping between the two phenomena." Furthermore, Julie Lee says: "To the lesbian, femaleness is the essence—and the only reality—in her life."

I am often asked whether, if lesbianism had been as publicly accepted in my youth as it is today, I would have continued my quest for sex reassignment. *Yes.* No qualifications. Unlike the lesbian, I did not want to be a woman and felt I should never have been one, that I could be content only in the male gender. The lesbians we know have no wish to change their sex. They want only to be women, and the idea of changing anything that might interfere with their woman-to-woman relationship is unthinkable to them. This is in complete contrast to my feelings: I have always wanted, will always want, only the male-to-female relationship.

Is transsexuality a continuum of heterosexuality or of homosexuality?

I think it is in the heterosexual area of the spectrum of human sexuality. And what significance has the question, after all? The transsexual and lover or spouse fondle and caress each other's bodies—doing all the arousing, loving, explorative physical things that humans have always done. Limited by their vanities and vulnerabilities, by their fantasies, their depth of trust in the mate, transsexuals have free or inhibited sex. They make strong or weak love. It is a matter of individuality and preference. And sexual activities will always differ between partners, whether heterosexual, homosexual, transsexual.

Because my kind of transsexual *has* gone through sex-change surgery—and because his partner *is* female—these couples think of their relationships as heterosexual.

And, to the sex-reassigned, a sanctioned marriage and children represent the conventional life-style. Once they are married, the urge for parenthood is almost universal among transsexuals. The desire to father a child is as great among female-to-male transsexuals as among other males who want a family. The possibilities are artificial insemination, or adoption, or ready-made families by a previous marriage.

In the 1960s it was not always easy to find a doctor who would listen to such cases, and most of our patients were unwilling to walk into an unsuspecting M.D.'s office and ask that the patient's wife be inseminated. First of all, the physician must test the husband's sperm—which the transsexual husband is quite incapable of producing. Then the physician must test the wife to see if her generative organs are functioning properly. An all-around embarrassment. In time our group found a doctor, a very sensitive human being, who understood the problem. His only requirement was, and still is, that the couple be married.

One of the most persistent transsexual debates still revolves around having children by artificial insemination donation (A.I.D.) or by adoption. My personal recommendation is the A.I.D. baby. Only the parents and the doctor need know of the insemination—prospective adoptive parents, on the other hand, must be interviewed and face possible rejection by agencies' screening.

Legal problems do loom in some states, however, for families who employ artificially inseminated pregnancy. Because legislative recognition and clarification of civil rights are still withheld, between 10,000 and 20,000 test-tube babies are born in a "legal no-man's land" each year in our country. The baby's potential claims are not clearly defined. But transsexual couples cherish the chance of a family experience—and they want the added joy of knowing the baby is growing in the mother's body.

Transsexuals lead lives very much as their heterosexual neighbors do, facing problems of living and propagating and dying. But, however similar life-styles may seem, transsexual problems often are extraordinary.

Julian, a doctoral student in research sociology, married Elaine, foreign-born. Their two-year-old, an A.I.D. baby, is the pride of the maternal grandparents, who do not know the circumstances of his conception nor Julian's transsexualism. His parents are just as proud, having accepted, with equanimity, Julian's sex change. The family's happiness was interrupted by a legal problem having nothing to do with the A.I.D. baby. It was with the Immigration Department, because of a precedent set in another state that a female-to-male transsexual and a female cannot marry because he lacks the equipment to function as a husband. Julian had had phalloplasty but balked at their request for a physical examination by a Public Health physician, believing his rights were challenged. Their case went to Federal court and they waited two years before receiving a favorable verdict. Now they plan to increase their A.I.D. family.

Despite this victory by the sex-reassigned, most couples still successfully conceal the fact that one of them is a transsexual. Nonetheless, they live under the shadowed past, fearful of public nonacceptance. These friends are representative of that group.

Karen and Stephen, lovers since undergraduate days, have Ph.D.s in clinical microscopy. Karen is in charge of a laboratory in a large hospital, Stephen teaches in a medical school and researches birth-linked defects. His goal is to become an M.D. as well. In spite of his successful phalloplasty, they both live in dread that Stephen's carefully guarded transsexualism may become known and endanger his standing in the medical world. They hesitate to plan a family. They live and work in the northern part of our country, are homeowners and active in church and community. His parents accept his sexual reassignment, but hers are less receptive.

Some husbands and wives, dedicated to careers, prefer their quietude to the voices of children. Our friends, Marcello and Sue, decided they had waited too long to start a family. A registered nurse with a master's degree, Marcello is a professor in a nurses graduate program in the Midwest. He and Sue have been together for almost twenty years. Both their families are religious and, in the beginning, found this liaison unacceptable, sex reassignment intolerable. Eight years ago the change was legalized and the couple married. Gradually the family attitudes have changed and today the parents are openly proud that Marcello is a doctoral student and that Sue has earned a master's degree. The couple own their home and find pleasure in the quiet academic life of the university.

A happy solution for some transsexual husbands is the ready-made family. And Kevin was lucky: He married a woman with very young children, who have always called him Dad. Two years prior to sex-change surgery, Kevin met and eventually lived with Sharon, who had been divorced, and her three small children. The couple hoped to marry in the Catholic Church, but Kevin was unwilling to concede to the physical examination his own priest requested. Marriage was solemnized by a Protestant minister. Kevin adopted the children. They lived on a small farm and, after returning from his job in town as a mechanic, he tended the cows for an elderly neighbor as a form of bartering for milk. Today the family owns a large farm and a modern house, with cows and goats and pet rabbits. The two sons and the daughter are growing and beginning lives of their own. A happy Catholic family, they are involved with Church and neighborhood, grateful that God has guided them through their more troubled years. The two older children know of their father's transsexualism, the younger one has not yet been told.

Roger, determined to be a parent, was more courageous than most transsexuals, with reinforcement from a father and mother who loved him. His was one of our most exceptional cases. He was reared in a tiny village in mid-America where there was never any talk of sex-change surgery or artificial insemination. As a five-year-old, *she* knew *she* would one day be a *man*. After high school graduation, the girl deliberately became pregnant and bore a baby girl. Leaving the baby with her parents, she went away for sex reassignment, then came home and claimed the baby. Within the year, he met Virginia, told her the amazing story and they were married and took the child to live with them. Today the child is eight years old and knows nothing of her father's girlhood. Roger says they're playing it by ear, that they'll face the problem if the time comes.

Impatient to live with the woman he loves, as my story shows, the transsexual may not wait for the sex change to be legalized. This arrangement is often flawed for both partners, since female-to-male transsexuals make a virtue of the conventional marriage.

Choice of partner is vitally important to any marriage, particularly to the transsexual. George is the cautious kind and refuses to jeopardize his new life-style with the wrong mate.

Searching for the perfect woman (he says he's waiting for my Becky!), George has no present plans for marriage or family. A real estate salesman, he is often in the community news and, because of this publicity, is fearful of eventual exposure as a transsexual. George is a deeply religious man and believes that God has shown him the way, through reassignment, to a happier life than he could ever have envisioned as a female. He is a member of the board of directors in his church and prominent in Bible study groups.

Every life has its own story. But few stories have greater poignancy than that of the transsexual and mate and their lives together and of their decision to have or not to have children.

One of my biggest regrets has been that I could never give Becky a child, that the two of us could not create a new life. In our earlier years I sensed that Becky missed not being a mother. Not in what she said but by the sadness in her eyes when she is around babies, in the way she fondles and soothes them and the way she looks on leaving them. She believes they sense her warmth and security, and it seems that they do, for she can stop a child's crying simply by holding it in her arms.

She always told me I'd be too strict as a father. But I believe that discipline and affection are the two basics in raising healthy, normal children. I communicate with children, talk with them, allay their fears, and, in a way, draw lines of discipline for them.

Nearly twenty years have gone by since the day Becky and I met at Renner's School for Women. We would no longer be young parents. Also, we cannot foresee what hardships might be in store for our children when they would learn that one part of our lives was secret from an unsympathetic public. Born a full generation later, could they be expected to understand our reasons? Would they believe us less than honest . . . even lose faith in our integrity?

Too many years have gone by, we concluded.

Today our lives are filled with the joys and sorrows of family and close friends and professional peers—and with the satisfaction that comes from helping others in finding their own sexual identity.

Keeping in touch with our former patients is one of the pleasures in our life. We return their phone calls, answer their letters—we comment on their latest news and photos of growing children, congratulate them on advancements in work and profession.

We were elated with a recent letter. In closing, our friend added these lines: "We've just planted two tomato plants. And we've named them Mario and Rebecca. . . . Do you mind?"

Mind? Who else gains immortality by having tomato plants named for them!

13

Phalloplasty

In time I learned about the experiments in Europe. New techniques were being developed to replace the earlier attempts at phalloplasty, which were unsatisfactory. One procedure had been to embed a piece of rib so that the neophallus remained erect. This was fine for intercourse—but what was one to do with it when not being used for that purpose?

From the time I had first considered sex-change surgery, I had investigated the creation of a phallus made from the patient's own tissue. Rumors that this type of surgery was being done in our own country were just that: rumors.

Today, techniques are considerably refined in the countries where phalloplasty is being done. Basically, this is what sex-change surgery consists of in our country today.

For a male-to-female, the first step in creating a vagina—called a *vaginoplasty*—is removal of the testicles. After a wait of some weeks, the patient returns for removal of penis and scrotum. The surgeon removes the skin, with its remaining nerve sensitivity, from the penis. He makes a pouchlike opening in the patient's body (approximating the vaginal entrance on the genetic female) between the urinary meatus—the point at which urine exits the body—and the anal sphincter. The outer skin of the penis is turned inside out and inserted to cover the canal of the new vagina. No attempt can be made to graft or construct any of the child-bearing organs.

In the female-to-male transsexual, the vagina and urinary system are left intact and a neophallus is created from the patient's own tissues, without any attempt at creating male generative organs. Simple as that may sound, it is a difficult procedure.

The female-to-male transsexual considering phalloplasty must recognize these problems inherent in creating, by plastic surgery, a penis through which urine may pass. In the genetic male, the base of the penis is on the mons, that hair-covered triangle at the groin. In the genetic female, the meatus is deep in the folds of the labia, below the clitoris and just above the vagina. If the plastic surgeon attempts to construct a penis through which urine will pass, which must attach to the female body in the appropriate male location, he must succeed in running a tube from the female meatus to the higher spot on the mons where the penis attaches.

The first of the surgeon's problems is the attachment of the artificial tube to the female meatus. There is only a fraction of an inch from the meatus to the interior sphincter, or ring-shaped muscle which controls the flow of urine. Therefore, the junction which must be created between the natural duct and the new artificial extension must be made in just that short distance. To move further into the body would be to interfere with the sphincter and cause the patient to lose urinary control. Only one plastic surgeon claims to have solved this problem. We know of one of his patients who stands to urinate, and the surgeon says he is one of five in the world who can do this.

The patient does not know his surgeon's carefully kept secret. The patient does know he has made five trips to the operating table—that the phallus measures only four inches—that he does not consider it cosmetically good, nor do others who have seen it. Furthermore, he had to choose between standing to urinate and performing sexually—and now he is giving second thoughts to his opting for the former and is considering another trip to the operating room.

The second difficulty is in developing an artificial duct which can carry urine the way the natural urethra does. The acidity of urine has so far damaged the materials employed. The perfect material would not only carry urine, but would not collapse at the point where the duct folds into the base of the penis hanging from the body. If disintegration of the duct does take place anywhere in its length, or if it collapses either at the juncture with the new penis or with the meatus, urine may leak, causing infection or the pulling away of the newly grafted tissue from the body itself. While these difficulties are as yet unresolved, transsexuals place their hopes in the ingenuity of the medical profession.

Adding cosmetic testes to the female-to-male is still in the experimental stage. The procedure is difficult since the vagina has not been closed. Attempts have been made to all but close this canal, but the opening was too tiny for cleansing and the build-up of secretions and the resultant odor necessitated abandoning the operation. The testicular implant is painful, expensive, and often quite unsatisfactory. In one procedure, special Teflon-covered steel balls are implanted in the labia majora. The resultant outpouching somewhat resembles a scrotum. But often the body rejects the steel balls and they may actually "pop out."

What is true even today is that phalloplasty can yield a cosmetically good penis, although without feeling of its own. This lack of pleasure or pain may subject it to accidents with zippers or radiators. The neophallus is constructed to erection size and remains that size at all times. But that is nothing more than an inconvenience, more than compensated for by the psychological benefit in having it. The permanent softness of the constructed phallus requires the use of a stiffener for intercourse. A plastic material, this is inserted into a slit in the natural flesh. This is the predominant procedure now employed, but plastic surgeons also experimenting with the implantation of a hydraulic system which will cause erection. A tiny pump about the size of a finger may be pressed by the patient, causing fluid

to flow into plastic tubes inside the new phallus, thereby stiff-
ening it. In the past, this technology, developed for use in im-
potent males, had been subject to failure because the body's
rejection mechanism acted against it. Whatever the technique
employed, no longer must a transsexual use a replica at the most
intimate times.

Phalloplasty, of course, cannot bring to the transsexual the
possibility of begetting a child. It cannot produce an organ rich
in the sexual feeling of the natural one. The tissue cannot
duplicate the erectile capacity, and there is, therefore, the
cumbersomeness of a new organ which is always the same size.
(When, after my surgery had healed, I first tried sleeping
prone, as was my former preference, I could not find a comfortable way to do it!)

These drawbacks, serious as they are, are minor when compared to the fulfillment phalloplasty brings.

Its greatest value is the psychological uplift. And this psychological stimulation can heighten the physical excitement
and pleasure. The neophallus is also, of course, a safeguard
against exposure.

My own experience with phalloplasty included both troughs
and peaks. The wait had seemed intolerable, but now, in the
early 1970s, Dr. Lake learned of a surgeon, Dr. Fogle, who was
creating a penis with the patient's own tissue. He had done
many such procedures on servicemen injured during the war,
and he had slides to prove his work.

Dr. Fogle was the first surgeon even willing to try in my case
and, somehow, his fee of $2,000 (it would have been more
without Dr. Lake's recommendation), staggering as it was,
seemed almost trivial as compared to other obstacles I'd faced.

I was never more excited! Yet now, suddenly, for the first
time—now that phalloplasty was within my grasp—I was
afraid. Afraid I'd somehow not measure up to what would be
expected of me as *man*. Afraid that, because of hormones, this
forced voice and body change was a regression back to puberty. Afraid of my newly heightened sexual desires and what
to do about them. Afraid of new relationships with women now
that they saw me as a male.

But the fears vanished as quickly as they had appeared. I'd dreamed of phalloplasty since my teens and now, in my thirties as the country entered the enlightened seventies, the dream was to become a reality.

What about shock from anesthesia?

Well, I'd survived it twice before, and I'd survive it again.

Dr. Fogle painted a rather gloomy picture. I credited him for his frankness but would not be deterred. I was never more optimistic, more determined to proceed.

Arrangements were made for surgery.

The very night before it was scheduled, I had an urgent call from Dr. Lake. "Mario," he begged, *"don't go through this. Even Dr. Fogle is uncertain as to the outcome. This whole thing is too chancy."*

"Dr. Lake, stop acting like a father. My decision is made. If it's the wrong one, I'm prepared to take the consequences."

"I'm talking to you as a friend. And as your doctor." His voice had a certain sadness as he repeated his warning: "Don't do it!"

His sadness weakened my determination for the briefest moment. "Don't worry, good friend. Everything will go well."

Becky and I had agreed that I should have this surgery while she was on vacation. I would recuperate at home and I had to have her near me. I was to lie flat on my back for at least three weeks, and Becky was the finest nurse I knew.

Tomorrow was The Day of Beginning.

While I was under local anesthesia, Dr. Fogle placed the sterile towels over my thigh and began the series of injections to anesthetize that area. My senses were numbed beyond feeling the pinprick, but the knife cut in my thigh sent an electrifying shock through my whole body. I could take pain. I'd had a mastectomy, a hysterectomy, and salpingo-oophorectomy, all without postoperative pain. And without benefit of any analgesic or pain-deadening medication after the surgery. But now the cut flesh burned, and Dr. Fogle reinjected the thigh still another time and then another. He continued while I fought against this torturous procedure by arching my body and picturing myself as a complete man.

The procedure, known as *stage one*—"creating the tube within the tube"—went like this: The surgeon made two parallel incisions, about four inches apart, in my upper thigh. He then sewed them back up. This was done so that the tissue between the two incisions would become accustomed to a lessened blood supply. The flesh between the two incisions would, in several weeks, be cut away from the body to form the new phallus. But now, a long, thin piece of skin was taken from my lower abdomen and wound—skin side in—around a fine rubber tube (about the thickness of a pencil), which was then forced under the fat, up the middle of the four-inch-wide oblong between the incisions. This rubber tube would eventually become the duct, inside the new phallus, which would lead urine out of my body.

My heavy sweat hampered the work of the surgeon's hands. I bit my lips until I could taste blood—and wasn't sure if my incoherent words were in prayer or blasphemy. I seemed to be drowning in my own sweat and choking on my own blood and guttural sounds.

Dr. Fogle wrapped my thigh in pressure bandages for immobilization and to stop bleeding, then dressed the abdomen.

This next procedure was *stage two:* After four weeks of bed rest, the stitches were removed from the two incisions on my thigh and the incisions reopened. All flesh down to the muscle between the incisions—including the rubber tube, which had earlier been inserted—was now lifted away from the thigh except at the top end near the groin and bottom end near the knee. A penis-like tube could now be formed by pulling together the two incised edges and sewing them on the underside. Since it was still attached to my thigh at either end, however, the tube resembled a suitcase handle. The gaping flesh underneath the newly constructed tube was sewn together and now both incisions were closed and expected to heal.

Trying to get off the doctor's table, I grew suddenly faint. I'd lost a great deal of blood, and somehow, today, the pain seemed even worse than it had four weeks ago. Was all this truly worth the male picture I'd fancied for myself?

Yes, yes! If the surgery worked it would be the realization of a dream.

Becky took me home and we endured another two weeks of pain, but with renewed hope. Sleeping on my back was trying, for I was accustomed to sleeping on my abdomen. But sleep was short, at intervals, and medication did little to relieve the pain. And I was puzzled: There had been no postoperative pain with the other surgeries. Why such torment with the phalloplasty?

This early period of recuperation was not uneventful. After the first seven or eight days I realized the dull, burning pain was changing to a throb. I told Dr. Fogle it felt infected.

"Oh, you nurses! Always worrying, worrying."

Toward the end of the second week, I asked if Becky could do a culture on the operative site. The doctor agreed.

With a sterile swab Becky took a small amount of fluid and sent it to the hospital lab. We were right: infection! I was put on a powerful antibiotic and this *seemed* to clear the problem. I returned to hospital duty, my leg still wrapped in pressure dressing and encased within the elasticized bandage. I sat with my leg elevated, trying to alleviate the pain, sweating profusely.

We returned to the doctor's office to have him tell us—no surprise!—that the incision on the thigh itself resulted in a gaping wound. (He withheld the fact that the infection had worked its way into the suitcase handle, too.) He said a skin graft was necessary, that our next step was to find the hospital.

But not one hospital in the metropolis, only a few miles away, would allow any type of transsexual surgery. These rejections from one of the largest cities in the world were beyond belief. Thus, Dr. Fogle was forced to take me into a ghetto area in another city (where such restrictions did not exist) for a skin graft.

Dr. Fogle decided on a spinal anesthetic. Injected into the lower spine, this form of anesthetic removes all sensation from the lower abdomen down through the toes.

In spite of all earlier experiences, somehow this time I was not afraid. Perhaps because this was a spinal and that is usually so effective. And because this time I refused to think of dying: I was too close to my goal to die now.

I spoke with the anesthesiologist as he placed me in a sitting position and inserted the needle in my lower spine. A friendly fellow, he occasionally broke into bits of Spanish song as he worked and this broke tensions and helped me to relax. I was fully aware of what was going on, as opposed to clouded memories with the earlier injections. And, still aware of the procedure, I talked with Dr. Fogle as he took a thin layer of skin from my left thigh. He was working with a *dermatome*, an instrument used for cutting or grafting skin—an instrument very much like the machine with which a butcher slices meat to desired thickness.

Maybe it's psychological, I thought, but suddenly I had this crazy yen to wiggle my toes. No feeling whatsoever, I'd no control over them. The frightening thought: Being paralyzed must be like this.

In a surprisingly short while I was back in my hospital bed, Becky at my side. It was four hours before I could wiggle my toes—and then, suddenly, it was as if my whole body were on fire. It was like a third-degree burn: even a slight touching of the covers, the twitch of a muscle, opening or closing an eye—to move was excruciating.

Becky stayed with me that night. We had full cooperation and unexpected kindnesses from staff and administration. They brought tea and crackers, pillows for Becky's comfort. Such hospital care and consideration for a transsexual patient was a rare thing to see, and very few nurses accord the respect I was shown here. Would that all transsexuals could experience this type of treatment in a general hospital.

For the first two days the pain came in waves but not so severely that I needed medication. I had only to lie quietly, and this was not difficult once I made up my mind to it. On the third day I was discharged to return home for three weeks.

The kindness of the staff at this ghetto hospital had greatly increased my confidence in life itself. Were these people kind in spite of living and working in the ghetto? Or because of it? The hospital was very small and almost everyone connected with it would look in and say "hi." If they were morbidly curious they concealed it and seemed to see me as they saw other males. They'd wish me well and be on their way.

Becky returned to work. I confined my physical exercise to

walking from bed to bathroom and back. By the third week I could shower. The skin graft seemed to have taken well and we could expect the wound on my thigh, which it covered, to heal.

This could not be said of the tube which was intended to become my new penis. The underpart of the tube was eaten completely through and had formed a ridge in the middle. The tube was shriveling, curling in on itself like a snail. Instead of the handsome phallus I had expected to grow on my thigh for later relocation, I had a disintegrating suitcase handle.

At our next postoperative visit, Dr. Fogle removed the dressing. Realizing that part of the tube was too damaged "to live," he asked my permission merely to cut higher on the suitcase handle, removing only the end of the tube which appeared to be diseased. He said he thought the rest of it could be saved and then excused himself for the moment.

Becky spoke up now. "Forget it, Mario. Don't give your permission. It's all broken—throughout the entire tube. I was waiting for Dr. Fogle to tell you this. . . ."

The doctor returned.

"I want the entire tube removed," I said. "As soon as possible."

I would not be a guinea pig! At that very moment I lost respect for Dr. Fogle: He was falsifying the picture. As dark as the picture was, I could have accepted the truth—a downright lie I could not accept. My intelligence was insulted. Furthermore, I questioned his medical ethics.

I had come out of all this pain, expense, and time with a scarred thigh and not an inch of progress toward a phallus.

I felt dejected. If ever I tried phalloplasty a second time, I resolved, I must be ninety-nine percent sure the surgery would work. I bore no ill feelings toward my doctor about the surgery, for he had warned me it was chancy. My complaints were confined to his hesitancy in handling the infection and to his saying the tube could be saved by working higher up on the thigh. Later, my discontent with Dr. Fogle was to increase for the simple reason that he continued these same procedures on others. I was to learn of no other patients who became infected, but even their net results were not good as compared to the heavy cost and almost unbearable suffering.

I cite one pitiful case: The tube was about the length and circumference of the patient's forefinger, the tube had a sprouting of hairs, the whole thing was as blanched as that on a corpse. The patient saw no remedy in his own future—other than a second phalloplasty.

Figuring my sixteen weeks' loss of time from work, plus Becky's work loss, plus cost of anesthesia and surgical fees, this surgery had cost us about $6,000. High price for the wisdom I gained.

I was to wait another four years to find the surgeon I'd trust for my second—and successful!—phalloplasty. Dr. Robertson was truly interested in what he was creating, he cared about me as a patient, he inspired my confidence and respect. The work was done in a fine Midwestern hospital, staffed with friendly and sympathetic personnel. Doctors and nurses and new acquaintances went to extremes in making my long stay there a happy one.

My surgeon is proud of his work. And I am proud of it. His techniques are the conventional ones that are withstanding the test of time. After having made two incisions about three inches apart, he quite literally turned my skin *inside out* to make the "suitcase handle" (with seam side up) on my abdomen (rather than on my thigh as the first surgeon had done), just below the navel to the middle of the mons.

He took the additional skin graft from the hip and thigh and covered the entire "suitcase handle" so that a neophallus was formed with natural skin both on the outside and surrounding an interior duct which would accommodate the stiffener for intercourse. This stiffener is a pencil-sized tube filled with silicone which is inserted into what would be the urethra in a real penis.

As a skin graft is applied, it lays down cells which generate new skin, and the top layer gradually sloughs away. The small irregular pieces of graft leave the neophallus with the appearance of having both small and large veins in it, exactly like an erect penis.

Like all skin grafts, mine was excruciatingly painful. The pain and sensations of burning were dulled by medication the first three days and, within fourteen days, the area from which skin was taken had healed.

Four weeks later, the surgeon cut the top of the tube away from under the navel and let it fall into position at the mons. And now he formed the *glans,* or head of the penis, by cutting a half-moon incision under the umbilicus as the tube was cut away from the body. Then the two edges were folded in to make the head. No skin graft was necessary for this procedure of creating the glans.

At the time of my second phalloplasty, I was one of eight patients. None of the others had postoperative problems. I was the exception. Driving home from the hospital, a new friend and I took a circuitous side trip to visit a former instructor of mine. Because of its swelling during these days, the only inconspicuous and less painful way I could wear my new penis was positioned against my abdomen. Apparently, the blood supply was not sufficient to reach the tip of the penis, for within the week after the trip that area turned dark, signifying death of the tissue.

Did this mean I might lose the entire penis? All that money and time—and pain—for naught?

I telephoned Dr. Robertson on an every-other-day average. He agreed that warm baths would stimulate circulation to the tube, but that it would not save most of the head from turning black and foul-smelling. So, nightly, I sat in the tub and, very slowly, cut away the dead tissue.

Talk about castration complex!

Psychologically, this cutting was almost impossible for me, yet it had to be done. And now newly formed skin of the graft on the undersurface broke through, leaving the tube with a large flattened effect from the middle of the penis to the top of the head. Eventually, I lost three-fourths of the head—and the exposed area was too large to cover over without another graft.

Becky could not bring herself to help me through the cutting-away period, and I felt quite alone and upset. Even though I really didn't want her to see it in that condition.

Three months passed, and then I returned to my surgeon for another skin graft of the entire tube plus repairs on the head. By the end of the second week (a week before I was to leave there), the doctor said the earlier graft had not taken because the swelling had persisted longer than expected before the latest surgery and worsened afterward. Apparently, in my own case, when skin is removed, that raw area of my body swells and breaks the graft before it has time to heal.

With this news I hit bottom, so to speak. I felt down as I never had before. My happiness seemed to dim out.

That night I called Becky. And my mood did an abrupt upward swing. How comforting her words: "Mario, I've been looking at your body for almost twenty years now. I'm happy with it. I know you want perfection: a perfect phallus. But be happy with what you have. I will be."

Of course I wanted to give her a perfect phallus. But her attitude helped me accept the fact that, while little in life is perfect, she was happy with me as I was and am.

I saw Dr. Robertson again the following morning, and his report was better than I'd expected: "Mr. Martino, we had been afraid you'd lose the whole thing—but now, we're sure everything will be all right."

There will be no more grafts. Not ever. We'll simply wait until the tube is completely flaccid, or relaxed—then, again, the undersurface of the graft (which did not "take") will be sewn together. I ask for nothing better.

So today I'm happy with what I have: a respectable phallus —three-fourths perfect. . . .

Now, I can tell myself, there is a new part of me—a part I have always conceived of myself possessing. It completes outwardly a picture of myself which I have always carried in my head. By day, whether working, driving, gardening, or relaxing, I sense always the presence of this outward acknowledgment of my maleness. And, by night, my new organ—for all its being less than perfect—is still deeply stimulating to both me and my mate, both psychologically and physically.

14

The Reassigned Life

Many female-to-male transsexuals do not choose to have phalloplasty *at this time* because of the difficulties involved and because some find the results of phalloplasty inadequate. They find that, after about six months on male hormones, the clitoris has usually grown too large to be contained within the protective lips or labia and now it resembles a miniature penis. Resting on the outside of the labia, the clitoris is very quickly stimulated and even the feel of the dildo is sexually exciting: Any movement reminds the patient that he has a semblance of the male organ. So equipped and stimulated, the female-to-male transsexual realizes to some degree the satisfaction of being male and achieving climax. And even the artificial penetration of his mate adds to his heightened sexual drive.

Many patients are very nearly content with such an arrangement. Many have no plans for phalloplasty because of the cost, sometimes as much as $10,000. The procedure requires several periods of hospitalization and loss of work time, and often it is no more satisfactory than a strapped-on dildo. The combination of enlarged clitoris and dildoe or phalloplasty seems to us an approximation of the normal male's response.

Because of their own insecurities and fear of the woman's rejection, many female-to-male transsexuals refuse to have a sexual relationship before reassignment by surgery. Still, after sex-change treatment the female-to-male may notice an increasing of the sex drive, the male-to-female a lessening. This reversal in sexual desire is attributed to hormones given to bring about the change from one sex to the other: estrogen for the male-to-female, testosterone for female-to-male. Studies also indicate that the male who turns to reassignment may have a lower sex drive than the average male.

The reassigned male-to-female reports anything from inability to experience orgasm to multiple orgasms. Postoperatively, the female-to-male reports ability to achieve climax and perform as a male. Three factors contribute to the ability of the reassigned, both male and female, to reach a satisfactory climax: the skill of the surgeon, the effect of the hormone injections, and the emotional/psychological makeup of the individual.

All transsexuals—female-to-male and male-to-female—must maintain hormone treatment for the rest of their lives. Because recent research indicates that with prolonged use of testosterone on genetic males for three conditions—eunuchism, scanty sperm, and menopause—liver tumors may result, the female-to-male is cautioned to have a liver function test at least once each year.

I know of no female-to-male who has reported an unsatisfactory sex life in the new gender. Even without phalloplasty, each attributes his satisfactory orgasms to the psychological change: Now he is at ease with himself—and having his mate respond to him as a male is a dream fulfilled.

With phalloplasty, some females-to-males claim a wild new urge to "sow oats," but, for the most part, they are content with mild flirtations and remain faithful to their wives.

Infrequently, though, marriage will crumble after this type of surgery:

Divorced, and the mother of two little girls, Dawn met Jerry prior to his surgery. She married him after his legal reassignment, in spite of the fact she considered herself lesbian. But she had underestimated Jerry, believing she could dissuade him from phalloplasty. Jerry was not to be deterred. Dawn retaliated by divorcing him, declaring she really wanted to love a woman—not a man! In time, Jerry remarried and is now happy with Barbara. They plan to have babies by artificial insemination. Jerry does not consider his second marriage as a rebound romance—rather he thinks of it as God's way of compensation.

Among the many female-to-male transsexuals we know, all wish to go on with phalloplasty eventually, although fewer than fifteen have actually done so because of the almost prohibitive cost. With the exception of Jerry and Dawn, all husbands and wives seem happy with the results.

While it seems all-important to the husband to bring a phallic representation to the marital bed, the wife who loves him will learn—rather, husband and wife will learn together—how to adjust, and they will find mutual enjoyment.

Nothing is more vital to harmonious copulation than the woman's feelings about her man: To her, the absence of male genitalia need not make him less of a man. As we have reported, many transsexuals have good, stable marriages. And enduring ones.

To look backward is to be urged forward. Many of yesterday's children were thrown into the despair of gender dysphoria because doctors had to guess in assigning a sex at birth when the baby had "ambiguous genitalia."

Until very recently only the most casual inspection of the newborn was used to issue the birth certificate, which, in turn, decrees whether the infant shall be regarded as male or female. With today's new scientific tools, however, medical teams can now rationally determine the sex of a newborn within about thirty-six hours immediately following birth. Is the baby a chromosomal female with ovaries (indicative of fertility) or a chromosomal male without ovaries? *Yet chromosomes alone do not define gender.* Many doctors believe the determination of sex is far more complex than the results of a chromosome test.

Emergence accomplished, at last I'm free to live as I wish and to tell my story.

It becomes the responsibility of the team, therefore, to assign the sex in which it believes the baby can grow and mature most comfortably. Our general awareness of chromosomes began with the controversy over the East German women swimmers. The issue also surfaced with the emergence of Dr. Renee Richards in tennis competition. Perhaps athletic commissions will accept these tests as authoritative, but the debate, which is certain to take place, will raise the level of public understanding of this medical frontier.

How has sex reassignment changed me?

I have always had a strong sex drive and with the rarest of exceptions have always been orgasmic. As everyone will recognize, attempting to describe or compare one's own orgasms is difficult. What I can say is that the pleasure I have had has always seemed to satisfy me, and that certainly remains true. I rather think that I have a higher intensity of sex-pleasure now than ever before. What this may be attributable to is of course open to interpretation. No doubt the male hormone testosterone which I take produces a broad range of effects. Certainly the enlargement of the clitoris is arousing. The fact that I am no longer troubled by the use of a dildo, an instrument not of my own flesh, but can feel that an actual part of my own body is involved in the sex act is a source of immense satisfaction to me. There is of course also the absence of the tension induced by those feelings of being trapped in the wrong body. Before my change, there were parts of my body I did not want touched, my breasts and vulva. Now those feelings are gone.

Shift of weight has been my most noticeable physical difference. I have long since stopped worrying about a beard and body hair, having become hirsute. The natural curves of the female body have flattened into a strong semblance of the male. Trousers that had fit around my waist before hormones almost reached my chest afterward, even though there was no appreciable weight loss.

I credit hormones as well as surgery.

Prior to reassignment, I was much more emotional. I cried freely, with tears sliding down my cheeks—but, for years now, I haven't cried at all. I still talk from the soul, and one can go no deeper than that.

I'm more gutsy now. I call a spade exactly what it is. If necessary, I am brutally frank. A completely masculine trait, according to the dictates of my Italian-American upbringing.
Unladylike before sex surgery, acceptable as part of a man's
expressing himself. Some outbursts I attribute to my Italian
temper: It may take hours to reach white heat, or mere seconds
for the verbal response to blue the air. Usually I hold my
temper in check, consider myself emotionally stable.

I'm more realistic today. More than thirty years have passed
since Jimmy Stewart was my idol. I cannot say I've used him as
a role model, at least what we see on the surface. About the
only time I can match his calm is during an emergency. I don't
walk slowly into things, I plunge. I like the good-guy image,
but not at the expense of what I believe. Idols are to be admired and learned from, but not at the expense of losing one's
own identity.

With maturity, one mellows or grows more inflexible. I like
to think my views have mellowed.

Today I see all the Misses Wilson in a more charitable light,
recognizing them as being so pitifully confused as not to be
held accountable. Perhaps, unknowingly at the time, I even
detested them because they had so ruthlessly (or so it seemed
then) left behind in the surgical theatre that which I worked
mightily to attain. When one works toward a goal for so many
years, this overcompensation immediately after sex-change surgery can, perhaps, be forgiven. We've worked at the visible
signs of our chosen gender and now, suddenly, with this release
from the hated bodies, we want to shout and wave the flags of
liberation.

We, as sex-changed persons, are what we've always wanted
to be. For the most part, the uncertainties are behind us, and
we are emerging from our private labyrinths into new identities of our own choosing.

Ten years ago I took a certain pride in being a male chau-
vinist, and this I attribute to my despair in having been born
with a female body. *But brains, talents, and skills are not defined by sex.* Becky exemplifies the women who work shoulder
to shoulder with their men. And I laud those women who support their families alone. And those women who excel in the

professions, in administration, government, and industry, and in stamina and moral fortitude.

Always one to excel, Becky cannot be surpassed as a marriage partner. She proves herself again and again.

When Becky and I first met, I was willing to fight her battles for her, but over the years I've had to face the fact that she fights her own battles or they remain uncontested. I am proud of her when she goes to bat for what she believes, annoyed when she allows others to take advantage of her good nature.

Becky is slow to anger. Our occasional spats revolve around her habit of bottling up her emotions, my excited verbalizing in response to get them unbottled.

Becky's reticence is a characteristic trait of her family. She has never been comfortable with the words, *"I love you"*—something a man needs to hear from the one person closest to him. This is the only imperfection in Becky's makeup to which I cannot reconcile myself.

Do I think of Becky as second to myself?

In no way! Becky is extremely bright, honest, moral, very giving of self. She is quiet, I am verbose. She is strong when I need to lean. She lifts my spirit just by being herself. I support her when she's misunderstood. Life works out for us, we each have something to offer the other.

Certain social restrictions crystallized after my change. No longer can I jump over to visit a married woman two or three times a week without a neighbor raising an eyebrow—or the husband questioning my motives.

I have learned to play the games that go on forever between male and female. As a male, it is socially acceptable for me to casually flirt or tell an off-color joke—as a female, I wouldn't quite dare.

I am no longer a man searching for himself. My search ended in finding that man I always knew myself to be. And so it is that I presume to qualify the theory: "Anatomy is destiny." With talents from a Power greater than mortal self, Homo sapiens is now radically changing the dictates of biology. We have advanced to an age in which anatomical alterations are not only a reality but scarcely a surprise.

Removing the procreative organs—and recreating the genitalia—is often equated with living under false pretenses, living a lie. Patients report that occasional friendships (begun after sex change) terminate instantly with self-revelation.

I have yet to master my vulnerability. I have yet to reveal myself to friends we've met since my change, some as dear to us as family members—to explain to them there is a part of my life they know nothing about. Will they feel betrayed? Would this revelation affect the children we know and love even more intensely?

How do I explain my reticence?

All sorts of accusations are hurled at some transsexuals. "I can never trust you again!" "If you aren't true to yourself, you can never be true to anyone else." "And you call yourself a good Catholic?" "I refuse to talk about it." "You turn me off!"

These are not responses that encourage self-revelation.

Why, even today, are people shocked and frightened and angered by sex-change surgery? Or even the mention of it?

The degree and range of adverse reactions relate proportionately to an individual's failure to understand the problem. As society becomes more open and recognizes the scope of conventional sexuality, the more accepting individuals will become of transsexualism.

Not to typecast, generally, the greater one's own securities, the more receptive the individual is to opposing views in all controversies. Big or small.

To care, we must first be informed. Far too little information has been disseminated. All too hush-hush. Those persons afflicted with the gender dysphoria syndrome are just beginning to come forward, most of them still too vulnerable to face the shock, the fright, the anger the prurient curiosity of a scandalized public. Our Puritanism is more ingrained than we might wish to acknowledge or even imagine.

For some, the thought of reversing the genitalia hits at the core of their own sexuality and shatters their faith in biological destiny.

Very often religious scruple is the excuse for nonacceptance. To some, the thought of sex amputation is repugnant: Recreation of the opposite genitalia is beyond any vestige of human dignity.

Sex reassignment was not accepted by the Catholic Church in the early sixties, nor is it accepted wholeheartedly today. But their doors are opening to dialogue on the complex implications. As controversy about organ transplants and blood transfusions, even choice of sex at conception, leads to reevaluation, it seems logical to assume that one day transsexualism will be generally recognized by medicine and church as a medical-psychological problem, not a religious-ethical one.

Will society ever accept, without equivocation, the sex-changed person? Will the medical profession ever totally solve the problems of this syndrome? Will the laws of our respective countries protect us?

Surely the answer to all three must be an unequivocal *yes*.

Transsexualism is not what I would have wished for myself, but, since I am what I am, I strive to turn this liability into an asset, to establish a bridge of understanding between our segment and society in the main.

Taking a last backward glance, I realize that in envying the boy's rich maturation period I also denied myself many of the riches the girl experiences in the same period. On the brighter side, I have experienced some of the best of both. I've been doubly blessed.

As the calendar years mark time, I more fully appreciate that good things can come of miscarried plans. No experience is lost: It fits into our individual pattern. Out of trauma comes reinforcement in the relationships with family and friends.

Getting my own life in order was the first requisite in what I am doing today. This has been my major accomplishment. Being able to say *I have achieved* is the ultimate reward.

By nature I am a positivist.

On occasion I am asked how I've succeeded in the light of transsexualism. My code is simple and one I've followed all my life: *I will not fail because of my problems. I will succeed in spite of them.*